Helping
Crime
Victims

Helping Crime Victims

Research, Policy, and Practice

Albert R. Roberts
Rutgers University

With contributions by:
Arlene Bowers Andrews
Harriet Bemus
Arnold Binder
Alan T. Harland
Eric Hickey
Beverly Schenkman Roberts
Cathryn Jo Rosen

SAGE Publications
International Educational and Professional Publisher
Newbury Park   London   New Delhi

For information address:

SAGE Publications, Inc.
2455 Teller Road
Newbury Park, California 91320

SAGE Publications Ltd.
6 Bonhill Street
London EC2A 4PU
United Kingdom

SAGE Publications India Pvt. Ltd.
M-32 Market
Greater Kailash I
New Delhi 110 048 India

Printed in the United States of America

Library of Congress: 90- 61079
ISBN 0-8039-3468-8 (cloth)
ISBN 0-8039-3469-6 (paper)

95 96 97 98 99 10 9 8 7 6 5 4
Sage Production Editor: Amy Kleiman

Contents

Foreword

As we begin the decade of the nineties, a growing and critical rediscovery of the impact of crime and the trauma of crime victims is in full stride in the United States. Society's responsiveness to crime victims has been demonstrated by enactment of federal and state criminal justice reforms, including the authorization of a federal crime victims fund—made up of federal criminal fines and penalties—which has provided steadily increasing support for crime victim assistance and compensation programs. While precursors of dramatic change date back to the sixties, most of the systemic advances have been accomplished in one short decade.

Helping Crime Victims offers readers the first opportunity to review the history of victimology, research on the nature of victim/witness assistance programs, and a detailed discussion of approaches to address the needs of crime victims in one text. Dr. Al Roberts presents this information, with contributions from seven other prominent professionals who have a range of clinical and academic backgrounds. The text provides a framework for the rapidly growing field of victimology.

Dr. Roberts points out that the study of victimology has evolved considerably since the researchers of the 1940s and 1950s postulated that in a large percentage of cases, the victim shares responsibility for his or her victimization. He is clearly one of the *new* victimologists who rejects the focus on victim facilitation of the crime and shared responsibility, and instead focuses on how to ease the pain of victims through effective assistance programs.

The notion of providing help to crime victims is a rather recent phenomenon. It originated in grassroots efforts in the 1960s and 1970s to assist victims of sexual assault and battered women. In the 1980s, national attention was focused on this subject when President Ronald Reagan appointed a Task Force on Victims of Crime that reached startling conclusions. The Task Force found that crime victims were often victimized twice—first by the crime itself, and then by the criminal justice system. Innocent victims were ignored, mistreated or even blamed for what happened. Traumatized by criminal and judicial proceedings they did not understand and relegated to serving as evidence at the convenience of the courts, the experience left victims unwilling to become involved again in the criminal justice system.

Dr. Roberts distinguishes between victim service programs that provide crisis counseling, shelter or other specialized treatment and victim/witness assistance programs whose major goal is "to alleviate the stress and trauma for victims and witnesses who testify in court." In late 1985 he initiated a nationwide study of more than 300 victim/witness assistance programs—all that could be identified at the time. He received an unusually high—60%—response rate to his survey and the results of his study are presented in Part II.

The study documents the history and the current state of the art of victim/witness assistance programs. The majority are located in prosecutors' offices, although some are located in police departments or social service agencies. Services provided to victims center on information about case status, the court process, and assistance in participating in judicial proceedings; referral of victims to social service and mental health agencies; and help completing crime victim compensation forms. While less than half the programs reported that they provide crisis intervention, the providers were more likely to be the police-based or social service agency programs.

The results of the national survey represent the first comprehensive examination of victim/witness assistance programs and the services that they offer. The detailed information describing organizational structure, staffing patterns, funding levels and sources, use of volunteers and services provided (e.g., witness notification) would be helpful to anyone interested in establishing or expanding such a program or preparing professionals to work in the criminal justice field. The study extends our body of knowledge by giving us important baseline information on the nature of services provided.

The early 1980s were marked by increased public attention on the rights and needs of crime victims; passage of landmark federal legislation, the Victim Witness Protection Act of 1982 and the Victims of Crime Act of 1984, and increased advocacy at local, state and federal levels. There has been so much progress in services to victims in the past decade, that it is easy to forget how young the field is. While programs have proliferated, too little research is available to guide program planners and policymakers. Dr. Roberts suggests that the time is ripe for more research and evaluation of program effectiveness.

Part III of *Helping Crime Victims* is a collection of specially written chapters
that offer insight into a number of clinical and programmatic aspects of victim
assistance and recovery. A forthright discussion of data regarding missing and
murdered children clarifies the scope of this problem. While the relatively small
numbers of stranger and serial offenders seem to be encouraging, the devastating
impact of such crimes upon families and communities motivates all concerned
to become more informed about prevention and appropriate response when
a child is missing.

The profound impact that victimization within families can cause is also described. Because of the violation of trust and chronicity that typically accompany incest, spouse abuse and elder abuse, recovery presents special concerns.
A discussion of the levels of assistance that should be provided to a survivor
of family violence is presented. In addition, a model approach to response and
treatment of battered women and their children is described in detail.

Despite advances in victim participation in criminal justice proceedings, restitution continues to be an underutilized potential resource to crime victims. Reasons
for this situation are explored in hopes that greater attention can be focused
on resolving practical problems that inhibit full implementation of presumptive
restitution in criminal cases.

Helping Crime Victims highlights the major criminal justice reforms which have
been accomplished in the last decade. At a time when the field has seen such
rapid growth, it is necessary to consolidate the knowledge base and evaluate
its policies and practices. This book fills a significant gap in the field, by system-
atically reviewing the principal methods and approaches employed in victim and
witness assistance. I am confident that victim advocates, service providers and
researchers, regardless of their discipline perspective, will be better prepared after
reading this book to critically assess and further enhance victim and witness
assistance services in the decade of the nineties.

— *Jane Nady Burnley*
Director, Office for Victims of Crime
U.S. Department of Justice

Preface

This volume has been prepared for use by informed citizens, victim advocates, social workers, program development specialists, criminal justice administrators, government officials, and legislators. Its aims are twofold:

(1) to report the complete findings of the first national survey of the organizational structure and functions of 184 programs or units serving crime victims and witnesses throughout the United States; and

(2) to offer the reader practical ideas and realistic strategies in the form of procedural guides and workable program components and services that seem to be effective in meeting the needs of crime victims.

This book was written to provide a stimulus, a factual knowledge base, and alternative approaches for those professionals dedicated to improving services for crime victims and witnesses.

After decades of neglect, crime victims are finally being recognized as a vulnerable and forgotten group of people who have rights and are in need of services. During the past 10 years, as a result of federal, state, and local initiatives, a host of victim service and witness assistance programs have been developed in cities and counties across the United States and Canada. Victim compensation programs now exist in 45 states and the District of Columbia; 44 states have crime victim bills of rights. In addition, there are now several thousand programs to aid crime victims, including general victim assistance centers, specialized services for elderly victims, and programs for victims of rape, domestic violence, and child sexual abuse.

This volume is a systematic, comprehensive, and up-to-date work on a rapidly developing area of criminal justice and social work—victimology and victim services. This book synthesizes the professional literature, research findings, treatment alternatives, and program and policy implications. The focus of the book is on the immediate and short-term psychosocial needs of crime victims and on specific services and treatment programs developed to meet their needs.

Part I of *Helping Crime Victims* focuses on the history and emergence of the field of victimology and on the development of victim compensation, family violence intervention programs, and victim/witness assistance programs. Part II reports on the first systematic study of the organizational structure and functions of 184 victim service and witness assistance programs. Part III includes an examination of programs, recovery services, and remedies designed to improve service delivery and lessen the trauma experienced by victims of rape, domestic violence, robbery, and other violent crimes. The Appendix provides a directory of 184 victim/witness programs, including their staffing patterns and specialized types of victim services.

The chapters in this volume examine numerous concepts, treatment alternatives, and victim service options that provide an overview and guidelines for helping crime victims to reduce the trauma experienced in the aftermath of traumatic events.

This book is written for students in victimology/victim services courses, as well as for service providers, clinicians, and law enforcement and criminal justice professionals. In recent years, there has been a proliferation of government documents, agency annual reports, journal articles, final reports, and training manuals on various aspects of crime victimization. To date, the task of pulling together and integrating the best of these materials in one volume has not been accomplished. For some time, professionals have been searching for a book that brings together the knowledge base on victimology, victimization, and victim assistance. This is the first book to provide a comprehensive body of knowledge on this topic.

It is highly likely that victimization in the home and on the street will continue to be a pervasive societal problem and will only continue to increase in the future. This will result in an increased need for student and staff training and for more programs and services to help crime victims.

Acknowledgments

There are many individuals who have given information, support, technical assistance, and encouragement on this project. First, I would like to acknowledge the early support and intellectual stimulation of two research psychologists: Dr. Lucy Friedman (executive director) and Rob Davis (director of research and information systems) at the Victim Services Agency (VSA) in New York City. I have benefited significantly from my work as project director and researcher at VSA during 1984. It was during 1984 that I began to realize how little we know about the psychosocial impact of victimization and the effectiveness of different types of victim assistance in facilitating the recovery of violent crime victims.

Because of my fervent interest in building our knowledge base on the effectiveness of victim service and witness assistance programs, I planned and initiated the national survey in 1985. I would like to thank the Office of Research and Sponsored Programs at Indiana University for awarding me a small grant in support of my nationwide survey of victim/witness assistance programs. I also appreciate the interest and encouragement of Dean Sheldon Siegel and Ann Gratz at Indiana University. I would like to thank the succession of three part-time research assistants who worked on different phases of this project: Laura Noblitt, for coding and tabulating the responses; Bobbi Sicardi, for preparing and typing the directory of 184 responding programs; and Vicky Sampson, for reviewing brochures and annual reports sent by many of the respondents and for working on and typing portions of the first draft of the study findings, particularly Chapter 6. Most important, I thank my wife Beverly for typing and editing portions of Chapters 1 through 5 of this volume. Bev's speed, diligence, and accuracy are truly remarkable.

My deep appreciation goes to all of the victim/witness assistance personnel who completed my questionnaire, shared their agency reports, and allowed me to interview them. Without their contributions, this survey would not have been possible. I am singling out three victim assistance professionals for special mention because of their careful reading, insights, and suggestions on the revision of my draft survey report. They are Karen Kurst, Rochester Police Department in upstate New York; Jeanette Atkins, Greene County Prosecutor's Office in Xenia, Ohio; and JoAnn Beaudry, Milwaukee County District Attorney's Office. In Indianapolis, the suggestions and technical comments of Marion County Prosecutor Steve Goldsmith, Ruth Purcell (coordinator of Marion County's Witness Assistance Program), and Deborah Daniels (former chief counsel in the Prosecutor's Office and currently a U.S. attorney) are greatly appreciated.

It would take too many pages to list the 200 victim advocates and program directors who completed the mailed questionnaire, shared quarterly and annual agency reports, or allowed me to interview them by phone or in person. However, I do wish to gratefully acknowledge the information, materials, and insights these individuals shared with me. Without their contributions this survey would not have been possible.

Special mention should also be made of the generous cooperation of several resource specialists and reference librarians: Mary Stanley, library science professor at Indiana University; Cindy Stein, formerly of the U.S. Department of Justice's Office of Victims of Crime; and Michaela Cohan of the National Organization for Victim Assistance (NOVA). These information and library specialists shared with me various directories of victim witness assistance programs as well as journal articles and several government documents. Their cooperation enabled me to make this study as thorough and up to date as possible. I greatly appreciate the encouragement, support, and guidance of Terry Hendrix (vice president) and Christine Smedley (editor) at Sage Publications. Finally, special thanks go to Amy Kleiman (production editor) for her care for detail in the final production stages of this book.

—*Albert R. Roberts*, D.S.W.
New Brunswick, New Jersey

PART I

Introduction

1

Introduction and Overview
of Victimology and Victim Services

Case 1

Just before Christmas, a young mother we shall call Janie and her 15-month-old daughter return to their apartment in the housing project after a long weekend spent visiting relatives. The lock doesn't operate properly. When Janie finally gets the door open, the shock is incredible. Every piece of furniture, all their clothing, food, presents, and even the Christmas tree have all been stolen.

Unfortunately, that was only the beginning of their horror story. Janie reported that the police were unsympathetic to her feelings. The victim was made to feel as though it had been her fault. She had to find another place to stay because she didn't feel safe in her own home. She felt raped, robbed of all the dignity that she had.

As Janie returned to her apartment a few days later, someone exited through the front door as she came in the back. She reported that the police were no more sympathetic this time.

Meanwhile, Janie had been referred to the Minneapolis Crime Victim Center by the Red Cross. There, a counselor was able to obtain two emergency checks for her for $80 to use on food and clothing and also informed her about furniture available from a regional center. Perhaps most important was the time the counselor spent, letting Janie know that she was not alone and that she was not at fault. The counselor also helped Janie to pursue a different rental unit. She came to realized that, despite the loss of all her possessions, she still had a great deal in her beautiful baby (M. Stendor, personal communication, July 1985).

Case 2

This is a description of the victimization of Sam, a 21-year-old automobile parts salesman who was robbed at gunpoint upon returning to his apartment building after a long day spent visiting accounts in the Bronx, New York. Sam talked about what happened:

> I walked into the building, and the perpetrator followed me. I thought he lived in the building. [Sam had lived there for only four months.] He put the gun to my head and asked for money. I gave him $169.00, then he took my coat, watch, glasses, and shoes. I was very upset. I was angry at the landlord for not having the building secure. The front door to the building had a broken lock and anyone could get in.

During the weeks that followed, Sam had several flashbacks, especially when entering the dark hallway in his building. He sued his landlord and went to the local victim service agency. The victim advocate helped him fill out victim compensation forms and, as a result, he was compensated for his monetary and property losses. He received crisis counseling and brief cognitive treatment once a week for five weeks from the clinical social worker. Sam's flashbacks abated, and he received $550 from the victim compensation board.

We live in a society in which millions of people are robbed, raped, beaten, shot, or stabbed each year. The prevalence rates of violent crime document the enormity of this problem. Recent data from the National Crime Survey show that there are more than six million crime victims in the United States each year, at a cost of approximately *$9 billion annually* (Bureau of Justice Statistics, 1987). According to a monograph by the President's Task Force on Victims of Crime (1982), somewhere in our nation a woman is raped every six minutes; two persons are robbed every minute; and two persons are shot, stabbed, or seriously beaten every minute. Our vulnerability to crime is made clear by recent studies that indicate that five out of every six American citizens will be victims of violent crime at some point in their lives (Bureau of Justice Statistics, 1987).

In addition to their physical injuries, crime victims experience financial and property losses, emotional distress, and psychological trauma. The research evidence documents the long-term and short-term psychological damage of victimization (Burgess & Holmstrom, 1979; Friedman et al., 1982; Kahn, 1984; Lee & Rosenthal, 1983).

After decades of neglect, victims of violent crimes are finally being recognized as a vulnerable and forgotten group of people who have rights and are in need of services. What are the existing services for the myriad victims of violent crime in our society? In years past, the pain and suffering of crime victims was generally met with indifference by court clerks, the police, and prosecutors and their staffs. But the ignorance and indifference of law enforcement and court personnel are being replaced by a genuine effort to correct the injustices that have been perpetrated against crime victims. During the past decade, as a result of federal, state, and local initiatives, a host of public and private victim assistance programs have been developed. Much of the credit for the proliferation of programs emerging in the 1980s should go to responsive legislators, victim advocates, social workers, prosecutors, and police administrators.

Victim service programs provide crisis counseling, emotional support, and concrete services such as emergency food coupons, financial aid, and replacement of broken locks in the aftermath of victimization. Witness assistance programs provide information on the status of cases as well as guidance and role-playing sessions to help witnesses overcome the anxiety and "stage fright" of testifying in open court.

A large number of crime victims are turning to victim service and witness assistance programs for help in coping with the crisis of being victimized. I recently conducted a national survey of the organizational structure and functions of 184 victim service and witness assistance programs. This survey showed that in 1984 respondents provided counseling and/or concrete services to 336,540 crime victims. The average number of victims served by each program was 1,829. Based on these findings, given that there are currently more than 600 victim/witness assistance programs nationwide, a fair estimate of the total number of victims served annually by all of programs would be 1,097,400, or close to 1.1 million. The considerable number of victims served indicates the large demand and crucial need for programs that serve victims and witnesses.

Federal Legislation and Funding

In recent years, the U.S. Congress has given recognition and support to the financial and service needs of crime victims, especially victims of family violence. For example, in 1982 President Reagan's Task Force on Victims of Crime made 68 recommendations for addressing the multiple problems of crime victims. The task force recommended that federal, state, and local governments, together with private agencies and organizations, develop a series of strategies to improve the plight of crime victims.

By 1984, Congress had implemented one of the principal recommendations of the 1982 task force when it passed the Victims of Crime Act (VOCA; P.L.

98-473). This federal legislation established the Crime Victims Fund, which provides grants to states to supplement funding to both state victim compensation programs and locally operated victim assistance programs. The total amount of the fund is fixed at a maximum of $100 million annually. The money comes from the many fines and forfeitures that are collected from offenders who have been convicted of federal offenses. Included in this fund are monies collected from federal fines, new penalty assessment fees for federal felons, forfeited bail bonds, and criminals' literary profits.

During fiscal year 1985, a total of $68.3 million was available. Of this amount, $23.6 million was given to state crime victim compensation programs, $41.3 million was available for grants to the states to support local victim assistance programs (providing assistance to victims of violent crimes, sexual assault, spouse abuse, and child abuse), and $3.4 million was for victims of federal crimes.

VOCA helps state-sponsored victim compensation programs through annual grants from the federal Crime Victims Fund. The U.S. Department of Justice (through the Assistant Attorney General's Office for Victims of Crime) also provides the states with grants for victim service and witness assistance programs. When applying for these funds, each state is required to certify that it is giving priority to the funding of local victim assistance programs that are aiding victims of sexual assault, spouse abuse, or child abuse.

The National Organization for Victim Assistance (NOVA) conducted a survey to determine the extent to which the states had a single- or multiple-victim focus during the first year of VOCA funding. NOVA found that while some comprehensive programs did receive funding, the majority of the funded applications were from single-focus groups. For example, in the state of Wisconsin, 85% of the applications were from groups serving victims of family violence. Of the 16 VOCA grant awards to Wisconsin programs, only two were to prosecutor-based witness assistance programs.

In Massachusetts, over half the VOCA grants went to battered women's programs and rape crisis centers. Some of the Massachusetts programs served more than one of the targeted groups (e.g., battered women's shelters that helped abused women as well as abused children). Only three program grants were awarded to general victim assistance programs serving all types of crime victims.

Each state receives a base amount of $100,000 annually to support victim assistance programs. The remaining funds available to the states are divided on a formula basis determined by each state's share of the total U.S. population. The VOCA allotments to three sample states are as follows: Massachusetts, $972,000; Pennsylvania, $1,890,000; Wisconsin, $817,000.

In order to understand the influences that have shaped the field of victimology, it is useful to review briefly the development of the past to determine the major milestones in victimology. Therefore, the next section of this chapter will examine the history of the victim and the emergence of the field of victimology.

History of the Victim

During primitive times, "social control," restitution, and revenge were handled by individuals who took the law into their own hands and, in effect, made the law and carried out the punishment in the form of revenge. The earliest form of social control was victim retaliation and personal reparation.

In early times, compensation and restitution were enforced for purposes of increasing the punitive sanctions against the criminal. For example, the Code of Hammurabi (1750 B.C.) was based on revenge and cruelty. In those times, it was not uncommon for a thief to have his hand cut off or for a rapist to be castrated. Sometimes the criminal's obligation was as much as 30 times the value of the damage caused. The Code of Hammurabi also required the victim's family and the entire community to take responsibility for helping the victim if the offender escaped or could not be found, and therefore could not be made to pay restitution (Schafer, 1968).

By the end of the Middle Ages, it was generally recognized that the person harmed must have recourse through the common law, rather than taking the law into his or her own hands. Unfortunately, because of the states' interest in "bringing the wrongdoer to justice" and punishing the criminal, victims' needs for compensation were often postponed or completely ignored (Mueller & Cooper, 1974, p. 86). Whenever the criminal act was treated as a crime against society, the civil remedy for damages was delayed until after the offender's trial, conviction, and sentencing. All too frequently, this resulted in the denial of any monetary or tangible personal compensation to the victim.

During the early 1700s, Indian tribes such as the Cheyenne and Comanches roamed North America, and they responded to crime victims as a collective or group (Debo, 1970; Fehrenbach, 1974). In tribal law, an offense against an individual was viewed as an offense against the individual's clan or tribe, and the victim's concerns were often taken over by the tribe. The tribe's response might have been a long blood feud, a vendetta, or monetary reparation. The main purpose of a blood feud was not the restoration of any moral order, but the restoration of the power of the tribe and the securing of conditions for its survival.

For centuries, victims of crime have had, in theory, the option of bringing tort actions against individuals who have wronged them through the commission of crimes. However, in practice, this potential civil remedy is usually of little value. According to Wolfgang's (1965) early research, in a large number of cases, the offender is not known to the victim; even when the offender is known, the victim often cannot afford the expense of bringing a civil lawsuit against him or her. Furthermore, since the overwhelming majority of offenders of violent crimes are unemployed and/or poor, civil judgements against such offenders are almost impossible to collect (Geis, 1967; Mueller, 1965). In addition, civil actions have often been subject to delays of several months or sometimes years; such delays can discourage litigants and dim their hopes of receiving any satisfaction if they pursue their cases.

Victimology

Scholarly interest in the study of the relationship between the criminal and the victim emerged in the 1940s with the pioneering studies of Mendelsohn, von Hentig, and Ellenberger, followed by Wolfgang in the late 1950s. From its origin to the present day, this field has had an interdisciplinary perspective.

Benjamin Mendelsohn (1940) coined the term "victimology" and proposed that this be a new field of study—not merely a branch of criminology, but a discipline that would be "the reverse of criminology" (Schafer, 1968, p. 42). A practicing attorney as well as a scholar, Mendelsohn asked his clients approximately 300 questions and concluded that a "parallelity" seemed to appear between the biopsychosocial characteristics of the offender and those of the victim.

In his classic book, *The Criminal and His Victim*, von Hentig (1948) explores the relationship between the "doer" (criminal) and the "sufferer" (victim). He postulates that in a large percentage of criminal cases, the victim shares the responsibility for his or her victimization. Such notions are repudiated by modern victimology research. He concludes that the personality characteristics of some crime victims may contribute to their victimization, while others may become victims because of the community in which they live.

Mendelsohn and von Hentig were the two pioneer victimologists to develop victim typologies. Mendelsohn (1956, pp. 25-26) classifies victims into six types based on the culpability of the criminal vis-à-vis the victim. His typology distributes responsibility or culpability along a continuum marked by the degree of the victim's contribution to the crime:

(1) "completely innocent victim"
(2) "victim with minor guilt" and victim due to his or her own ignorance

(3) "victim as guilty as the offender" (e.g., voluntary victim)

(4) "victim more guilty than the offender" (e.g., the provoker or imprudent victim who encourages someone to commit a crime)

(5) "most guilty victim" and "victim who is guilty alone" (e.g., the violent perpetrator who is killed by another person in self-defense)

(6) simulating and "imaginary victim" (e.g., the paranoid, hysterical persons or senile individuals)

von Hentig's (1948) typology includes 13 categories and is based on psychological, social, and biological factors. Schafer (1968, pp. 43-44) lists von Hentig's categories as follows:

(1) the young

(2) the female

(3) the old

(4) the mentally defective and other mentally deranged

(5) immigrants

(6) minorities

(7) dull normals

(8) the depressed

(9) the acquisitive

(10) the wanton

(11) the lonesome and the heartbroken

(12) tormentors

(13) the blocked, exempted, and fighting

Henri Ellenberger (1954), a prominent psychoanalyst, focused his research on the psychological relationship between the criminal and the victim. In his book, *Relations*, he states that it is important for criminologists to focus special attention on what he refers to as "victimogenesis" rather than on "criminogenesis." He urged criminologists to study the potential dangers to which victims are subjected because of their occupation, social class, or physical condition.

The first systematic study of victim precipitation was conducted by Wolfgang (1958, 1959) and focused on criminal homicides committed in the city of Philadelphia and recorded by the Philadelphia Homicide Squad from January 1948 to December 1952. Most research conducted prior to Wolfgang's sociological analysis of criminal homicide studied either the victim or the offender. Wolfgang was the first to study the victim and the offender as separate and distinct entities and as "mutual participants in the homicide" (Wolfgang, 1967, p. 17). During the study period of 1948 to 1952, there were a reported 588 homicide victims. Since in some cases several people were involved in committing a homicide, a total of 621 persons were arrested and taken into custody.

Wolfgang is credited with coining the term "victim-precipitated homicide" to refer to those cases in which it has been found that "the victim is a direct, positive precipitator in the crime—the first to use physical force in the homicide drama" (Wolfgang, 1967, pp. 24, 72). The Philadelphia study found that just over one-fourth (150 or 26%) of the 588 homicides were victim precipitated.

When comparing the victim-precipitated (VP) group with the non-victim-precipitated cases, Wolfgang (1967, pp. 86-87) found "significantly higher proportions of the following characteristics among VP homicide":

- Black victims
- Black offenders
- male victims
- female offenders
- stabbings
- victim-offender relationship involving male victims of female offenders
- mate slayings
- husbands who are victims in mate slayings
- alcohol in the homicide situation
- alcohol in the victim
- victims with a previous arrest record for assault

Hepburn and Voss (1968) studied victim-precipitated homicides in Chicago and reported that 38% of the murders they studied involved victim precipitation. Mulvihill, Tumin, and Curtis (1969) prepared a staff report for the National Commission on the Causes and Prevention of Violence (NCCPV) based on their study of five major crimes of violence in 17 cities, in which they analyzed a 10% sample of all police reports. For those cases cleared by arrest, the researchers conclude that the percentages of victims sharing responsibility with the offenders due to facilitation, precipitation, or provocation are as follows: homicide cases, 22%; aggravated assault cases, 14%; armed robbery, 11%; forcible rape, 4%; unarmed robbery, 6% (Curtis, 1974).

Silverman (1974) and other criminologists have noted how discrepancies and cultural differences can result in different perceptions and indicators of victim precipitation. Silverman points out that it is almost impossible to replicate studies of victim precipitation because of the latitude of interpreting and assigning motives to the victim.

Emergence of Rape Crisis Centers
and Battered Women's Shelters

By the mid-1970s, the women's liberation movement had begun to correct the myth that the female victim of rape had in some way provoked the assault against her. Women's groups, women's counseling centers, and rape crisis centers were developed by grass-roots organizations in local communities and at major universities and medical centers across the United States. Numerous magazine and newspaper articles, books, and research studies were published giving recognition to the prevalence of rape in society and to the need to report rapes to the police. With pressure from feminist leaders and victim advocates, women became more willing to report rapes to the police, law enforcement officers became more sensitive and understanding of rape victims, and hospital emergency room staff, social workers, and prosecutors developed coordinated crisis intervention programs for the victims.

By the late 1970s, rape crisis centers were developed as a result of federal funding from the now-defunct Law Enforcement Assistance Administration (LEAA) and from the National Center for the Prevention and Control of Rape (of the National Institute of Mental Health). Emergency shelters and crisis intervention programs for battered women received substantial staffing support as a result of funding from the Comprehensive Employment and Training Administration (CETA) (Roberts, 1981). Other funding sources for victim services were community development and ACTION grants and state human service block grants. Most of these funding sources have been dismantled or significantly cut back as a result of the Reagan administration's fiscal cuts. During the early 1980s, family violence and victim assistance programs in several states had difficulty staying open, and those that could not locate alternative funding had to close (Roberts, 1990).

The victims' movement is now well established and on solid footing. In recent years, through state general-revenue grants and innovative state-authorized funding sources, family violence and victim assistance programs have received increased and stable funding. As of 1989, 48 states had provisions for the funding of domestic violence intervention programs, 34 states had funding mechanisms for general victim service and victim/witness assistance programs at the local level, and 25 states had provided funding for local sexual assault crisis services. The primary state mechanisms for raising funds designated for family violence and victim assistance programs include the following:

Fixed penalty assessment on convicted offenders of criminal offenses and/or
traffic offenses
variable penalty assessments levied by judges on convicted felons
a surcharge on all criminal fines
state income tax check-offs
bail forfeiture funding, marriage, divorce, birth, and death certificate surcharges
wages earned by convicted offenders
notoriety-for-profit laws
alcohol taxes

Recognition of the need for and actual establishment of crisis intervention
for survivors of the battering syndrome has increased dramatically since the
mid-1970s. While there were only seven emergency shelters for battered women
and four police-based crisis intervention programs nationwide in 1974, by 1987
there were more than 1,250 emergency shelters and crisis services for battered
women and their children (Roberts, 1990).

A small number of victimologists continue to build on the original investigations of von Hentig, Mendelsohn, and Wolfgang by studying how victims may
contribute to their own personal vulnerability and victimization. These researchers
focus on such issues as determining victim proneness, the frequency of shared
responsibility, and victim facilitation, precipitation, and provocation. Recently,
a growing group of victimologists have been involved in studying the many ways
of lessening the physical, psychological, medical, and financial losses of violent
crime victims. This new breed of victimologist has begun to study the effectiveness of domestic violence programs, sexual assault treatment programs, victim services, and witness assistance in lessening victims' trauma and in facilitating
the recovery process. These researchers are also beginning to evaluate the effectiveness of private and state-operated programs to compensate victims for their
medical and financial losses.

Victim Compensation Legislation

During the 1960s, legislation was enacted to provide monetary compensation to crime victims, particularly victims of violent crime. The writings of
Margery Fry (1957), an English penal reformer, have been recognized as a strong
early influence in urging society to compensate crime victims as a matter of
social welfare policy.

Pioneer victim compensation legislation was adopted in New Zealand in 1963.
Known as the New Zealand Criminal Injuries Compensation Act of 1963, it

resulted in the formation of the Crimes Compensation Tribunal, consisting of three members with discretionary powers to consider claims and make awards to victims who were injured as a result of any of the crimes specified in the statute (Enker, 1974). In August 1964, Great Britain established an administrative board with power to assess and award monetary compensation to crime victims (Schafer, 1968, pp. 121, 123).

The first American legislation to aid crime victims was enacted in 1965 when California passed the first statewide victim compensation legislation. This act enabled a crime victim to obtain monetary compensation for sustained injuries and medical expenses. Dependents of murder victims were also eligible for compensation. Several other states followed by passing their own victim compensation legislation: New York in 1966, Hawaii in 1967, and Massachusetts in 1968. These three victim compensation programs are based, for the most part, on the state welfare or public assistance approach rather than on requiring offenders (who are often destitute) to pay back or provide monetary compensation to victims for their crimes. By 1983, 38 states had enacted victim compensation legislation and statewide programs. As of 1989, 45 states and the District of Columbia have provided victim compensation through statewide programs for victims of violent crime. The states still without victim compensation programs are Maine, Mississippi, New Hampshire, South Dakota, and Vermont (C. Edmunds, legislative specialist, NOVA, personal communication, August 7, 1989).

Much criticism has been leveled at victim compensation practices, particularly when the programs were in their infancy, because of the extremely small number of victims who knew about and applied for compensation and the even smaller number of victims who actually received these funds. Elias (1984) has charged that less than 1% of all violent crime victims had applied for compensation and that only about one in three had received payment—reimbursement that was generally inadequate for the losses sustained.

Although problems still persist, victim compensation programs have increased the number of awards made in the past few years. For example, during the 1988 fiscal year, the Ohio Crime Victims Compensation Program had approximately $18 million to allocate to victims. While this would appear to be a sizable amount of money, the low number of victims applying and the high rate of denials resulted in over two-thirds of the funds not being awarded. Of the 2,749 victims who applied for compensation during the 1987 fiscal year, less than half (47.6%, or 1,310 persons) were given compensation, for a total disbursement of $4.9 million, or an average award of $3,740 (Fiely, 1988).

McCormack's (1989) study of New Jersey's Violent Crimes Compensation Board found that only about 8% of the 45,000 persons who were victimized by violent crime in 1987 had filed compensation claims. McCormack believes that a primary reason for the small percentage of claims filed is that New Jersey has only two Compensation Board offices. He recommends that additional community-based offices be opened in high-crime urban neighborhoods so that victims can have improved access to compensation claim services.

Victim Service and Witness Assistance Programs

Where do we stand now, more than a decade after the beginning of the victims' movement? Victim/witness programs exist all over the country, with more being developed every year. The ignorance and indifference of court personnel are being replaced by a genuine desire to correct the injustices that crime victims suffer. What can victims across the country expect from their local services?

I designed the National Survey of Victim Service and Assistance Programs to assess our current position and to calculate how far we have to go. Although services for the perpetrator have been available for more than a century, general services for victims of violence have become available only since the mid-1970s. At the end of 1975, there were just 23 victim programs in the United States; by 1986, that number had grown to more than 600.

Origin of the Study

I began the study by looking at the history of victim programs. A number of the early victim/witness assistance programs received their initial funding from the now-defunct Law Enforcement Assistance Administration, a federal agency. During the mid-1970s, prosecutors' offices developed victim programs in a number of major metropolitan areas. Other victim service programs cropped up in county or city law enforcement agencies and, to a lesser extent, in family service agencies and not-for-profit organizations. However, the most significant proliferation of victim/witness assistance programs occurred in prosecutors' offices. After the demise of LEAA, these programs were funded by county or state allocation (such as Title XX block grants).

Over the years, a difference evolved between victim *service* programs and victim/witness *assistance* programs. The former focused primarily on providing victims with crisis counseling and referral to community services but also provided a range of additional services, such as accompaniment to court, repair or replacement of broken locks, and emergency financial aid.

In contrast, victim/witness assistance programs tried to alleviate the stress and trauma of victims and witnesses who testified in court. For example, prior to the court date, program staff might accompany victims to an empty courtroom to orient them to the physical layout of the court and to familiarize them with courtroom procedures. Other services might include transportation to court, child care during the court appearance, apprising the victim of the progress of the case, and referral to social service agencies.

At the time the study began, the information available on both types of programs generally consisted of a list of program names and addresses. Though many programs provided brochures describing their services, no national survey had been conducted of the organizational structures, functions, and services provided by these newly emerging programs. This study provides the first national perspective. It examines trends, patterns of program development, and the current state of the art in victim services.

Types of Services Provided

Eleven types of services were identified by the responding programs. The services provided most frequently are as follows:

explaining the court process (131, or 71.2%)

making referrals to other agencies (126, or 68.4%)

providing court escort (120, or 65.2%)

helping the victim fill out victim compensation forms (118, or 64.1%)

educating the public (112, or 60.9%)

advocating with an employer on behalf of the victim (111, or 60.3%)

providing transportation to court (109, or 59.2%)

Only a small percentage of respondents indicated that they were providing the following three services:

repairing or replacing broken locks (23, or 12.5%)

providing emergency money or food vouchers (15, or 24.4%)

providing child care while the parent is in court (69, or 37.5%)

Funding

According to the report of the President's Task Force on Victims of Crime, since 1980 victim advocacy services within the justice system have doubled (U.S. Department of Justice, 1986). The number and size of victim/witness programs have increased with funds provided through federal and state legislation and through local or county budget appropriations. Many programs that were originally staffed primarily by volunteers became eligible for funding under the provisions of the federal Victims of Crime Act of 1984 and the Justice Assistance Act of 1984. Furthermore, since 1982, laws have been enacted in 21 states providing for crime victim services.

Fines charged to perpetrators of federal crimes have been a significant new source of funding for local programs. In 1985 alone, $41,270,000 was collected through this method under the Victims of Crime Act. These funds, shared by the states on a population formula basis, have enabled many state programs to expand their services to crime victims. For example, in 1986 the state of Illinois more than tripled the amount it had previously spent on victim aid.

The survey respondents were asked to identify their sources of funding and the proportion of their operating budget supplied by each source. A total of 84% (154) of the programs provided information on their sources of funding. While many of the programs had more than one funding source, many relied heavily on public funding in the form of state block grants and county general-revenue funds. In fact, 95% of the respondents indicated that they received all or a substantial part of their monies through state or county funds.

The responding program with the highest budget (more than $3 million annually) was the Victim Services Agency in New York City. A total of 13 respondents reported annual budgets in excess of $300,000.

Staffing

The predominant staffing pattern consisted of full-time professionals. Three-fourths of the programs had small staffs of one to five full-time employees. Of those programs with larger staffs, 16% employed six to ten workers and the remaining programs had eleven or more employees.

The highest degree earned by most coordinators was a bachelor's (44%) or a master's (42%) degree. At the bachelor's level, 96% of the degrees were B.A. or B.S. and 3% were social work degrees. At the master's level, M.A. or M.S. degrees were held by 55%, social work degrees by 32%, and public administration degrees by 8% of the coordinators.

The professional degrees earned by staff were reported by 163 programs. The largest proportion, 48%, held bachelor's degrees. Social work degrees were held by 25% of staff members, with 15% having M.S.W. degrees and 10% having B.S.W. degrees. Master's degrees in criminal justice, guidance and counseling, or sociology accounted for another 13%, while 4.4% had J.D. degrees. Almost 8% did not have college degrees.

Estimating the size of staff based on the number of paid employees could be deceiving. Many programs supplemented staff through the recruitment and training of volunteers. Slightly more than half (52.1%) of the programs studied used volunteers. Programs with smaller paid staffs had a tendency to rely on volunteers. Most of the victim services that recruited volunteers had fewer than ten volunteers on staff at a time.

Conclusion

The development and expansion of victim compensation and victim assistance programs have come a long way during the past two decades. With the rapid proliferation of programs nationwide during the 1980s, it is easy to forget that we are really just beyond the early stages of program development. Hardly any local, regional, or national evaluations have been conducted on victim compensation or victim assistance programs. The time seems ripe for planning and conducting a national evaluation of victim assistance programs. It is important to determine which types of services are most effective in reducing symptoms and increasing the recovery of crime victims.

I believe that the first step in planning regional and national evaluation studies is to publish baseline information on the programs currently in operation throughout the United States. The full findings of my national survey of the organizational structures and functions of 184 victim and witness assistance programs are presented in Chapters 2 through 6 of this book. These chapters document the wide variation that exists in the delivery of services among different types of victim and witness assistance programs. The three primary types of program auspices are county prosecutor-based, police-based, and not-for-profit agencies. As will be shown, the programs have a number of self-reported strengths and problems. The strengths include providing personal and immediate assistance to victims 24 hours a day, assisting victims in completing victim compensation forms, orienting witnesses to the criminal court process, and providing court escort. The major problems of the programs studied include insufficient funding to hire needed staff, lack of adequate office space, and attrition of volunteers.

References

Amir, M. (1971). *Patterns in forcible rape*. Chicago: University of Chicago Press.

Bureau of Justice Statistics. (1987). *Lifetime likelihood of victimization* (Technical Report NCJ 104274). Washington, DC: Government Printing Office.

Burgess, A. W., & Holmstrom, L. L. (1979). Adaptive strategies and recovery from rape. *American Journal of Psychiatry, 136*, 1278-1282.

Curtis, L. (1974). Victim precipitation and violent crime. *Social Problems, 21*, 594-605.

Debo, A. (1970). *A history of Indians of the United States*. Norman: University of Oklahoma Press.

Elias, R. (1984). Alienating the victim: Compensation and victim attitude. *Journal of Social Issues*, *40*, 128-137.

Elias, R. (1986). *The politics of victimization*. New York: Oxford University Press.

Ellenberger, H. (1954). Psychological relationships between the criminal and his victim. *Revue Internationale de Criminologie et de Police Technique*, *2*, 103-121.

Enker, A. N. (1974). A comparative review of compensation for victims of crime. In I. Drapkin & E. Viano (Eds.), *Victimology: A new focus* (Vol. 2, pp. 121-138). Lexington, MA: D. C. Heath.

Fehrenbach, T. R. (1974). *Comanches: The destruction of a people*. New York: Alfred A. Knopf.

Fiely, D. (1988, April 15). After the crime: Court has millions for victims, *if* they can get it. *Columbus Dispatch*, p. F13.

Friedman, K., et al. (1982). *Victims and helpers: Reactions to crime*. New York: Victim Services Agency. (mimeo)

Fry, M. (1957, July 7). Justice for victims. *Observer* (London), p. 8.

Geis, G. (1967). State compensation to victims of violent crime. In President's Commission on Law Enforcement and Administration of Justice (Ed.), *Task force report: Crime and its impact—an assessment*. Washington, DC: Government Printing Office.·

Hepburn, J., & Voss, H. (1968). Patterns of criminal homicide: A comparison of Chicago and Philadelphia. *Journal of Criminal Law, Criminology and Police Science*, *59*(4), 499-508.

Kahn, A. S. (Ed.). (1984). *Final report of the American Psychological Association Task Force on the Victims of Crime and Violence*. Washington, DC: American Psychological Association.

Lee, J. A. B., & Rosenthal, S. J. (1983, December). Working with victims of violent assault. *Social Casework*, pp. 593-601.

Mendelsohn, B. (1940). Rape in criminology. *Giustizia Penale*.

Mendelsohn, B. (1956, July-September). The victimology. *Etudes Internationals de Psycho-Sociologie Criminelle*, pp. 25-26.

McCormack, R. J. (1989, April 1). *A perspective on United States crime victim assistance*. Paper presented at the annual meetings of the Academy of Criminal Justice Sciences, Washington, DC.

Mueller, G. (1965). Compensation for victims of crime: Thought before action. *Minnesota Law Review*, *50*, 213-221.

Mueller, G. O. W., & Cooper, H. H. A. (1974). Society and the victim: Alternative responses. In I. Drapkin & E. Viano (Eds.), *Victimology: A new focus (Vol. 2, pp. 85-102)*. Lexington, MA: D. C. Heath.

Mulvihill, D., Tumin, M., & Curtis, L. (1969). *The offender and his victim* (Staff report prepared for the National Commission on the Causes and Prevention of Violence). Washington, DC: Government Printing Office.

National Organization for Victim Assistance. (1983). *The victim service system: A guide to action*. Washington, DC: Author.

National Organization for Victim Assistance. (1986, 1987). *Victim rights and services: A legislative directory*. Washington, DC: Author.

President's Task Force on Victims of Crime. (1982). *Final report*. Washington, DC: Government Printing Office.

Roberts, A. R. (1981). *Sheltering battered women*. New York: Springer.

Roberts, A. R. (1986). Policies, programs, and services for victims of violent crimes. *Emotional First-Aid*, *3*(3).

Roberts, A. R. (1990). *Crisis intervention handbook: Assessment, treatment and research*. Belmont, CA: Wadsworth.

Schafer, S. (1968). *The victim and his criminal*. New York: Random House.

Silverman, R. A. (1974). Victim precipitation: An examination of the concept. In I. Drapkin &
    E. Viano (Eds.), *Victimology: A new focus (Vol. 1, pp. 99-109)*. Lexington, MA: D. C. Heath.
U.S. Department of Justice, Office of Justice Programs. (1986). *A report on the President's Task Force
    on Victims of Crime: Four years later*. Washington, DC: Government Printing Office.
von Hentig, H. (1948). *The criminal and his victim: Studies in the sociobiology of crime*. New Haven,
    CT: Yale University Press.
Wolfgang, M. E. (1958). *Patterns of criminal homicide*. Philadelphia: University of Pennsylvania Press.
Wolfgang, M. E. (1959). Suicide by means of victim precipitated homicide. *Journal of Clinical and
    Experimental Psychopathology and Quarterly Review of Psychiatry and Neurology, 20*, 335-349.
Wolfgang, M. E. (1965). Victim compensation in crimes of personal violence. *Minnesota Law Review,
    50*, 229-241.
Wolfgang, M. E. (1967). *Analytical categories for research in victimization*. Munich: Kriminologische
    Wegzeichen.
Wolfgang, M. E., & Ferracuti, F. (1967). *The subculture of violence*. London: Tavistock.

PART II

National Survey of the Organizational Structure and Functions of 184 Victim Service and Witness Assistance Programs

2

Background, Functions, and Services
of Victim Service and Witness Assistance Programs

What services exist for the myriad victims of violent crime in our society? In years past, the pain and suffering of crime victims was generally met with indifference by court clerks, the police, and prosecutors and their staffs. However, this insensitivity is now being replaced by a genuine desire to correct the injustices that have been perpetrated against crime victims. Much of the credit for this new outlook should go to responsive prosecutors, police administrators, and victim service and victim/witness assistance programs.

Background Information

A number of the early victim/witness assistance programs received their initial funding from the now-defunct Law Enforcement Assistance Administration (LEAA). During the mid-1970s, these programs were developed by prosecutors' offices in a number of major metropolitan areas. Some victim service programs were also developed by county or city law enforcement agencies and, in a small number of cities, programs were developed by not-for-profit social service agencies (in conjunction with local prosecutors' offices and/or police departments). Across the nation, the most significant proliferation of victim/witness assistance programs has been in prosecutors' offices. After the demise of LEAA, these programs were funded by county or state allocations (such as Title XX block grants, general state revenues, and penalty assessments and fines on criminal offenders).

There is a clear difference between victim service programs and victim/witness assistance programs. The former focus primarily on providing victims with crisis counseling, concrete services, and/or referral to community services. To a limited extent, victim service programs offer a range of additional services, including the provision of volunteer advocates to accompany victims when testifying in court, repair or replacement of broken locks, and emergency funds.

In contrast, the major goal of victim/witness assistance programs is to alleviate the stress and trauma for victims and witnesses who testify in court. For example, prior to the court date, program staff may accompany a child or elderly victim to an empty courtroom to orient the individual to the physical layout and courtroom procedures. Other services may include transportation to court, child care while the victim or witness is appearing in court, apprising the victim of the progress of the court case and changes in the trial date, and referral to social service agencies.

The information that has been made available on the nation's victim/witness assistance programs to date consists primarily of listings of programs' names and addresses (though many of the programs do disseminate brochures describing their services). However, a national survey that reviews and analyzes the organizational structure, functions, and services provided by these programs has not previously been published. This study provides the first national perspective on victim/witness assistance programs. It examines trends, patterns of program development, and the current state of the art.

Survey Methodology

A listing of 312 victim and witness assistance programs was developed by cross-indexing two lists of such programs: a listing obtained from the U.S. Department of Justice's Office of Crime Victims and a membership directory provided by the National Organization for Victim Assistance (NOVA).[1]

A detailed four-page questionnaire was developed, pretested (with four administrators of victim assistance programs in Indianapolis and Cincinnati), revised, and mailed with a cover letter to 312 programs during the first week of November 1985. Within a month after the mailing, the post office had returned seven questionnaires because the addressee was unknown. The result was a sample of 305 victim assistance programs. A follow-up letter and another copy of the questionnaire were sent to the nonrespondents in early December 1985. By the summer of 1986, a reply had been received from 184 of the 305 programs constituting the study sample—a 60.3% response rate. Of the 184 respondents, there were 127 prosecutor or state's attorney-based programs, 23 nonprofit social service or criminal justice agency programs, 13 police-based programs, 8 county probation-based programs, and 13 other types of programs (see Table 2.1).

TABLE 2.1: Auspices of Responding Programs (N = 184)

	Number of Programs	Percentage
City or county prosecutor	107	58
State's attorney	21	11
Nonprofit social service agency	20	11
Police department	13	7
County probation department	8	4
County criminal justice or social service agency	5	3
Hospital	3	2
Nonprofit criminal justice agency	3	2
U.S. Attorney's Office	1	0.5
Miscellaneous	2	1
No information given	1	0.5
Total	184	100

The study examined whether the programs operated independently or were a unit/program of a large agency. The overwhelming majority (156, or 84.7%) were separate components or relatively autonomous units of larger agencies. Generally, the result was more secure and stable county or city funding and a greater reliance on paid staff. In contrast, many of the independent grass-roots victim assistance organizations relied heavily on volunteers and private donations.

The respondents were from all parts of the United States and represented a wide geographic distribution. There were respondents from 42 states, representing all 12 major regions of the United States. Those states with the largest number of responding programs were California (30), Wisconsin (19), New York (11), New Jersey (10), Florida (10), and Ohio (9). The following states were underrepresented, having no respondents: Arkansas, Idaho, Louisiana, Mississippi, North Dakota, South Dakota, Vermont, and West Virginia.

With regard to demographics, the victim assistance programs were distributed across jurisdictions that varied considerably in total population. The two largest areas were New York City and Los Angeles County, California, with populations of 8 million and 5 million, respectively. The two smallest jurisdictions were Eddyville, Kentucky (population 2,000), and Crescent City, California (population 3,000). Of the responding programs, 55 were located in large metropolitan areas, with populations over 500,000. Of these, 7 programs were in highly populated cities, that is, cities with populations of 2 million or more.

At the other end of the continuum, 40 programs were located in small towns with populations of 60,000 or fewer. The remaining 89 programs were in small and medium-sized cities with populations ranging from 61,000 to 499,000.

Responses were received from administrative directors and coordinators of victim assistance programs in all 12 regions of the United States. The most representative regions were Region V, the Great Lakes states, with 39 programs; Region IX, western states, with 37 programs; and Region II, northeastern states, with 21 programs. Those regions with a dearth of victim assistance programs, which were somewhat underrepresented, were Region VI, southwestern states, 6 programs; and Region VII, midwestern states, with 4 programs. Table 2.2 depicts the responses by region and state.

All respondents indicated that they provide assistance to witnesses and/or victims of crimes. The responding programs represent a cross-section of victim service and witness assistance programs in urban, suburban, and rural areas in all parts of the United States.

Recognition of the victim's need for crisis counseling, social services, court advocacy, and financial compensation is a recent phenomenon. Whereas services for the perpetrator have been available for more than a century, services for victims of violent crimes have been available only since the 1970s. At the end of 1975 there were only 23 programs serving crime victims; by 1987, that number had grown to over 600 nationwide. The study data indicate that more than four-fifths (81.7%) of victim/witness assistance programs were developed between 1977 and 1985.

Information collected from the 184 completed questionnaires, as well as from interviews with staff at the victim service and witness assistance programs in Cincinnati, Indianapolis, Minneapolis, St. Paul, and New York City, indicates that there are several key organizational characteristics and functions of the programs. These were used as the primary categories for the analysis, as follows:

the year the program began
the total number of victims served
the services provided by the programs
the location and type of crisis intervention
methods and auspices of witness notification systems
child-care services
specialized services for elderly victims
services related to elder abuse and neglect
sources of referral
sources of funding
staffing pattern
educational background of staff

TABLE 2.2: Regional Representation of Victim Assistance Programs Surveyed

Region	Number of Programs	Region	Number of Programs
Region I		Region VI	
Connecticut	1	Arkansas	0
Maine	3	Louisiana	0
Massachusetts	4	New Mexico	2
New Hampshire	1	Oklahoma	2
Rhode Island	1	Texas	2
Vermont	0	Total	6
Total	10		
		Region VII	
Region II		Iowa	1
New Jersey	10	Kansas	1
New York	11	Missouri	1
Total	21	Nebraska	1
		Total	4
Region III			
Delaware	1		
District of Columbia	1	Region VIII	
Maryland	5	Colorado	5
Pennsylvania	6	Montana	2
Virginia	6	North Dakota	0
West Virginia	0	South Dakota	0
Total	19	Utah	2
		Wyoming	1
Region IV		Total	10
Alabama	1		
Florida	10	Region IX	
Georgia	3	Arizona	3
Kentucky	4	California	30
Mississippi	0	Hawaii	2
North Carolina	2	Nevada	2
South Carolina	2	Total	37
Tennessee	1		
Total	23	Region X	
		Alaska	1
Region V		Idaho	0
Illinois	3	Oregon	7
Indiana	2	Washington	7
Michigan	5	Total	15
Minnesota	1		
Ohio	9		
Wisconsin	19		
Total	39		

staffing, annual budget, and number of victims served in relation to the size of the city where programs were located

the programs' self-reports of strongest features, major problems, and needed changes

The Year the Program Began

We have come a long way from 1969, when the first program was developed (see Table 2.3), to the present, when there are over 600 victim service and witness assistance programs nationwide (NOVA, 1987). The trend in the number of programs established each year reflects growing recognition of the needs of victims and witnesses. Increased availability of information about the needs of victims, lobbying efforts by victim coalitions, and new legislation on state and federal levels have resulted in a steady development of new programs.

Table 2.3 shows the program's year of origin as reported by 179 of the 184 responding programs. The first such program—located in the courthouse at Yakima, Washington—was developed in 1969. The second program, called the Crime Victims Center of Chester County, Pennsylvania, began in 1972. By the end of 1974, nine more programs had been established in the following cities: Boston, Massachusetts; Dayton, Ohio; Des Moines, Iowa; Gainesville and Miami, Florida; Pittsburgh, Pennsylvania; Portland, Oregon; and San Pablo and Santa Monica, California. The mission of four of these nine early programs was to provide crisis intervention services to rape victims, while the other five programs were developed with the broader mission of serving all victims of violent crimes. Of the five general victim assistance programs, three were developed by county prosecutors and the remaining two were under the auspices of a county social service department.

Twelve (6.9%) programs began in 1975 (e.g., Milwaukee, Wisconsin, and Brooklyn, New York) and fourteen (7.8%) more began in 1977. In its 1977 Statutes, California established its Victim/Witness Assistance Program by funding six full-service assistance centers with the help of a supplemental grant from LEAA. The purpose of these pilot centers was "to provide ways of improving the attitudes of these citizen victims/witnesses toward the criminal justice system and to provide for faster and more complete recovery from the effects of crime" (California Victim/Witness Assistance Program, 1985). By 1978, ten additional California agencies developed and began operating victim/witness centers with LEAA funds. Wisconsin, in May of 1980, became the first state to enact a "Victim/Witness Bill of Rights," which enabled state reimbursement of up to 90% for county expenditures for victim/witness programs (Chapter 950, Wisconsin Statutes). The greatest number (over two-fifths) of responding programs were developed during the four-year period from 1978 to 1981, when a total of 74 new programs began.

TABLE 2.3: Years Programs Began

Year	Number of Programs	Percentage[a]
1969	1	.5
1972	1	.5
1974	9	5.0
1975	12	6.7
1976	9	5.0
1977	14	7.8
1978	19	10.6
1979	21	11.7
1980	14	7.8
1981	20	11.1
1982	14	7.8
1983	17	9.4
1984	17	9.4
1985	11	6.1
Total	179	99.4

a. Percentages are based on 179 responses.

Background on Federal and State Funding
for Programs Serving Crime Victims

In 1975, the National District Attorneys' Association (NDAA) developed eight victim/witness assistance programs in prosecutors' offices, all of which were funded by the Law Enforcement Assistance Administration. The success of these programs resulted in an NDAA (1987) recommendation to the nation's prosecutors "that every prosecutor focus such attention on the needs of victims and witnesses in their respective jurisdictions."

Information from the American Institutes for Research 1980 national assessment of victim/witness assistance projects indicated that the majority of the projects that developed between 1974 and 1979 received their initial funding from LEAA (Cronin & Bourque, 1981). In 1980, with the demise of LEAA, federal grants to victim assistance programs declined. Existing programs tried to make up for the loss of LEAA monies by requesting county or city funding, but local governments were frequently unable to allocate sufficient funds. As a result, there was a significant reduction in the programs' budgets, and certain services had to be discontinued (e.g., child care for witnesses' children and lock repair for burglary victims).

In the early 1980s, soon after the LEEA funding cuts, a number of states enacted legislation to fund programs aiding victims and witnesses. For example, the Nebraska Legislature passed a bill that created and funded the Nebraska Crime Victim and Witness Assistance Program and established a "bill of rights" for victims and witnesses of crimes; the National Organization for Victim Assistance published a comprehensive model of services for victim/witness assistance programs in 1981.

Several federal and state initiatives led to the growth and increased funding of victim service programs between 1982 and 1985. In 1982 the federal government brought nationwide attention to the needs and rights of victims and witnesses when the President's Task Force on Victims of Crime issued a report that recommended actions at federal, state, and local levels. The Victim/Witness Protection Act of 1982 was passed. This act also required the U.S. attorney general to develop additional guidelines and legislative proposals to aid federal victims and witnesses.

The Federal Comprehensive Crime Control Act of 1984 created major reforms throughout the federal criminal justice system. Federal funding for the improvement of state and local victim/witness assistance programs became available through the Victims of Crime Act and the Justice Assistance Act, parts of the 1984 Comprehensive Crime Control Act.

Between 1981 and 1985, 28 states were able to make some provision for the funding of general victim or victim/witness services (as distinguished from the targets of special funding such as services to victims of child sexual assault, domestic violence, or child abuse) through local victim/witness programs. The trend among state legislatures has been to raise the funds for these programs and services by earmarking a percentage of penalty assessments and/or fines on criminal offenders to these programs. Of the 28 states, 19 fund victim services through penalty assessments and fines, while the remaining 9 states fund victim services through general state revenues (M. Young, executive director, NOVA, personal communication, December 1985).

By 1986 the funding and stability of victim service and witness assistance programs had increased dramatically. This was largely the result of increased public awareness and growing support from police, prosecutors, judges, and state and local victim rights coalitions. The National Organization for Victim Assistance, the President's Task Force on Victims of Crime, and passage of the Victims of Crime Act also played significant roles. With the commitment and recognition of legislators and the federal government of the victims' rights movement had come a marked increase in the size and visibility of local programs.

Types of Services Provided

The services provided by victim/witness assistance programs are listed in Table 2.4. The overwhelming majority of programs indicated that they provide five or more of the eleven services listed in the questionnaire. The four most fre-

TABLE 2.4: Services Provided by Programs

Type of Service	Number of Programs	Percentage
Explain court process	131	71
Make referrals	126	69
Provide court escort	120	65
Help with victim compensation applications	118	64
Public education	112	61
Assist with employers	111	60
Provide transportation to court	109	59
Provide crisis intervention	99	54
Provide child care	69	38
Provide emergency money	45	25
Repair locks	22	12

NOTE: 184 respondents supplied 1,063 responses.

quently mentioned services are explaining the court process (131, or 71%), making referrals (126, or 69%), providing a court escort for the victim (120, or 65%) and helping the victim fill out victim compensation applications (118, or 64%).

The three service areas with the fewest responses were providing child care while the parent appeared in court (69, or 38%) providing small amounts of money on an emergency basis (45, or 25%), and repairing or replacing broken door locks (22, or 12%). Some respondents recognized the need for such services as repairing locks, but stated that there was no money in their budgets to pay for them.

Explaining the Court Process

Lack of knowledge about court processes and procedures can cause confusion and emotional stress that ultimately discourages the victim/witness from participating in the legal system. In order to ensure successful prosecution of criminal offenders, it is imperative that the victim/witness gains an understanding of what to expect from the justice system and what is expected of him or her at any point in the court process. The more informed the witness, the better he or she is able to assist in the prosecution process. In this survey, the most frequently reported service (provided by 131, or 71.2%, of the programs) was explaining the court process.

Many victim/witness programs provide victims and witnesses with a pamphlet that informs them of their rights, introduces the program, emphasizes the importance of their participation in the justice system, and outlines the court process. The pamphlet may also include information on the roles of courtroom personnel (judge, assistant district attorney, defense attorney, bailiff, and so on), suggestions to aid the individual on the witness stand, and answers to practical questions (directions and map to the courthouse, availability of parking and bus service, what to do with children). The pamphlet may be given to the victim/witness by the police or by a crisis intervention worker at the scene of the crime or be available at information desks in police and court buildings.

Questions about the court process, what will happen next, and case-specific questions such as the bail status of the defendant or fear of retaliation are addressed in a number of ways, including a notification letter, the initial screening conference, and/or telephone contact initiated either by the victim/witness or by the victim/witness assistance program. Many court-related concerns and questions are addressed during the course of court proceedings through personal contact with an advocate.

Preparation for court generally occurs prior to the first court appearance. An advocate meets with the victim/witness to outline the legal proceedings that will occur in court that day and describes what to expect and what will be expected of him or her. In some programs the advocate shows the victim/witness the empty courtroom, explains the duties of court personnel, and points out the location of each in the room. In other programs the advocate accompanies the individual to court on the day when the testimony will be given, to provide information and support.

The advocate helps the victim/witness to overcome fear or uncertainty that could interfere with the testimony by providing specific information on the court process. The advocate provides advice on issues such as how to conduct oneself in court (neat dress, respectful attitude, careful listening to and answering of questions, remaining calm, telling the truth) and what to expect (the usual length of time on the witness stand, the types of questions that will be asked). The advocate also answers any questions the victim/witness may have, such as whether the courtroom will be open to anyone and whether the defendant will be in close proximity to the victim in court. In addition, the victim/witness may prepare for court through a role play in which the advocate poses the types of questions that the attorneys are likely to ask.

Court Escort

Court escort originally meant providing transportation to and from court. Today this service includes accompanying the victim/witness to and from the courtroom and remaining with the individual to provide moral support and to explain and interpret court proceedings. Escort services are especially appropriate for a victim/witness who is (a) intimidated or harassed by the defendant or the defendant's friends, (b) elderly, (c) handicapped, or (d) reluctant to leave home or distressed about participating in court. Domestic violence, sexual assault, and child abuse victims often request the companionship and support of an advocate or volunteer in the courtroom. Court escort, when necessary or requested, is provided by 65% of the respondents.

In Savannah, Georgia, volunteers for the Victim/Witness Assistance Program perform the following court escort duties:

> Volunteers accompany victims and witnesses to courtroom on the day they are to testify; sit with them in the witness waiting rooms off the courtrooms until time to testify; and sit with them in court when appropriate and when desired. Volunteers also accompany them to the Assistant D.A.'s office for interview, to wait during court breaks, bring lunch to them if they do not feel like going out publicly just after testifying, etc.

Individuals who act as court escorts must have a thorough knowledge of all stages of the criminal justice process and must respect witness confidentiality.

Transportation to Court

Of the survey respondents, 109 (59%) offer transportation services to ensure that witnesses will appear in court. The cost of transportation, difficulty in finding parking near the courthouse, difficulty in locating the proper building, and public transportation inconveniences may present obstacles to court appearance. Providing victims/witnesses with transportation services minimizes court delays due to their late arrival or nonappearance.

Services for those who are able to provide or find their own transportation may include reimbursements for mileage expenses, conveniently located reserved parking spaces, and free tokens or tickets for use of public transportation systems. Some alternative source of transportation for victims and witnesses include volunteers (accident insurance required), police officers, and local service agencies (such as the local Area Agency on Aging) that provide transportation services for their clients. In several cities, taxi companies have been persuaded to donate free taxi services for elderly or handicapped persons.

Transportation may also be provided by an advocate/volunteer as part of an escort service, involving transportation to and from the courthouse and staying with the victim or witness throughout the court proceeding.

Public Education

Public education is an important vehicle for helping crime victims. The public must be made aware of the availability of services offered by victim/witness assistance programs for these services to be utilized fully. Of the responding programs, 102 (61%) indicated that they were engaged in public education.

The primary goal of public education is to acquaint the general public with agencies that offer help or information to victims of or witnesses to a crime. Victims need to be treated with understanding by representatives of the criminal justice system or of other helping agencies with whom they come in contact after a crime has been committed. Public education can also lead to improved attitudes regarding the reporting of criminal acts, prosecuting the lawbreakers, and being willing to testify in court.

Public education efforts may focus on one or more of the following issues:

(1) awareness of the availability of the program and the services it offers

(2) awareness of issues confronted by victims and witness

(3) awareness of the trauma/crisis aspects of victimization

(4) information on crime prevention and self-defense

Educational presentations, which are generally designed either for the general public or for agency staff, utilize a variety of approaches:

(1) The public usually receives information by means of the following:
   (a) newspaper articles and advertisements;
   (b) television and radio ads, news coverage, and talk shows;
   (c) brochures distributed in the community; and
   (d) presentations to schools and community groups and to businesses.

(2) Agencies and organizations that are directly or indirectly involved with victims and witnesses receive information by means of
   (a) newsletters and brochures;
   (b) presentations at in-service and continuing education sessions; and
   (c) presentations and contacts made at regional or national conferences on victim issues.

The Maricopa County Attorney's Office Victim Witness Program in Phoenix, Arizona, considers public awareness a key part of the program. Its educational efforts directed toward the general public included the following:

(1) periodic public service announcements, talk shows, and interviews on television and radio regarding the Victim Witness Program, victim rights, and issues affecting victims

(2) presentations by advocates to schools, community and civic organizations, preschools, and parent-teacher associations

(3) advocate participation in a variety of workshops and conferences

(4) participation each spring with other agencies in local crime-prevention fairs held at three or four different sites, which includes distributing literature and responding to questions about the criminal justice process, sexual assault, child sexual abuse, and prevention

The program conducts community awareness and training programs for other agencies and individuals in three ways:

(1) It distributes a quarterly newsletter, *The Victim's Voice*, to approximately 275 agencies, legislators, and citizens who work with or are concerned about victims of crime. Each issue addresses a different type of offense or topic of interest to victims; for example, two issues have focused on domestic violence, one on the scope and dynamics of the offense, the other on the impact on the victim and issues in treatment. Other topics included crisis intervention and services in the community, homicide and the effects on the surviving family members, and the need for victim compensation.

(2) It provides ongoing training to agencies that work with victims the Center Against Sexual Assault, the Rape and Battery Hotline, Maricopa County Adult Probation Department, Child Protective Services, and the Maricopa County Sheriff's Office.

(3) It cosponsors a conference on child sexual abuse for attorneys and community professionals who work with child sexual abuse victims and/or offenders.

Public education is also considered an important element in community relations by the Racine County Victim/Witness Assistance Program in Racine, Wisconsin. Educational community relations projects have included the following:

(1) coordinating a display at the Regency Mall center during Victim Rights Week, April 1985, featuring

    (a) representatives and printed information from community groups that could assist victims

    (b) a neighborhood watch and home safety display coordinated by the crime-prevention departments of five police agencies

    (c) fingerprinting of children by the Racine Police Department

    (d) presentation of information brochures and slide project by Victim/Witness Programs staff, and

    (e) presentation of annual citizens' awards for outstanding witness cooperation by the district attorney's office;

(2) making 16 presentations to over 600 people in a eight-month period based on a ten-minute slide show depicting the criminal justice process in Racine County; and

(3) supplying information for newspaper articles and radio public service announcements aired by a local station at least once a day.

Educational efforts conducted by this program for agencies and organizations directly or indirectly involved with victims and witnesses have included the following:

(1) taping a 20-minute training video with the cooperation of the Racine Police Department for viewing by all officers (the purpose of which was to clarify the Victim/Witness Program and what it does, and to give some insights into victims' reactions to crime)

(2) participation by the coordinator of the program with other community social service agencies in communication projects such as a task force on domestic violence and a committee on sexual abuse and neglect

(3) participation by the district attorney and the Victim/Witness Program at the 1985 Judges Conference on Criminal Law and Sentencing

Assistance with Employers

The cooperation of a victim/witness may be affected by his or her concern over salary losses and negative employer attitudes due to absences at work. The individual may lose work time because of injuries and/or emotional trauma resulting from the criminal attack, follow-up investigations, and court appearances. Of the programs responding to this study, 60% (111) indicated that they intervene with employers on behalf of victims/witnesses. However, it should be recognized that programs do not intervene with every client; also when they do contact employers, they may meet with resistance and lack of cooperation.

Ideally, employers will agree to grant victims/witnesses time away from work and to pay them their regular wages (less any witness fees received). In many situations, the victim/witness merely shows the employer the subpoena and is granted release time from work to testify. However, it is advisable for victim/witness programs to arrive at an agreement with large companies that will apply to all of their employees. The National Organization for Victim Assistance (1983) suggests the following steps for developing agreements with employers:

(1) Send an initial letter to employers with information on what your program does and the importance of having witnesses involved in the criminal justice process. It is helpful to have the initial letter signed by a prominent public official (mayor, district attorney, police chief, etc).

(2) Follow the letter with a personal visit from the program director to the employer. The director should outline the consequences of criminal victimization to an individual (the victim of crime is likely to experience stress which may be a source of problems in the work environment as well as in everyday life). . . . He should mention the positive effects of providing a victim with recovery time following

a serious attack. He should then discuss the benefits of witness cooperation in prosecution and suggest that making the criminal justice system work benefits not only the community but business as well.

(3) After clearly stating the issue, the director should ask the employer to set a policy for the company which allows flexible recovery time for a victim and allows paid time off for witnesses. (p. 67)

An offer by the director to minimize absenteeism of subpoenaed employees by placing them on a telephone alert system may make an agreement more attractive to the employer. A draft agreement should be ready for signing during this visit if the employer agrees to the proposition (NOVA, 1983).

Similar contact can be made with small businesses, though creative arrangements may be necessary for businesses (such as retail or service) that rely heavily on employee attendance. Some suggestions include arranging for employees within the business to trade working hours to free the victim/witness for court and calling on retired workers with appropriate skills to fill in on a volunteer basis for the victim/witness. Labor unions may also assist in making substitute arrangements for union members who have to appear in court.

Referrals

Many victim/witness programs provide limited crisis intervention and short-term counseling through telephone coverage and personal contact with victims. A total of 123 programs (69%) stated that they make referrals for services to help victims recover from the traumatic impact of crime. In most communities a network of social service and criminal justice agencies (state, local and private) stands ready to provide services that are not covered by victim/witness programs. For the most part, only short-term assistance is needed. However, the victim's immediate needs, such as for shelter, food, clothing, transportation, medical assistance, and financial assistance, are often met through referral.

According to the Middlesex County D.A.'s Office Victim/Witness Service Bureau in Cambridge, Massachusetts, "The greatest percentage of crime victims do not require long-term, extensive services such as clinical treatment, or psychotherapy." However, some individuals, especially victims of extremely violent crimes, may need referrals for long-term assistance in such areas as individual or group therapy, family counseling, legal assistance, and assistance with medical and rehabilitation problems. These cases may require several months of monitoring and follow-up.

The referral process consists of (a) assessing the victim's needs, (b) locating appropriate helping agencies and making arrangements (appointments and possibly transportation) for the individual to receive needed services, and (c) making follow-up contact with service providers to determine that the needs of the victim are being met. The delivery of services through referral is enhanced when advocates cooperate with other agencies in the community to coordinate information about the services they provide. For example, the Sacramento County Victim/Witness Program in California coordinates its service with 46 referral agencies. Referrals are made according to service emphasis in three categories:

(1) physical/financial assistance (housing, food, clothing, financial assistance, transportation, health care, employment/training)
(2) emotional assistance (long-term counseling, legal counseling, family counseling, handicapped and disabled services, crisis counseling)
(3) State Board of Control Victims of Violent Crime Compensations assistance (assistance in completing and filing victim compensation application)

The Erie County D.A.'s Office Victim/Witness Assistance Program in Buffalo, New York, refers victims who need food, clothing, emergency shelter, or transportation to the following social service agencies:

Buffalo Council of Churches
Catholic Charities
Community Action Organization
Erie County Department of Social Services
Goodwill Industries
Hamen House
Salvation Army
Child and Family Services

Finally, the Green Bay, Wisconsin, Victim/Witness Assistance Program provided the following list of agencies to which referrals may be made:

community counseling agencies or counselors
Crisis Intervention Center
Sexual Assault Center
Family Violence Center
financial assistance
food/shelter
legal services
private attorneys
Department of Social Services
Legal Help Line

Job Service Programs
medical care
area law enforcement agencies
city attorney
small claims court
Parents of Murdered Children support group
Consumer Protection (landlord/tenant issues)
Office of Protection and Parole
Clerk of Court Office (for restraining order injunctions)

Emergency Financial Assistance

In the aftermath of a property-related crime, some victims—especially the elderly and indigent persons—may need emergency financial assistance. Burglary victims, especially the elderly and indigent persons living on fixed income, may need immediate financial assistance to buy food or to replace stolen prescription medications or other essential items. Individuals who were financially needy prior to becoming crime victims may find themselves in dire straits after the traumatic event. Unfortunately, many programs (75.6%) are not able to provide emergency money.

Those programs that can provide emergency monetary aid often do so at the discretion of the victim advocate, either at the crime scene or immediately following the crime. Another approach is to offer assistance after a formal needs-assessment interview.

Several programs responding to this study provided information about emergency financial assistance. Specific from three of these programs appear below.

Indianapolis, Indiana. The Indianapolis Police Department Victim Assistance Program can provide emergency financial assistance, though other available community resources are first pursued as sources of emergency funds. If other sources are not feasible, the coordinator has two in-program sources of funds that are utilized at her discretion on a case-by-case basis:

(1) A $2,500 contingency fund provided for a period of one year by a VOCA grant contains specified accounts for food, shelter, transportation, and small home repairs. All authorized expenditures are made by staff members. For example, a victim in need of emergency food makes a request for specific items, and a staff member makes the grocery purchases and delivers them to the individual in need.

(2) A memorial fund provides $50 in cash each month for small emergencies. At the discretion of the coordinator, a staff member makes all emergency purchases for the victim: for example, a meal, cab fare, or replacement of stolen medication

Chesapeake, Virginia. The Chesapeake Sheriff's Victim Assistance Program includes an Elderly Victim Assistance Program, which provides limited emergency financial assistance (up to $200 and referral services to (a) elderly victims, and (b) victims, regardless of age, whose income is at or below the poverty level. The criteria for receiving financial assistance include the following:

- The crime must be reported to the police within 72 hours.
- The victim must apply for compensation within two weeks.
- The victim must cooperate with the police and the commonwealth's attorney in a prosecution attempt.
- The victim must sustain a personal loss.
- Losses must be documented by records of ownership (personal property) or medical records in the case of injury.
- Losses must not have been insured.
- The victim must be a resident of Chesapeake.

None of the money used for the Elderly Victim Assistance Program is city-government budgeted; it comes from an annual fund-raising barbecue, a major social event for the city.

San Francisco, California. The District Attorney's Victim Witness Assistance Program has an emergency fund that is used only in the absence of another community resource, and then only in the case of emergency. "Emergency" is defined as any immediate financial intervention in response to a victim's basic needs, such as temporary shelter, food, transportation, clothing, and medical care, including prescription medicines, eyeglasses, or dentures. The fund is used only after the crime has been verified with local law enforcement. Emergency assistance, in the form of goods or services, is limited to no more than temporary subsistence. In some cases the assistance is considered a loan, and full or partial repayment is expected; in other instances it is an outright gift. An individual victim may not draw on the emergency fund for more than three crime incidents.

The San Francisco program has developed specific procedures and safeguards for management of the emergency fund. This fund is separate from regular grant allocations and has its own account. The county requires that the fund operate on a noncash basis via bills submitted to the county controller, who handles all money; purchases are made through a credit system with local merchants. The district attorney has sole authority to make payments from the emergency fund.

Repair of Broken Locks, Windows, and Doors

The crime victim may need immediate help securing his or her home in order to feel safe; repair or replacement of broken doors, windows, and locks can protect the individual from further victimization. However, only a small number of the responding programs (23, or 12.5%) offered lock repair. Examples include the following:

- Appleton, Wisconsin: On referral by the Police Department, high school service club members make repairs for property victims who have no insurance.
- Waukeshaw, Wisconsin: Any victim of a burglary is eligible for lock installation services. The victim pays the program's low cost for a single-cylinder deadbolt lock, but receives free installation.
- Garden City, New York: An emergency locksmith replaces or repairs locks damaged during a burglary for handicapped, elderly, or low-income victims.

Help with Victim Compensation Applications

Many victims suffer undue financial insecurity and/or loss because they do not know about victim compensation or because they are unable to make a proper claim. Nearly two-thirds of the responding programs (118, or 64%) provided help to victims in completing victim compensation applications.

As a result of legislation passed by individual states, victims of specified crimes in 45 states and the District of Columbia offer compensation awards to reimburse victims and their survivors. Victims can apply for and receive state-administered funds that reimburse them for specified crime-related expenses not paid for by insurance or other collateral sources. State victim compensation programs provide reimbursement for expenses arising from personal injury to a victim or a "Good Samaritan" as a direct result of a crime. Compensation may be made for medical bills, loss of wages, loss of future earnings, and, in a growing number of states, expenses related to psychological treatment necessitated by the crime. Dependents of a victim who has died are eligible for compensation for burial expenses, loss of support, and other crime-related expenses. Some states provided partial compensation for loss of or damage to property such as doors, windows, locks, or other residential security devices. Awards vary from state to state, ranging from an often-specified $100 minimum to a frequently declared limit of $10,000-$15,000. Several states, however, do allow awards of up to $25,000, and Alaska awards up to $40,000 (Anderson & Woodard, 1985, p. 226).

Each state has its own eligibility regulations and procedures for victim compensation. The victim, a dependent, or any other eligible claimant may apply. Generally, the offender need not have been apprehended or convicted for compensation to be paid. Claims that have been filed are reviewed by state boards of commissions, established by state legislation, which determine the awards.

Many individuals fail to receive compensation because they do not know it is available or because they are unable to make a proper claim. Therefore, it is imperative that all agencies and professionals who have contact with victims inform them of the availability of victim compensation funds.

The role of the advocate in filing victim compensation claims is extremely important in (a) providing information, (b) assessing victim eligibility for compensation, (c) helping the victim to pursue other avenues of repayment such as insurance, (d) assisting in filling out compensation application forms, (e) helping victims assemble itemized receipts necessary for claims, and (f) monitoring the progress of claims.

Generally, a victim is considered to be ineligible if he or she

(1) was an accomplice to the crime;
(2) was related to or living with the perpetrator;
(3) failed to cooperate with police (or was injured while in custody of a law enforcement official);
(4) was injured as a result of an auto accident;
(5) failed to report the incident to law enforcement officials within a specified time period (usually 48-72 hours);
(6) failed to file the claim within a specified period of time after the incident (usually 1-2 years);
(7) has insurance or other sources that will pay for economic losses (Anderson & Woodard, 1985, p. 223-226; NOVA, 1983, pp. 70-71).

A major change that was accomplished through the reauthorization of VOCA in 1988 was the *expansion of crime victim compensation* to include victims of domestic violence, drunken driving, and out of state residence (effective October 1, 1990).

In some instances the advocate will determine that claims are questionable. NOVA's 1983 publication, *The Victim Service System: A Guide to Action*, proposes the following guidelines for filing questionable claims:

In assisting victims with victim compensation claims, advocates should not try to second-guess eligibility decisions. While it is prudent to make sure victims who are patently ineligible do not make application, on judgmental questions involving victim contribution, family exclusion, and the like, it is best to describe the problem to the victim, then if he wants to file, to leave the decision to the compensation decision makers. (p. 72)

Victims may need the advocate's reassurance that they are correctly providing the necessary information. Many victims, especially the elderly and those suffering emotionally due to victimization, need direct help in completing the forms. This assistance, along with help in assembling itemized receipts required by the board in order to make awards, is an invaluable service.

Several programs responding to the survey provided information on the history, organization, funding, and procedures for filing claims for their state compensation programs. The Wisconsin program is outlined below.

The Wisconsin Crime Victim Compensation Program. Wisconsin's Crime Victim Compensation Program became operational January 1, 1977, under the auspices of the Department of Industry, Labor and Human Relations. In July 1980, legislation transferred the program to the Wisconsin Department of Justice.

The rationale for "awards for the victims of crimes" is set forth in the Wisconsin Statutes as follows:

> The legislature finds and declares that the state has a moral responsibility to aid innocent victims of violent crime . . . . It is the intention of the legislature that the state should provide sufficient assistance to victims of crime and their families in order to ease their financial burden and to maintain their dignity as they go through a difficult and often traumatic period. It is also the intention of the legislature that the department should actively publicize the crime victim compensation program and promote its use. (Wisconsin Statutes, Chapter 949. 001, 1983, p. 5430)

Individuals who may be eligible for awards from the Crime Victim Compensation Program include (a) the innocent victim (or the person responsible for the care of that victim) of a compensable violent crime who was injured as a result of that crime, (b) the "Good Samaritan" who was injured "while attempting to aid a crime victim, or attempting to aid a police officer" (Office of Crime Victim Services, 1984, p. 36) and (c) the dependent(s) of a victim or "Good Samaritan" who dies as a result of the crime.

To be eligible for an award, the victim must meet the following requirements:

- The incident must have been reported to the police within five days of its occurrence, or within five days of the time when a report could reasonably have been made.
- The application must be made within two years after the date of the personal injury or death.

- All other sources of assistance must have been exhausted, including court-ordered restitution, public assistance, private insurance, and workers' or unemployment compensation.
- The crime must be one of the compensable crimes presented in the statute.
- The applicant must cooperate with law enforcement officials in their investigation of the crime (Office of Crime Victim Services, 1984, pp. 36-37).

The victim may be ineligible for compensation if he or she

- "is the parent, child, brother, sister, or spouse of the offender or lives in the same household with the offender" (persons related to the offender may receive compensation if it is in the interest of justice);
- "committed a crime which caused or contributed to his/her injury";
- engaged in conduct that substantially contributed to the injury or death or in conduct that the victim could have reasonably foreseen could lead to injury or death;
- "has not cooperated with appropriate law enforcement agencies" (Office of Crime Victim Services, 1984, p. 37); or
- "was injured as an adult passenger in a drunk driver's vehicle and knew the driver was under the influence of an intoxicant, or had a blood alcohol concentration of 0.1% or more" (Office of Crime Victim Services, 1984, p. 34).

A Wisconsin resident who suffers injury or death resulting from a crime that occurred outside the state of Wisconsin is eligible for compensation by the Wisconsin Crime Victim Compensation Program if the state or territory in which the act occurred does not have a law providing for the compensation of victims of crimes. The resident has the same rights and must meet the same eligibility requirements as if the act had occurred in the state of Wisconsin. The Department of Justice maintains records of compensation legislation in other states and territories. Upon request, the department will assist Wisconsin residents in determining whether or not they qualify for compensation.

The maximum award for an individual's injury or death is $10,000. Any award made by the Crime Victim Compensation Program is reduced by the amount of any payment received, or to be received, as a result of the injury or death from other sources. Examples of other sources are insurance payments, workers' compensation and unemployment compensation, public funds, and restitution or any payment for or on behalf of the person who committed the crime. Compensation awards are made for economic losses such as those incurred through medical treatment, work loss, reasonable funeral and burial expenses up to $2,000, and reasonable replacement value up to $100 for any clothing that is held for evidentiary purposes (Office of Crime Victim Services, 1984).

Emergency awards may be made to victims if the department determines that an award will probably be made and that the claimant will suffer undue hardship if immediate payment is not made. Emergency awards are limited to compensation up to $500 or for funeral and burial expenses up to $2,000 and are deducted from the final award made to the claimant. If no final award is made, the claimant is required to repay the emergency award.

The Crime Victim Compensation Program attempts to complete the processing of claims within 90 days of the receipt of information. The actual length of time required depends, however, upon the cooperation of all information providers. Claims procedures are outlined below.

(1) The victim receives a compensation application form from one of several sources: a law enforcement agency (law enforcement agencies are required, by law, to provide applications to every potential claimant), a district attorney's office, a hospital, or a victim/witness support program.

(2) All applications for compensation are sent to the Department of Justice's Crime Victim Compensation Program, where they are reviewed and screened for eligibility. Additional information required for claims meeting the minimal requirements of the program includes the following: police reports describing and verifying the crime; medical reports and bills related to the incident (the victim is responsible for gathering and forwarding all medical bills to the department); information regarding work loss and when the victim returned to work; other collateral sources such as medical or disability insurance, unemployment or workers' compensation, compensation won in civil suits, restitution, and public assistance.

(3) Victims are notified of the findings of the program. Those eligible for compensation are informed in writing of the amount and the specifics of the award. An appeal of the decision may be filed.

(4) Payment is made directly to the appropriate service provider and/or to the victim.

(5) Additional awards may be made on a claim as the victim incurs additional incident-related medical treatment (Office of Crime Victim Services, 1984, pp. 37-39).

According to the 1983-1984 *Annual Report* of the Office of Crime Victim Services, Wisconsin Department of Justice, three major groups are involved in the functioning of the Crime Victim Compensation Program. The first of these is the Wisconsin Crime Victims Council. The nine members of this statutory body are appointed by the attorney general to three-year terms. The purpose of the council is to study the needs of Wisconsin's crime victims and to make recommendations regarding these needs. Council activities focus on (a) increasing the sensitivity of the criminal justice system to the plight of crime victims and witnesses and (b) promoting and strengthening the coordinated participation of all agencies in order to provide effective assistance to all victims. Some council activities include "training for criminal justice system personnel, promoting funding for victim services, educating various constituent groups about victim/witness rights and services, seeking support from the business community, doing general public outreach, promoting various crime prevention programs, monitoring pending legislation and proposing new legislation" (Office of Crime Victim Services, 1984, p. 71).

The council also distributes a crime victims' newsletter in Wisconsin, as well as in other states and Canada, to more than 3,300 individuals. In Wisconsin, the newsletter is sent to all judges, victim service agencies, police chiefs and sheriffs, public libraries, news media, legislators, district attorneys, and special interest victims' coalitions and organizations. The newsletter's twofold purpose is to increase awareness of crime victim issues and to facilitate communication among local organizations (Office of Crime Victim Services, 1984).

The second group involved in the functioning of the Crime Victim Compensation Program is made up of 17 county victim/witness assistance programs, the Milwaukee County Sheriff's Office County Witness Protection Unit and the Wisconsin Department of Justice Victim/Witness Assistance Program in Madison, Wisconsin. The major focus of this group is to provide information and direct services to victims.

The third group is composed of the staff of the Crime Victim Compensation program who handle all applications for compensation. During the 1983-1984 reporting period, the program had a staff of seven: the executive director, three claims specialists, two investigators, and a clerical support person. Automated claims procedures were being implemented at that time for more efficient handling of the increased number of applications.

Statistical information for the State of Wisconsin's Crime Victim Compensation Program for the period July 1, 1983 through June 30, 1984, is presented below (all data are from the Office of Crime Victim Services, 1984).

Summary of Claims

claims pending as of 7/1/83	569
claims received 7/1/83 through 6/30/84	1273
total claims	1842
total initial awards granted	559
total claims denied and/or closed	498
pending as of 6/30/84	785
total	1842
total dollar amount of awards granted, 7/1/83 through 6/30/84	893,860.15
average amount per award	1,599.03

Claims Summary by Age of Victim

Age	Number	Percentage
1-10	53	4.2
11-15	57	4.5
16-20	225	17.7
21-25	275	21.6
26-30	168	13.2
31-35	139	10.9
36-40	71	5.6
41-45	50	3.9
46-50	45	3.5
51-55	35	2.7
56-60	34	2.7
61-65	27	2.1
66 +	94	7.1

Summary of Applicants by Sex

Sex	Number	Percentage
male	693	54.5
female	580	45.5
total	1273	100.0

Breakdown of Award Expenses

Type of Award	Amount ($)	Percentage
medical expenses	519,452.87	58.1
lost wages	179,691.77	19.1
funeral expenses	146,975.97	16.4
loss of support	35,443.10	4.0
clothing	7,012.75	.8
attorney fees	5,971.13	.7
emergency award	1,256.56	.1
total	893,860.15	100.0

Initial Crisis Intervention Procedures

When asked to provide information on their initial procedures, approximately two-thirds of the programs indicated that they provided crisis intervention. The respondents mentioned six main methods of crisis intervention: phone/hot line, phone and in person, in person only, at crime scene, home visit, and at the hospital. Data related to crisis intervention methods are presented in Table 2.5.

TABLE 2.5: Location of Crisis Intervention

Method	Number of Programs	Percentage[a]
In person only	32	26.4
Phone and in person	26	21.4
At crime scene	22	18.1
Phone/hotline	16	13.2
At hospital	15	12.3
Home visit	10	8.2
Total	121	99.6

a. Percentages were calculated based on 121 responses.

Of the 121 programs that responded to this question, 32 (26.4%) provide face-to-face crisis intervention in their offices. An additional 26 (21.4%) indicated that they provide both telephone and in person counseling; 47 (39%) reported that they provide immediate emergency response to the victim in crisis. This timely and critical emergency response takes place at the crime scene, in the hospital emergency room, or at the police station or the victim's home. Of those respondents who provide an emergency response to the victim, almost one-half provide crisis intervention and advocacy at the crime scene. Other respondents indicated that they meet or assist the victim at the hospital, while only a small number (10, or 8.2%) provide crisis intervention in the home.

Many crime victims, especially those who are elderly, handicapped, socially isolated, or lacking transportation, will not get the help they so urgently need unless home visits by victim counselors are provided. Unfortunately, most of the programs do not provide home visits because of staff shortages and/or the high cost of liability insurance. In addition, some programs may not recognize the need for and potential of home visits in facilitating the victim's recovery.

To illustrate the most frequently utilized crisis intervention methods, the initial procedures of five of the respondents are presented below.

Victim Assistance Services (Glendale, Arizona). Police officers may call the crisis worker in any situation where it is felt that the victim may benefit from immediate professional intervention. After regular business hours the worker is paged and responds to the scene within 30 minutes. The worker assesses the victim's needs, provides support, accompanies the victim to the hospital or the police station, contacts the victim's support system, and links the victim to appropriate resources.

The Crime Victims' Center of Chester County, Inc. (West Chester, Pennsylvania). The call is responded to immediately either by telephone counseling (information, options counseling, or the like) or, in most cases, by immediate escort to police or medical facilities. The counselor remains with the victim during medical procedures and the police interview. Counseling is provided to the victim's family and friends as well. Where appropriate, a team approach is arranged with children's services or mental health agencies.

Victim/Witness Division—Green County Prosecutor's Office (Xenia, Ohio). Crisis intervention is provided on a 24-hour basis immediately following the initial report to police, hospital, or self-referral to the division. At the time of intervention, the victim receives crisis counseling, support, advocacy, and information on the medical, police, and prosecution procedures that will possibly be taking place.

N.C.C.J. Santa Clara County Victim Witness Assistance Center (San Jose, California). Victims are notified of the agency's services by a police officer or are called to the scene by the police. A staff member responds in person as needed and interviews victims to assess their needs. If great stresses are present, an emergency psychologist is contacted through another agency. The staff provides any needed material care such as food, shelter, transportation, clothing, and cash.

Victim/Witness Assistance Program (Hollister, California). In this program the following steps are taken in crisis intervention:

(1) Calm the victim and assure of safety.
(2) Outline services and resources available and begin delivery of emergency assistance services (transport to shelter, change locks, give money from victim fund).
(3) Provide peer counseling.
(4) Help victim develop an action plan for the future.

Witness Notification

The term *witness notification* refers to the process by which victims and witnesses are informed that a formal criminal or misdemeanor complaint has been filed. This process is also used to inform individuals of the day and time they will be expected to testify. Ideally, a witness notification system provides a witness with ongoing information about the status of the case as long as it is in the courts. A notification system generally provides the following information:

When a formal criminal or misdemeanor complaint is filed, the victim/witness is informed of the case number, the defendant's name, and the criminal court process that will be followed (a complete victim impact statement is requested at this time).

When a court date is scheduled, victims and witnesses are notified of the day and time they should appear in court (along with the location of the court) and are informed about what to expect during the court proceedings.

If the court time is changed, the date is postponed, or the case is canceled, notification is made.

When a final disposition is made, the victim and all witnesses are informed of the court's decision.

According to the Erie County Victim/Witness Assistance Program in Buffalo, New York, clients most often request the following information:

• incarceration status of defendants
• specific trial and hearing dates
• reasons for cases not being brought to trial
• locations and contact numbers for prosecutors and judges
• trial outcomes

During 1983-1984, Erie County program staff and workers provided case status and other court-related information to more than 1,900 victims and witnesses.

To a large extent, staff size and financial constraints dictate the method chosen for witness notification. Availability and ease of locating the victim/witness also determine the method of notification. Though there is a need for efficiency in informing a large number of persons of the status of their cases, this must always be balanced against the need for sensitivity in recognizing the suffering of crime victims. In addition, persons who are testifying may need to make special arrangements to take time off from work, locate a babysitter, or arrange for transportation. Therefore, it is important that all information related to a court appearance be communicated to the victim/witness as promptly as possible.

Since witness notification systems provide information pertaining to the scheduling of court dates and the time when testimony will be taken, it would be expected that most programs based in prosecutors' offices would have such a system, while those affiliated with hospitals, local police departments, and social service agencies would not. The survey found that a witness notification system had been developed in 146 of the responding programs. Almost all (94%) of the programs based in prosecutors' offices had some type of procedure for notifying victims and witnesses of the date and time scheduled for their testimony in court.

The 31 programs that did not have a notification system (Table 2.6) can be grouped under five categories. Due to the initial crisis intervention focus of their services and their location, all of the hospital-based programs and 8 of those

TABLE 2.6: Auspices of Programs with No Notification Services

	Number of Programs	Percentage of Similar Programs
Nonprofit social service agency	9	45
Police department	8	62
City or county attorney	6	6
Hospital	3	100
County social service or criminal justice agency	2	40
Miscellaneous	3	
Total	31	

in police departments did not perform court-related notification services. Several police departments reported that notification was handled by the D.A.'s office. Others with no notification services included 9 of the responding social service agencies and 2 of the responding county social services or criminal justice agencies. Of the responding programs under the auspices of city or county attorney's offices, 6 reported that they provided information to victims and witnesses but had no notification services because another office performed this service.

The year when each witness notification system began. Of the 146 programs that have a witness notification system, 135 provided the year of the system's origin. Table 2.7 shows that close to two-thirds of the systems have been initiated since 1980. There has been a steady growth in the number of these systems since 1975, when the first one became operational.

Witness notification methods. The different notification methods used by the responding programs are listed in Table 2.8. It should be noted that 27 programs use more than one method. Most of the programs use phone calls or letters, alone or in combination, to notify individuals. Other methods used, though to a lesser extent, are notification in person, contact by computer or recording machine, and notification by subpoena.

Combination of telephone and letter. The combined use of phone and letters is the method of witness notification used by 69 (47%) of the respondents. Personal telephone contact with the victim is extremely beneficial, particularly if the contact is made by a victim advocate who will be assigned to the case throughout the court proceedings. In addition to providing court- and program-related information, telephone contact allows the program to establish a personal link with the victim, to show someone cares about the victim's welfare and needs, to begin to determine what kind of services the victim requires, and to give the victim an opportunity to express feelings about the crime. However, in many large urban areas contact with all crime victims is impossible and notification by letter becomes necessary. When it is not feasible to have telephone con-

TABLE 2.7: Years Witness Notification Systems Began

Year	Number of Programs	Percentage[a]
1975	5	3.7
1976	11	8.1
1977	9	6.6
1978	9	6.6
1979	13	9.6
1980	14	10.3
1981	11	8.1
1982	14	10.3
1983	13	9.6
1984	16	11.8
1985	20	14.8
Total	135	99.5

a. Percentages are based on a total of 135 responses.

tact with all victims, it is suggested that program staff select those persons who are having particular difficulty coping with the traumatic event and apprise them of court scheduling by telephone.

At the Pima County Victim/Witness Program in Tucson, Arizona, the individual is notified by telephone or letter of the prosecutor's decision to initiate a case. During the progress of the case the following information is provided to the individual: who is in charge, how to verify when and where he or she will be needed in court, how to get input into the judge's presentencing reporting, and details about the final disposition of the case. The individual can also call the service to find out the current status of the defendant, such as whether he or she has been apprehended and whether he or she is in jail or out on bail.

Notification solely by phone. A total of 32 (22%) of the programs surveyed notify by phone only. Providing telephone notification to all victims/witnesses is feasible only in areas with relatively low crime rates. It would be impossible for workers in major cities to make all notifications by personal phone calls. To illustrate, the Victim-Witness Call-Off Alert used in Appleton, Wisconsin, provides telephone notification. A witness scheduler telephones victims/witnesses and police witnesses with advance notice of court appointments as well as of any changes or cancellations. The telephone alert system allows witnesses who can be reached by phone on the date in question to continue working until they are called on to testify.

Notification solely by letter. Notification by mail only was reported by 28 (19%) programs. In large cities where the volume of criminal cases is large, or in understaffed offices, notification by letter is a frequently used method. For ex-

TABLE 2.8: Witness Notification Methods

Method	Number of Programs	Percentage[a]
Phone and/or letter	69	47
Phone only	32	22
Letter only	28	19
In person	19	13
Contact by computer or recording machine	14	10
Subpoena	11	8
Total	173	
No notification system	31	
No information given	1	

a. Percentages were calculated based on 146 respondents. Some respondents use more than one method of witness notification.

ample, the Victim/Witness Assistance Program of the Attorney General, Providence, Rhode Island, has a systematized letter notification process to inform victims of felony crimes of the status of their superior court felony cases. Types of notification letters sent by this program include initial notification letters (1,666 sent from January 1985-January 1986), warrant letters (135 sent in the same period), passed-for-trial letters (503 sent), and disposition letters (333 sent). In all, 2,637 letters were sent by this program in 1985.

Each notification letter used by this program begins with case reference information (including case number and charges) and ends with information about the Victim/Witness Assistance Program: telephone number, office hours, how to call with questions (e.g., have case number and defendant's name available when calling), and the procedure to use to inform the program of address and/or telephone number changes. The victim is advised to keep all letters for future reference.

The initial notification letter is sent to each victim once a defendant has been arraigned in superior court. The victim is notified of the date the arraignment was held, the defendant's pleas, and bail status. The pretrial conference date is given. The victim is informed of his or her right to attend this conference, to "tell the court about the impact of the crime before a plea negotiation is accepted and a sentence is imposed by the judge," and to be informed of the status and disposition of the case. Enclosed with the notification letter are a Notice to Victim Form, which allows the victim to accept or reject his or her right to attend the pretrial conference, and a Victim Impact Statement. The victim must return the enclosures within ten days or the program assumes the victim is not interested in exercising his or her rights.

In cases when the defendant fails to appear for arraignment, a warrant letter is sent advising the victim that he or she will be notified when the defendant is arrested and brought before the court.

The passed for trial letter notifies the victim of the trial date and provides explanations of possible continuance or disposition by plea negotiation. Further notification is then made by the Department of the Attorney General or the Victim/Witness Assistance Program.

Three different types of disposition letters are used by the program:

- *Disposition letter*: This includes the date the case was disposed of in superior court, the defendant's plea, and the sentence.
- *Trial-guilty letter*: This includes trial date, jury's guilty finding, and sentencing date. The victim is advised of his or her right to address the court prior to sentencing and is encouraged to contact the Victim/Witness Assistance Program to make arrangements.
- *Trial-not guilty letter*: This includes trial date, the fact that the jury found the defendant not guilty, and an explanation of the principle of "beyond a reasonable doubt."

In all letters sent, the Victim/Witness Assistance Program stresses the importance of victim participation in the court process and thanks the individual for his or her cooperation and assistance.

Notification in person. A total of 19 (13%) programs reported the practice of in-person notification. Personal notification by a victim advocate may be necessary for any number of reasons. Witnesses may be reluctant to participate in the court process. Many victims of violent crimes need the assurance of safety and support provided by advocate involvement. Elderly victims who have difficulty reading and/or talking on the telephone should be notified in person. A substantial number of residents of large cities such as New York do not have telephones because they cannot afford them. Many of these same residents are foreign-born and communicate primarily in their native language. In-person notification may be the most effective method for cases such as these.

Programs must occasionally send police officers to provide notification. An individual who has been threatened by the defendant or others associated with the defendant may respond positively to the protection associated with a police officer. Other reluctant individuals may respond to the official law enforcement role of the police officer. When a victim or witness has moved from the recorded address, in-person efforts to locate and notify the individual are often required.

In-person notification is the method of choice for the Butte County Victim/Witness Assistance Program, in Chino, California. Due to its focus on personal outreach, the program initially attempts to reach the victim/witness in person. The purposes of the contact are to identify and explain the program, do a needs assessment, offer services and/or referral to other agencies, and provide criminal justice system information. If it is not possible to make personal notification, telephone and mail notification are the alternatives.

Notification by machine. A method of witness notification used by 14 (10%) of the respondents was contact by computer or recording machine. Since this form of contact is extremely impersonal, it is not recommended for initial contact with victims of violent crimes. A recording machine is often used to inform witnesses of changes in court time or date, adjournments, or cancellations.

In Sheboygan, Wisconsin, the D.A.'s office attempts to notify victims/ witnesses by phone. In case they cannot be reached, they are instructed during earlier contacts to call a designated number the evening before the trial and listen to a tape-recorded message that lists the cases that will be heard the next day. If the case is not mentioned, the individual must contact the advocate or the telephone number provided by the program to obtain new information about the scheduling or status of the case.

In Milwaukee, Wisconsin, a recorded message that lists all cases that will not go on as scheduled the following day is available after office hours. A short message in red ink is attached to each subpoena that states:

> Sometimes cases must be postponed at the last minute. We will try to call you if you will not be needed. If you have not been called by the court date, please call 278-4687 after 5:00 p.m. the evening before the case is scheduled. A recorded message will tell you if your case is cancelled.

The staff emphasizes that this recorded message is a supplement to, not a substitute for, telephone recall of witnesses.

Notification by subpoena. Witnesses are notified by subpoena by 11 (8%) of the programs. In Yakima, Washington, witnesses receive subpoenas in the mail approximately two weeks before the date set for a jury trial. The subpoena tells when and where to appear and what to bring to court. The victim/witness is instructed to write or call the prosecuting attorney's office with any questions. The individual is advised of the existence of a Victim Assistance Unit, which is available to help with any problems related to the case, and a copy of the program's "Tips for Witnesses" pamphlet accompanies the subpoena.

Child Care

Table 2.9 displays responses to the question: Do you have a program for the children of victims/witnesses? Only slightly less than one-third (57, or 31%)

TABLE 2.9: Child Care

	Number of Programs	Percentage[a]
Response to question: Do you have a program for the children of victims and witnesses?		
No	127	69
Yes	57	31
Total	184	100
In-house versus privately contracted child care		
Number of programs providing in-house child care	52	91.2
Number of programs providing privately contracted child care	5	8.7
Total	57	99.9
Type of liability insurance		
Provided by victim/witness	2	7.1
Provided by city/county	23	82.1
Provided by contracted day-care provider	1	3.5
Miscellaneous insurance		
Seven Hills	1	3.5
NASW	1	3.5
Total	28	99.7
Children served in 1984 by the 57 programs		
Programs serving 1-25 children	8	29
Programs serving 26-50 children	4	14
Programs serving 51-199 children	5	18
Programs serving 200-299 + children	11	39
Total	28	100

a. Percentages are based on varying numbers of respondents, depending on how many answered particular items. Only 28 respondents indicated the number of children they served in 1984. Percentages do not all add to 100 because of rounding.

of the respondents reported having programs for the children of victims and witnesses. Most of these programs consist of short-term child care, limited to the time spent by the victim/witness in consultation or in court, but several programs are intended as more than child care—they are designed to meet the special needs of children who are victims of or witnesses to violent crimes.

Provision of child care during the time the individual is participating in the justice system can be an important service for the parent. In this survey, programs for the children of victims and witnesses ranged from informally provided in-house babysitting, to use of day-care centers or other contracted providers, to structured programs for children who themselves are victims of or witnesses to crime. Regardless of the number of children served, the child-care situation presents a unique opportunity to provide services to young individuals who are in need of support. The lives of victims' children are affected by their parents' emotional reactions, losses, physical injuries, and disruptions of usual routines. In addition, the children may have witnessed the crime. A child-care program designed to meet the special needs of these children can be an especially valuable service for the entire family.

Ideally, child care is provided in a pleasant play area or room equipped with toys and books, and is supervised by a caring adult with training in the issues of victimization. In a safe, calm, positive atmosphere, children can be given the opportunity to express their feelings about the victimization. As a result of observations made by the adult caretaker, referrals may be made for those children who demonstrate the need for counseling. This service to the children may be as important as relieving the parents of the burden of making their own arrangements for child care at this difficult time.

Of those programs offering child care, 91% provided it in-house, using victim advocates for staffing or enlisting available staff (e.g., secretary or receptionist) or help from volunteers. Specifics from several programs include the following:

- In 1984 approximately 250 children were served by seven advocates who handle child care as part of their caseload in the Maricopa County Attorney's Office, Phoenix, Arizona.

- The Los Angeles, California, City Attorney's Victims of Crime Program employs two full-time staff to provide in-house child care. Some 2,000 children were served in 1984.

- The Sonoma County Victim Witness Project, located in the Probation Department, Santa Rosa, California, provides child care by appointment as much as possible Monday through Friday, 8:00 a.m. to 5:00 p.m., primarily for victims.

- Approximately 210 children were provided care in 1984 by the Multnomah County Victim's Assistance program in Portland, Oregon. In-house short-term care was provided in the victim/witness lounge.

Long-term care is usually arranged with local day-care providers. The remaining 5 programs (9%) handle child care through a private contractual arrangement. For example:

- In Hollister, California, the San Benito Victim/Witness Assistance Program served 120 children in 1984 (390 victims were seen). The program arranges for, transports children to and from, and pays for temporary child care in licensed centers and homes. Payment comes from a local victim fund or from local Respite Care Funds.

- The Outagamie County Victim/Witness Assistance Program, Appleton, Wisconsin, contracts with the Appleton YMCA Drop-In Day Care Center. Child-care services were provided for approximately 16 victims in 1983. When the center is closed program staff provide direct child care.

Several respondents reported special programs for children who are themselves victims or witnesses:

- The South Lake Tahoe (California) Branch Victim/Witness Center has a "wee witness room" for child witnesses where court orientation is provided. Child care is done by referral.
- In West Palm Beach, Florida, the Palm Beach County Victim/Witness Service has a counselor for children of homicide victims who have witnessed crimes, and so on.
- Two staff members provided therapy (not child care) for 30 children in 1984 at the Rape Crisis Center of West Contra Costa, San Pablo, California.
- In Greensboro, North Carolina, the Turning Point: Victim Assistance, a nonprofit social service agency providing rape and family abuse prevention services, served approximately 250 children in 1984. Their program for children is not babysitting for parents who are in court. Rather, it is a crisis nursery that serves child victims as well as children of victims. It is primarily a free drop-in nursery for preschool children of families in stress, providing a "time-out" place during troubled times and helping parents learn how to cope with the demands of young children. Staffing ratio is a maximum of five children to one staff member.

The expense of liability insurance seems to be a factor in the ability of a program to offer child care. Only twenty-eight programs responded to the question, How is liability insurance handled? City/County government was the provider for 23 (82%) of these programs.

Only half (27) of the programs providing a program for the children of victims and witnesses provided information on the number of children served in 1984.

- In Lihue, Hawaii, the Kuaui Victim-Witness Program served 5 children in 1984 (1,600 victims were seen). Care was provided by volunteers or by day-care centers used on a rotation basis.
- Victim Services Agency, New York City, operated six programs for children with a range of staffing patterns. In 1984 more than 3,000 children were served; more than 100,000 victims were seen by the program.

Conclusion

This chapter has highlighted the major findings of the national survey of victim/witness assistance programs with regard to the availability of different types of victim services. The goal has been to examine the extent to which the 184 responding programs provide specific types of services. Many of the respondents seem to provide immediate attention to victims and witnesses by means of witness notification of upcoming hearings or trial dates; court advocacy, transportation, and escort services; and referral to community agencies. The most frequently provided services available to crime victims who make contact with a victim assistance program are court advocacy and information; court escort; public education; referral to health, mental health, or social service agencies; and assistance in completing victim compensation applications. The services provided least frequently are crisis intervention in the home, emergency funds for destitute victims, child care for parent(s) appearing in court, and repair or replacement of broken door locks. The challenge for victim assistance programs is to recognize the critical needs of crime victims for all the types of services identified and to develop ways to meet these needs.

Note

1. Highly specialized victim assistance programs, such as child sexual abuse treatment programs and battered women's shelters, were excluded from the mailing list.

References

Anderson, J. R., & Woodard, P. L. (1985). Victim and witness assistance: New state laws and the system's response. *Judicature, 68*(6), 223, 226.

California Victim/Witness Assistance Program. (1985, May). *Program guidelines*. Sacramento: Author.

Cronin, R. C., & Bourque, B. B. (1981). *National Evaluation Program phase I report: Assessment of victim/witness assistance projects*. Washington, DC: U. S. Department of Justice.

National District Attorneys Association, Victim Witness Coordination Program. (1987). *The directory of prosecutor-based victim assistance programs* (2nd ed.). Alexandria, VA: Author.

National Organization for Victim Assistance. (1983). *The victim service system: A guide to action*. Washington, DC: Author.

National Organization for Victim Assistance. (1986, 1987). *Victim rights and services: A legislative directory*. Washington, DC: Author.

Office of Crime Victim Services. (1984). *Annual reports, 1982-1983, 1983-1984*. Madison: Wisconsin Department of Justice.

3

Specialized Services for
Elderly Crime Victims

The Case of Mr. S[1]

The Victim Assistance Office received a call from the police department requesting help for Mr. S, age 81, who had been robbed at knife point in his apartment on a very hot afternoon. The counselor arrived just as the police officer was leaving and was told that the apartment was extremely warm and that Mr. S was quite shaken. The officer had doubts about whether the counselor could get Mr. S to talk about the experience.

Repeated knocking on Mr. S's door produced no response from him. A neighbor, hearing the knocking, came over to say that "Smitty" was hard of hearing and was also reluctant to open the door to strangers. Finally, Mr. S did open the door a crack and peered through. Talking through the crack in the door, Mr. S said that because of the extreme heat, he was not wearing any clothing. Mr. S wanted complete details as to the purpose of the counselor's visit before he would put any clothes on and let her in. She praised him for his caution. The temperature in the city had been in the low 90s for the past week and the apartment was 15 to 20 degrees hotter than that, with no fan or air conditioner in sight.

In a congenial and sympathetic manner, the counselor alternately talked with and listened to Mr. S. At first, he denied that the robbery had upset him and he refused to discuss it. However, he eventually reached a point where he was willing to describe what had happened. On the day of the robbery, Mr. S had left the door to his apartment open because it was so hot and he was trying to get a breeze. A young man in his late teens brought his bicycle through the front door of the apartment building. Seeing Mr. S's front door open, the man put his bike down in the elderly man's doorway and asked him to watch it for him. Mr. S said that he was a little apprehensive, but he agreed to watch the bike. The stranger was gone for less than a minute when he returned to Mr. S's door. He burst into the room and pulled a knife from his pocket. The intruder forced Mr. S to tumble over his bed onto the floor—the first of numerous times that Mr. S was either thrown or fell to the floor. The intruder rummaged through virtually everything in the room in search of money. Mr. S dramatized how the robber tore the victim's pants to get to his wallet when no money could be found anywhere else. After taking $20 in cash, the robber left.

The counselor asked Mr. S what Victim Assistance could do to help him prevent a reoccurrence of such a situation. Together, they decided that if he had a fan, the door would not need to be open and the comfort level in the room could be improved. The counselor took him to a discount store, where she used Victim Assistance funds to purchase a large floor-model fan for him. After leaving her business card and telling Mr. S to call her if he needed anything, the counselor departed.

The impact of crime is often severe for the elderly victim. Those who live on fixed or limited incomes are often least equipped to deal with monetary or property loss. The theft of $25 from a poor elderly victim living on social security or a small pension check represents a much greater relative loss than the same amount stolen from an employed person. All too often, elderly crime victims have no bank accounts (or limited savings) from which they can withdraw funds in an emergency. Unless they receive emergency funds or food vouchers from a local victim assistance program, they often have to wait a month for their next social security check. Physical conditions associated with aging, such as osteoporosis, can mean that elderly victims who are hurt may take longer to heal and are more likely to suffer from internal injuries than are younger victims. They are also more likely to need hospital care. Furthermore, crisis reactions to victimization may be more severe in the elderly, leading to acute and chronic anxiety, denial of problems, depression, withdrawal, and increased isolation. For these reasons, special programs and specialized services for the elderly are recommended to help reduce the economic, physical, and emotional impacts of victimization (Miron, Goin, Keegan, & Archer, 1984; National Organization for Victim Assistance, 1983).

The American Psychological Association Task Force on the Victims of Crime and Violence suggests that special programs may be useful in reducing elderly victims' fear of subsequent victimization and in focusing their attention on concrete actions they can take to regain a sense of control (Kahn, 1984). Elderly victims can be helped through services and activities such as the following:

- transportation and escort to stores, public health clinics, hospitals, and banks
- provision of a special police unit that responds to cases of senior burglaries, robberies, purse snatchings, and assaults
- training youth to help elderly victims
- establishment of neighborhood block watch programs and neighborhood building patrols
- arrangement for new locks on doors and windows of elderly burglary victims
- provision of 24-hour hotlines and daily telephone reassurance
- making information and referral services available
- installation of video monitors in elevators and corridors of large apartment buildings

Selected Programs Serving Elderly Victims

Some of the programs surveyed indicated that they recognize the special needs of the elderly victim. A total of 70 (38%) programs reported that they provide specialized types of services for the elderly, such as home visits (12 respondents), transportation (18 respondents), court escort (8 respondents), emergency home repair and replacement of broken locks and doors (6 respondents), and emergency monetary support (5 respondents). Some program directors who did not report offering specialized services for this group stated that they offer the elderly the same services offered to all victims, but they indicated that the elderly require more of these services or need them more often. Descriptions of services provided by respondents ranged from general statements such as "special treatment" or "extra attention" to separate programs that provide a specially trained senior advocate and specialized services for elderly victims. Most programs providing special services to senior citizens seemed to recognize the need for extensive support through telephone counseling, outreach, visits, and/or referral to community senior citizen centers.

Characteristics of several programs specifically designed to serve elderly victims and witnesses are described below.

Milwaukee, Wisconsin. Court Watch is a separate program that provides information, support, and assistance for older adult victims and witnesses throughout the court process. It is sponsored by the Milwaukee County Executive Office on Aging in cooperation with United Way's Information Service for the Aging and the Victim/Witness Services Unit of the District Attorney's Office. Court Watch is staffed by older adult volunteers who monitor all criminal cases involving older adult victims and witnesses. The volunteers are trained to provide information, support, and assistance at all stages of the court process. According to a pamphlet distributed by the Milwaukee County Executive Office on Aging, a Court Watch volunteer's responsibilities include the following:

- staying with the victim in court and during waiting periods, if the victim desires
- providing directions and escort within the courthouse complex
- being available to provide information about the court process and related matters when the victim comes to court or calls the program
- providing information about other community services available to victims of crime in Milwaukee County

Pittsburgh, Pennsylvania. The Center for Victims of Violent Crime provides specialized comprehensive advocacy services and prevention education programming for the elderly. Services provided include home visits, accompaniment throughout the criminal justice system, and presentations designed to meet a variety of seniors' concerns.

Most cities without special programs for the elderly reported that they offered a variety of special services for the elderly in addition to their regular services. Some of these are listed below:

- Specialized training for staff and volunteers who provide services and support to the elderly:
  - Advocates receive special training on issues of elder victimization, elder abuse, and protective agencies (Cambridge, Massachusetts).
  - One individual is employed part-time (20 hours per week) as a "senior victim of crime" assistant, to provide services and community education programs (Santa Ana, California, CSP, Inc., Victim/Witness Assistance Program).
  - A special volunteer group works with elderly persons to provide crisis intervention, emergency monetary support, and referrals (Leesburg, Virginia).
- Cooperative effort with other agencies, such as the Department on Aging or Adult Services:
  - Utilize staff from the Brown County Department of Social Services to provide court escort, transportation, temporary shelter, and financial assistance (Green Bay, Wisconsin).
  - Attempt to mobilize community resources and interact with the victim's support network, including family members, clergy, and so on (Wilmington, Delaware).
  - Work closely with the Adult Protective Services Department to find temporary shelters (Houston, Texas).
- Services for elderly victims:
  - Outreach within 24 hours of the crime, whether arrest has been made or not (Savannah, Georgia).
  - Special phone and letter outreach offering counseling, home visits, case information, advocacy, and so on (Glendale, Arizona).
  - Services to victims within their homes (Santa Rosa, California).
  - Emergency financial assistance (Leesburg, Virginia).

- Extensive elder abuse service (White Plains, New York).
- Emergency assistance up to $200 (Chesapeake, Virginia).
- Special programs for elderly fixed-income victims (San Jose, California).
- Team effort of the Georgia State Bar, Young Lawyer's Section, and the Victim/Witness Unit for working with the elderly (Marietta, Georgia).
- Home visits, greater emphasis on the issues of physical safety (Greensboro, North Carolina).
- Support group (West Palm Beach, Florida).
- Assistance in filing medicare claims or other insurance forms (Helena, Montana).
- Crime prevention, locks, compensation, counseling (Rochester, New York)
- Elderly are considered "special needs" cases and receive service priority, regardless of the crime (Salem, Massachusetts).
- Special court-related services:
  - Special transportation for special needs, volunteer support services (Salt Lake City, Utah).
  - Transportation to court (Cincinnati, Ohio).
  - Access to wheelchairs for court appearances (Napa, California).
  - Court escort, transportation, and follow-up on criminal court cases; extra attention (San Francisco, California).
  - Close telephone and personal contact throughout the time the case is in the court system (Roanoke, Virginia).

Elder Abuse and Neglect

Most of the victim assistance programs in this national survey have not focused attention on meeting the needs of elder abuse victims. Elder abuse is a major social problem affecting large numbers of elderly persons, a problem that, for the most part, has been hidden until the decade of the 1980s.

The U.S. House of Representatives Subcommittee on Health and Long-Term Care estimated the number of assaults on the elderly at 1.1 million annually (Pepper, 1985). Gerontologists, victimologists, medical social workers, and family violence researchers agree that elder abuse is one of the most underreported crimes in our society. There are a variety of reasons that many elderly victims of battering do not report incidents of abuse to the authorities:

(1) The feelings of guilt and shame at having raised children who are physically abusing them prevent many elderly victims from acting. They choose to suffer in silence rather than face the embarrassment of having others know.

(2) An elderly parent may fear that the adult child will retaliate with increased and more intense maltreatment if the abuse is reported.

(3) An elder abuse victim may fear that if he or she reports the abuse, the caretaker will be arrested and then incarcerated. The removal of the caretaker from the home could result in the victim being placed in a nursing home.

(4) The most frequent victims of battering and neglect are aged 75 and older, and these persons are more likely to be disoriented, confused, impaired, and incapable of taking care of their own physical needs than their younger (65-74 years of age) counterparts. Some members of this age group are unaware of what is going on around them and are also unfamiliar with procedures for reporting elder abuse.

(5) Victims of elder abuse do not report the abuse because of their hope that the most recent incident of abuse was the last one and that it will not be repeated.

The 75-and-older age group is the fastest-growing segment of our population. There are currently approximately 26 million persons in the United States over 65 years of age. It is estimated that this number will increase considerably, to almost "67 million by the year 2040. During the same period, those over 85 years of age, currently about 2.2 million, will increase to 13 million" (Steinmetz, 1988, p. 36). With regard to the health limitations of the elderly, chronic diseases of the heart and circulatory system afflict more than half of the over-65 age group. Strokes (cerebral hemorrhages or blockages) are a primary cause of impairment and death in the "old-old," those over 75 years of age. It has been reported that 81% of seniors over 65 years of age have one or more chronic diseases or conditions that severely limit their daily activities (Schaie, 1982). Sociologists Pillemer and Finkelhor's (1987) study of 2,020 elderly persons (who were living on their own or with their families) in Boston indicates that elders in poor health are three to four times more likely to be abused than those in good health. It has been predicted that with the rapidly increasing numbers of frail elderly people in our society, the incidence of elder abuse and neglect will also rapidly increase.

With growing numbers of vulnerable elderly individuals victimized by abuse in their homes, the need for the planning and development of services for this group has become evident. All too often, the burden of investigating suspected cases of elder abuse and providing medical, legal, housing, and social services to the victims of elder abuse falls on the state's division of Adult Protective Services. The protection and provision of services for victims of elder abuse and neglect should be the joint responsibility of a network of community agencies, including victim assistance programs, family violence programs and shelters, police departments, visiting nurses' associations, in-home respite care programs, hospital senior care programs, and senior community centers. Unfortunately, only 15 of the 184 victim assistance programs in the current national survey indicated that they intervene on behalf of elder abuse victims and work with an elder abuse network or coalition of agencies in their community.

Several of the larger victim assistance programs have a full-time staff specialist assigned to work only with victims of elder abuse and other crimes against the elderly. For example, the Victim/Witness Assistance Program of Santa Ana, in Orange County, California, has a "senior victim of crime specialist" on staff. This individual is available to help senior citizens who have become crime victims. The senior victim of crime specialist assists victims of elder abuse in obtaining court-ordered protection through restraining orders and services available in the community, and provides continued follow-up contact to assure that needs continue to be met. The senior victim of crime specialist maintains close working relationships with community and government agencies serving seniors as part of the effort in Orange County to provide a broad network of services to the older citizen. (A complete job description for this position is presented below.)

The community education efforts of this staff person include frequent visits to senior centers throughout the county. There, he or she may make both formal and informal presentations on a variety of topics including elder abuse, crime prevention, and victim services. The specialist also presents other programs on similar topics to the community at large in an effort to educate the public about the needs and concerns of "seniors".

Job Description:
Senior Victim of Crime Specialist

Responsibilities

Under the supervision of the program assistant director, the senior victim of crime specialist is responsible for the provision of extended services to elderly victims of crime.

Principal Duties

- Assess client needs, accurately analyze case and take appropriate action.
- Provide assistance, information, referral, emergency assistance, and follow-up on cases to ensure client welfare, and complete service delivery.
- Accompany senior victims of crime to court when appropriate.
- Provide outreach to community groups and the community at large.

- Maintain education and cooperative relations with senior centers, police department, Department of Social Services, Adult Protective Services, Council on Aging, senior citizen community centers, and the criminal justice system.
- Handle all emergencies in a quick and calm manner.
- Provide emotional support to reduce trauma associated with being a victim or witness of crime.
- Establish and maintain clear and concise client files, including completion of information and referral forms, progress notes, and indexing.
- Maintain confidentiality of victims and witnesses.
- Maintain effective communications with individuals of various socioeconomic and cultural backgrounds.
- Evaluate and maintain cooperative relations with community service agencies. Maintain and update knowledge of resources and the process for providing appropriate client referrals.
- Establish and maintain professional and cooperative relations with the court and court personnel, law enforcement agencies, community agencies and the community, and all other resources of senior victims of crime.
- Provide presentations to the community, agencies, and service providers to educate them on victim trauma, rights, and available program services.
- Coordinate participation in local community fairs, workshops, and programs relating to victims of crime and victim witness rights.
- Collect accurate monthly data and all other statistics required for program implementation and progress.
- Participate in the development of procedures, techniques, and projects within the program.
- Participate in staff training and supervision and other appropriate meetings as necessary.
- Respond to all other program and client needs at the request of the program coordinator and assistance program coordinator, and do all other work required.

The following are three examples of services for seniors who are abused or neglected.

- Stevens Point, Wisconsin, has an elderly abuse network that makes referrals to the Human Services Department or Commission on Aging.
- In Springfield, Massachusetts, the Protective Service Agency for the Elderly reports abuse to the D.A.'s office and state police and victim/witness staff investigate. Other elderly victims are provided with transportation and other services as requested.
- Project S.E.A.R.C.H. (Seek out Elderly Abused Reaching out for Care and Help) in White Plains, New York, is a collaborative effort by the Westchester County

Office for the Aging and Victims Assistance Services of Westchester, Inc. It provides information and direct assistance to persons 60 years of age or older who may be the victims of abuse or neglect. A trained worker at the Westchester County Office for the Aging screens calls coming into the Project S.E.A.R.C.H. Help Line.

Conclusion

It has been projected that as many as five out of every six Americans will be crime victims one or more times during their lives. They will experience stress and short-term disequilibrium in the aftermath of the victimization, but most will survive and recover. Elderly crime victims may be the most vulnerable and isolated of victims. They have a strong need for support networks, and for concrete services. Therefore, it is imperative that aging crime victims be linked immediately with concerned relatives or friends, self-help groups for crime victims, and/or victim advocates. Their recovery and healing processes can be greatly facilitated by sensitive, concerned family members, friends, and/or victim advocates.

Note

1. I would like to acknowledge Professor Ray Koleski for preparing this case illustration.

References

Kahn, A. S. (Ed.). (1984). *Final report of the American Psychological Association Task Force on the Victims of Crime and Violence*. Washington, DC: American Psychological Association.

Miron, H. J., Goin, L. J., Keegan, S., & Archer, E. (1984). *The National Sheriffs' Association guidelines for victim assistance*. Alexandria, VA: National Sheriffs' Association.

National Organization for Victim Assistance. (1983). *The victim service system: A guide to action*. Washington, DC: Author.

Pepper, C. (1985, May 10). *Elder abuse: A national disgrace* (Opening statement at the hearings before the U.S. House of Representatives Select Committee on Health and Long-Term Care). Washington, DC: Government Printing Office.

Pillemer, K. A., & Finkelhor, D. (1987, June). *Domestic violence against the elderly*. Paper presented at the Third Conference on Family Violence, Durham, NH.

Schaie, K. W. (1982). America's elderly in the coming decade. In K. W. Schaie & J. Gerwitz (Eds.), *Adult development and aging*. Boston: Little, Brown.

Steinmetz, S. K. (1988). *Duty bound: Elder abuse and family care*. Newbury Park, CA: Sage.

4

Organizational Issues

Generally, three major issues affect the organizational stability, growth, and effectiveness of victim service and witness assistance programs: (a) the commitment and support of the parent agency (e.g., county prosecutor's office or county police department); (b) sources and level of funding; and (c) number and skill levels of staff. All three of these organizational issues are interrelated and affect the nature and extent of services available to victims and witnesses. For instance, sponsorship or auspice determines which agency and chief administrator have overall administrative authority over the victim program. The parent agency also influences the selection of primary funding sources, indirect matching funds, and the type of staffing pattern. The number of staff resources needed, in turn, affects estimates of program costs and the actual amount of funds requested. The sources and amount of funding received by each program determine the number of full-time staff who can be hired and their salaries.

Annual Budget Totals

The size of the 1984 annual budgets for victim/witness programs varied enormously, from a low of $500 to a high of $525,000, with an average program budget of $172,813. Overall funding for the 184 programs in this survey increased by 16.4% in 1985, from $31.8 million in 1984 to $37.9 million (see Table 4.1).[1] Because of the growth phase these victim/witness programs are experiencing, and the federal VOCA grants received by a number of the programs in 1986, $37 million was viewed as a low estimate of 1986 funding.

TABLE 4.1: Budgets

Total Allocations ($)	Number of Programs		Percentage[a]	
	1984	1985	1984	1985
Under 50,000	44	43	39.6	34.9
50,000-99,000	31	33	27.9	26.8
100,000-149,000	8	11	7.2	8.9
150,000-199,000	9	14	8.1	11.3
200,000-249,000	6	3	5.4	2.4
250,000-499,000	9	13	8.1	10.5
500,000-999,000	3	5	2.7	4.0
7,000,000	1	0	.9	0
9,000,000	0	1	0	.8
Total	111	123	99.9	99.6

a. Percentages for 1984 are based on 111 responses; percentages for 1985 are based on 123 responses.

Funding Sources

Of the survey programs, 84% (154) gave information on their funding sources and the approximate percentage of budget covered by each source. Many programs had more than one source of funding. Almost all of the responding programs (95%) received state and/or county funding. The most frequently reported funding source was state grants (43%), followed by county general revenue (33%). These two funding sources accounted for 80-100% of the programs' budgets in 1985. A 50/50 split between county and state funding sources was reported by 12% of the respondents; 7% of the program received the revenues collected from state penalty assessments and fines.

Federal grants and city government funds provided some portion of the funding for 10% and 4.5% of the programs, respectively. A small number of programs reported receiving partial funding from the local United Way, foundation grants, fund-raising events, or donations.

Brief descriptions of the sources and amount of funding received by four different programs serve to illustrate the multiple sources of funding of some programs, as well as their heavy reliance on county and state government grants (see Table 4.2).

The Center for Victims of Violent Crime, Pittsburgh, Pennsylvania, is a private, nonprofit social service corporation. Since 1974 it has been providing comprehensive victim services for the 131 communities that make up Allegheny County, through a coordinated effort between the center and the office of the district attorney. The center reported the following multiple funding sources for the 1984/1985 fiscal year:

TABLE 4.2: Funding Sources

Source	Number of Programs	Percentage[a]
State grants	66	42.9
County general revenue (80-100%)	51	33
County and state (50/50)	18	11.7
State penalty assessments/fines	11	7
City government	7	4.5
United Way	7	4.5
Federal grant	16	10.3
Department of Criminal Justice Service's	3	
Justice Assistance Act	3	
Title XX	2	
Victim of Crimes Act of 1984	2	
Human Service Development Fund	1	
Mental Health Systems Act	1	
community development block grant	1	
unspecified	3	
Private foundations	7	4.5
Junior League	2	
Area Fund of Dutchess City	1	
Z. Smith Reynolds	1	
Lutheran Social Services	1	
unspecified	2	
Other	10	5.4
private donations	5	
fund-raising events	2	
local banks	1	
hospitals	1	
church and community sources	1	
Total	193	

a. Percentages are based on 154 respondents.

Source	Amount ($)	Approximate Percentage of Budget
county general revenue	66,805	28.4
state government	65,294	27.8
city grant	20,379	8.7
federal grant (NIMH)	11,545	4.9
other grants	11,851	5.1
other support and revenues	59,016	25.1
total support and revenues	234,890	100.0

Government funding accounted for 70% of the total support and revenue. A combination of contributions, revenue, and in-kind donations made up the remaining 30% of funds received. In-kind donations of property, materials, and services supplied 21% of the total support and revenue. Contributions, accounting for 8% of the total funding, were made by individuals, through Donor Option/United Way, and in the form of grants from local businesses and other local groups. Revenue, primarily from interest and speaking engagements, added 1% of the funding total. Some of the local business and other groups supporting the Pittsburgh Center for Victims of Violent Crimes are the Alcoa Foundation, Mellon Bank, Monroe Business and Professional Women's Club, Pennsylvania Coalition Against Rape, Pittsburgh Press, Program to Aid Citizen Enterprise, Urban League of Pittsburgh, Inc., Western Psychiatric Institute and Clinic, and 3M Company.

The Crime Victim Centers program, developed by the Minnesota Citizen Council on Crime and Justice in 1976, serves seven counties from six locations in the Minneapolis/St. Paul metropolitan area. In 1985 the program consisted of three full-time centers, two satellite offices that were open on a part-time schedule, and one metrowide mobile unit. The program reported the following sources of funding in 1985:

Source	Amount ($)	Approximate Percentage of Budget
state government		
(Department of Corrections)	112,380	50
United Way	104,756	46
private foundation	2,236	1
general and individual contributions	6,538	3
total	255,910	100

The State Department of Corrections is the primary source of funding, with United Way funding a close second.

The Savannah, Georgia, Victim/Witness Assistance Program, located in the District Attorney's Office of Chatham County, became operational in August 1983. At that time, the county was the only source of funding, providing $43,000 for a Victim/Witness Assistance Office staffed by a full-time director, a full-time assistant, and a part-time clerk-typist. By 1984 the program's budget had grown to $65,715, of which 82% came from the county, and 18% from the Junior League.

The Fresno (California) County Victim/Witness Service Center, affiliated with the Probation Department and located in the courtroom, receives office space and equipment from the county. Its entire budget ($154,620 for fiscal year 1984-1985) was funded by the state restitution fund from payments of fines and penalty assessments.

Since 1980, victim advocacy services within the justice system have doubled. The number and size of victim/witness programs have increased due to funds provided by federal and state legislation. Programs that were primarily volunteer efforts in the past are now eligible to receive funds under the provisions of the federal Victims of Crime Act (VOCA) of 1984. During the 1985-1986 and 1986-1987 fiscal years, VOCA funding provided major incentives and support for increasing local victim assistance efforts. In 1985-1986, $41.3 million was allocated to the states to bolster local victim assistance programs. In addition, $23.6 million was allocated to state victim compensation programs. Also, laws enacted in twenty-one states since 1982 are providing funds for services to victims of all crimes.

Federal criminal fines and penalties generated a total of $41,270,000 collected in 1985 under the Victims of Violent Crime Act. These funds, shared by the states on a population formula basis, have enabled many state programs to expand their services to crime victims significantly. For example, as a result of the federal grant to Illinois, that state has been able to more than triple the amount spent on victim aid in 1984. In New York, the grant has doubled the state's expenditures.

Staffing Patterns

Most victim/witness assistance programs operate with a relatively small number of full-time staff. At the time of the survey, nearly three-fourths (121, or 74.2%) of the programs employed five or fewer full-time staff members. Unfortunately, of the 163 programs providing information about their staffs, 19 reported having no full-time positions (see Table 4.3). Part-time workers, deputy prosecutors, and volunteers were most often mentioned by these services as constituting the staff.

Programs with larger numbers of staff generally served large, highly populated cities. A total of 26 programs reported between 6 and 10 full-time staff positions, while only 11 reported having between 11 and 20 full-time staff. Only 5 of the programs (3%) reported having 21 or more full-time staff members, and these tended to be located in the highly populated, high-crime areas of the

TABLE 4.3: Size of Staff

Number of Staff Members	Number of Programs	Percentage[a]
1-5	121	74.2
6-10	26	15.9
11-13	7	4.2
14-16	0	0
17-20	4	2.4
21-24	3	1.8
35 +	2	1.2
Total	163	99.7

NOTE: A total of 19 programs have no full-time staff; they are staffed by part-time workers, deputy prosecutors, and the like. The question was left blank by 2 responding programs.

a. Percentages are based on 163 responses.

country, such as Miami, New York, and Los Angeles. These programs were as follows:

- Palm Beach County Victim/Witness Services (county criminal justice agency), West Palm Beach, Florida (population 940,000)
- Victim/Witness Assistance Program (state attorney), Miami, Florida (population 2,000,000)
- Los Angeles City Attorney Victims of Crime Program, Los Angeles, California (population 3,300,000)
- CSP, Inc., Victim/Witness Assistance Program (nonprofit criminal justice agency), Santa Ana, California (population 1,933,000)
- Victim Services Agency (nonprofit social service agency), New York, New York (population 8,275,000)

Volunteers

Many programs rely on volunteer assistance to provide needed services. More than half of the total respondents (96, or 52%) reported that volunteers constituted part of their staffing pattern. Table 4.4 shows the number of volunteers used by these programs. While approximately one-third (34%) of the programs used one to four volunteers, almost half (46%) of the programs had ten or more volunteers.

Programs with smaller paid staffs had a tendency to rely heavily on volunteers. For example, volunteer participation enabled programs to provide services to victims in such communities as the following:

TABLE 4.4: Number of Volunteers

Number of Volunteers	Number of Programs	Percentage[a]
1-4	33	34.3
5-9	18	18.7
10-19	18	18.7
20-29	7	7.2
30-39	7	7.2
40-49	7	7.2
50-59	1	1.0
60-69	3	3.1
185	1	1.0
300	1	1.0
Total	96	99.40

a. Percentages are based on a total of 96 responses.

- Savannah, Georgia, Victim/Witness Assistance Program (D.A's Office): population 200,000; 1,600 victims served in 1984; 2 full-time paid staff members; 50-60 volunteers

- Xenia, Ohio, Victim/Witness Division-Greene County Prosecutor's Office: population 130,000; 314 victims served in 1984; 4 full-time paid staff members; 25 volunteers

- Sanford, Florida, Seminole County Sheriff's Department Victim Services: population 23,000; 300 victims served in 1984; 1 full-time paid staff member; 10-14 volunteers

- Greensboro, North Carolina, Turning Point: Victim Assistance (nonprofit social service agency): population 350,000; 1,500 victims served in 1984; 2 full-time paid staff members; 12 volunteers

Volunteers also helped provide services in programs located in the following cities:

- Santa Ana, California, CSP, Inc., Victim/Witness Assistance Program: population 1,933,000; 8,790 victims served in 1984; 35 full-time paid staff members; 60 volunteers

- Houston, Texas, Police Department Crisis Team: population 2,410,000; 1,902 victims served in 1984; 12 full-time paid staff members; 40 volunteers

- Pittsburgh, Pennsylvania, Center for Victims of Violent Crimes (nonprofit social service agency): population 1,500,000; 1,376 victims served in 1984; 11 full-time paid staff members; 20 volunteers

Educational Background

More than 90% of the 541 staff members in victim/witness assistance programs had at least bachelor's degrees. Of that group, more than one-fourth (28%) also had graduate degrees, usually in social work, sociology, criminal justice, or counseling. A small group (21, or 4.4%) had J.D. degrees, and 2 had Ph.D. degrees. The professional degrees earned by staff are presented in Table 4.5.

Program coordinators. A total of 86% of the coordinators of the reporting victim/witness assistance programs held bachelor's or master's degrees, with the numbers split almost evenly (44% and 42%, respectively) between the two. Law degrees (J.D.) were held by 7.6% of the coordinators, while one held a Ph.D. Two coordinators were nondegreed workers: a deputy sheriff and a paralegal worker.

At the bachelor's level, coordinators nearly always held B.A. or B.S. degrees (96%), while 3% held social work (B.S.W) degrees and one position was filled by a registered nurse.

At the master's level, M.A. or M.S. degree holders were still employed more often (55%), but social workers (M.S.W.) were highly represented (32%). Of the master's-level coordinators, 8% held degrees in public administration, while 4% of these positions were held by persons holding M.Ed. degrees. The educational backgrounds of all program coordinators are shown in Table 4.6.

Primary Sources of Referral

The primary sources of referral to the responding programs are shown in Table 4.7. Each program identified its four most frequent sources, with 1 being the most frequent. Seventeen primary sources of referral are listed in Table 4.7.

Overall, the most frequent source of referral was police departments (152 total responses). District attorney's offices/assistant prosecutors were named by a total of 80 programs, followed by social service agencies (76 total responses).

The Sacramento County D.A.'s Victim/Witness Assistance Program is an example of the above response pattern. The program reported a total of 400-500 victim referrals per month. "Law enforcement" was named as the most frequent referral source. Police referred or brought victims to the program between 8:00 a.m. and 3:00 p.m. on the day following the victimization. The second most frequent referral source, "prosecuting attorneys," referred victims to the program as charges were filed. These two sources accounted for the majority of victim referrals. Public and private social service agencies were named as third and fourth most frequent sources, respectively.

The Erie County District Attorney's Office Victim/Witness Assistance Program in Buffalo, New York, lists the Buffalo Police Department as its number

TABLE 4.5: Number of Staff by Highest Degree Earned

Highest Degree Earned	Number of Staff Members	Percentage[a]
B.A./B.S.	259	47.8
M.S.W.	82	15.1
M.A./M.S.	72	13.3
B.S.W.	56	10.3
J.D.	24	4.4
A.A.	12	2.2
Ph.D.	2	.3
R.N.	1	.1
Other:		
high school +	27	4.9
paralegal	6	1.1
Total	541	99.5

a. Percentages are based on 541 responses.

one source of referral. During 1983-1984 the police department referred 10,309 crime reports on a next-day basis. Referrals directly from crime scenes were increasing. The program's 1983-1984 annual report listed the following primary referral sources: police, 65%; district attorney, 15%; warrant clerk, 10%; self-referral, 10%.

A total of 44 programs listed self-referrals/walk-ins as a primary source of referral. It is not clear how these victims were made aware of the victim/witness programs and their services. Some may have had previous firsthand experience with the criminal justice system. Some may have received information from other agencies or programs but were not directly referred by these programs. Other agencies and programs listed as sources of referral in Table 4.7 are as follows:

- hospitals/hospital emergency rooms (41 responses)
- community mental health and crisis centers (27 responses)
- other victims, family members (26 responses)
- battered women's shelters (20 responses)
- public information advertising (18 responses)
- rape and sexual assault services (15 responses)
- attorneys (14 responses)
- county departments of children and youth (11 responses)
- victim advocacy groups (11 responses)
- Department of Human Resources (10 responses)

TABLE 4.6: Educational Backgrounds of Program Coordinators

Highest Degree Earned	Number of Coordinators	Percentage[a]
Associate level	7	4.4
Bachelor's level		43.9
B.A./B.S.	66	
B.S.W.	2	
R.N.	1	
Total	69	
Master's level		42.0
M.A./M.S.	36	
M.S.W.	21	
M.P.A.	5	
M.Ed.	4	
Total	66	
J.D. level	12	7.6
Ph.D. level	1	.6
Other—no degree		1.2
deputy sheriff	1	
paralegal	1	
Total	2	
Total	157	99.7

a. Percentages are based on 157 responses.

Staffing, Annual Budget, and Number of Victims Served in Relation to City Size

Respondents were asked to provide information concerning the total number of full-time staff members, their 1984 budget, and the number of victims served in 1984. The size of full-time program staff varied from none to 24 full-time employees.[2] The 1984 budgets ranged from $500 to $525,000, with a mean of $172,813. The number of victims served in 1984 by each program ranged from 217 to 6,790 (excluding the New York program that reported serving approximately 100,000 victims).

It was predicted that the most populated cities would have the highest number

TABLE 4.7: Primary Sources of Referral

Source	Most Frequent	Second Most Frequent	Third Most Frequent	Fourth Most Frequent	Total Responses
Police departments	95	35	12	10	152
D.A.s/assistant prosecutors	39	23	10	6	80
Social service agencies	5	20	26	25	76
Self-referrals/walks-ins	7	9	16	12	44
Medical/hospital E.R.s	4	17	18	2	41
Community mental health and crisis centers	2	10	10	5	27
Other victims, family members	1	4	8	13	26
Battered women's shelters	3	4	10	3	20
Public information/advertising	1	4	4	9	18
Outreach letters	9	3	3	0	15
Rape and sexual assault services	0	7	4	4	15
Attorneys	3	1	5	5	14
State departments of children and youth	1	6	2	2	11
Victim advocacy groups	0	4	3	4	11
Departments of Human Resources	1	4	3	2	10
Probation officer felony screenings	0	2	5	3	10
24-hour hot lines	0	1	1	0	2
Total	171	154	140	105	570

of victims of violent crimes; therefore, if programs were developed based on community needs alone, the programs with the largest budgets, staffs, and numbers of victims would be in the ten largest responding cities. Likewise, the ten smallest cities would have the victim service or witness assistance programs that served the smallest numbers of victims and had the smallest budgets and full-time staffs. (See Tables 4.8-4.10.)

Of the 184 responding programs, 176 gave complete information on their full-time staffing patterns. In order to determine whether the funding, staffing, and victims served by each program varied by the population of the city in which the program was located, an analysis was made based on five types of cities: small towns (populations 60,000 and below), small cities (populations 61,000-275,000), medium-sized cities (populations 276,000-499,000), large cities (populations 500,000-1,999,000), and major cities (populations 2,000,000 and over).

TABLE 4.8: Program Respondents in Ten Cities with Populations Between 700,000 and 851,000

City	Population	Number of Full-Time Staff	Auspices	Number of Victims Served in 1984	1984 Budget ($)
Upper Marlboro, MD	700,000	7	state's attorney	500	170,000
Monroe County, NY (Rochester)	702,000	1	prosecutor	1,805	153,000
DuPage County, NY	725,000	1	state's attorney	650	—
San Francisco County, CA	735,000	6	prosecutor	2,815	218,009
Rochester, NY	750,000	5	police department	5,079	78,644
Indianapolis, IN	765,000	4	police department	2,700	99,000
Marion County, IN (Indianapolis)	765,000	7	prosecutor	—	—
Orlando, FL	800,000	3	police department	594	—
Memphis, TN	810,000	3	state's attorney	4,200	—
Hackensack, NJ	845,000	2	prosecutor	200	50,000
White Plains, NY	850,000	4	nonprofit	1,712	—
Nashville, TN	851,000	4	prosecutor	—	75,000+

SOURCE: U.S. Department of Commerce, Bureau of the Census (1982).

TABLE 4.9: Programs in the Ten Smallest Responding Towns

Town	Population	Number of Full-Time Staff	Auspices	Number of Victims Served in 1984	1984 Budget ($)
Eddyville, KY	2,000	0	state's attorney	—	1,000
Crescent City, CA	3,000	1	nonprofit	21	16,666
Lakeport, CA	4,000	2	prosecutor	100	50,000
Valdez, AK	7,500	3	nonprofit	130	—
Meadville, PA	16,000	1	nonprofit	200	39,000
Bend, OR	17,000	1	prosecutor	900	23,000
Black River Falls, WI	17,000	0	prosecutor	500	4,007
South Bend, WA	17,000	0	prosecutor	1,500	5,000
West Chester, PA	17,000	6	nonprofit	385	123,000
Brunswick, GA	18,000	0	nonprofit	15	500

SOURCE: U.S. Department of Commerce, Bureau of the Census (1984).

TABLE 4.10: Program Respondents in the Ten Largest Cities

City	Population	Number of Full-Time Staff	Auspices	Number of Victims Served in 1984	1984 Budget ($)
New York, NY	8,275,000	337	nonprofit	100,000	7,000,000
Los Angeles, CA	3,300,000	24	prosecutor	15,000	612,000
Garden City, NY	2,606,000	1	county social services agency	548	22,718
Baltimore, MD	2,500,000	6	state's attorney	—	157,589
Houston, TX	2,410,000	12	police department	1,902	219,250
Greater Miami, FL	2,000,000	23	state's attorney	40,000	—
Santa Ana, CA	1,933,000	35	nonprofit	8,790	499,961
St. Louis, MO	1,788,000	6	prosecutor	—	70,000
Dade County, FL (Miami Beach)	1,626,000	17	prosecutor	5,072	773,000
Phoenix, AZ	1,509,000	13	prosecutor	4,302	350,000
Pittsburgh, PA	1,500,000	11	nonprofit	1,376	160,781

SOURCE: U.S. Department of Commerce, Bureau of the Census (1982).

Program Auspices

The responding programs were grouped according to auspices and size of city (see Table 4.11). Of the 184 respondents, 176 formed six major auspices categories. The auspices of the remaining respondents (hospital, 3; U.S. attorney, 1; compensation program, 1; membership/study group, 1; no information, 2) were excluded from this analysis because of their uniqueness and highly specialized focus.

The greatest number of programs (106, or 60%) were based in city or county prosecutors' offices. Nonprofit social service or criminal justice agency programs made up the second largest category (23 programs, or 13%). State's attorney-based programs (21, or 12%) followed closely, and 13 (7%) police-based programs, 8 (5%) county probation-based programs, and 5 (3%) county social service or criminal justice agencies completed the categories. A look at the numbers of respondents by size of city reveals that there was a large number of responses from small cities and a small response rate from major cities. The small city category contained close to one-third of all responses (56, or 32%). The large city and small town groups also had large numbers of respondents, 27% and 23%, respectively. A total of 25 responses (14%) came from medium-sized cities. Only 7 (4%) responses came from major cities. Several large population areas were served by more than one program.

Variations in Staffing and Total Number of Victims Served

Tables 4.12 through 4.17 examine programs in each auspices category in relation to the total number of full-time staff members, the annual budget, and the number of victims served. Distribution is by size of city.

For purposes of comparing programs, it was necessary to eliminate those that did not provide complete information in all areas. Therefore, the number of programs used for each auspices category is smaller than the total respondents for that category as reported in Table 4.11. In some instances the data presented for size of city are based on only one or two responses. It is difficult to make any definitive statements based on such a small sample. However, some trends are evident in the data when the tables are examined as a whole.

One would expect that as the size of a city increases, the number of staff, budget, and number of victims served would also increase. In general, the data show that the average number of full-time staff increases as size of city increases. The average 1984 budget also increases as size of city increases, except in several categories where only one program provided complete information.

The surprising finding occurs under the category of he average number of victims served in 1984. Larger cities do not appear to serve greater numbers

TABLE 4.11: Program Auspices in Relation to Size of City

Size of City (population)	Prosecutor-Based	State's Attorney-Based	Police-Based	Nonprofit Agencies	County Probation-Based	County Agencies	Total	Percentage
Small town (60,000 and under)	23	4	2	7	4	0	40	23
Small city (61,000-275,000)	42	4	4	3	1	2	56	32
Medium-sized city (276,000-499,000)	16	2	2	3	1	1	25	14
Large city (500,000-1,999,000)	23	9	4	9	2	1	48	27
Major city (2,000,000+)	2	2	1	1	0	1	7	4
Total	106	21	13	23	8	5	176	
Percentage	60	12	7	13	5	3		100

SOURCE: U.S. Department of Commerce, Bureau of the Census (1982).

of victims. Table 14.12 shows that the average number of victims served by prosecutor-based programs increases through the medium-sized city category. The large city category shows a drop of almost 1,200 in the average number of victims served in 1984. This drop occurs even though the average number of full-time staff and average budget are considerably higher for the large city group than for the medium-sized city group.

Tables 4.13 and 4.14 have only one or two responses for each city size category. These limited data, however, illustrate the same drop in number of victims served. Table 4.13, which shows state's attorney-based programs, illustrates that the small cities serve the greatest average number of victims. This number drops for medium-sized cities and drops again for large cities even though the latter two categories show larger budgets and staffs. Police-based programs (Table 4.14) show an increase in the average number of victims served in 1984 through medium-sized cities, a leveling off at large cities, and a drop for major cities.

Only nonprofit agency programs (see Table 4.15) show the expected increase by size of city in all categories, with the exception of small city budget. A drop in small city average budget results in a small increase in average number of full-time staff and average number of victims served in 1984.

Tables 4.16 and 4.17 present single responses for each city size category. As shown in Table 4.16, small cities served the greatest number of victims in 1984, while Table 4.17 shows that medium-sized cities served the greatest number of victims in 1984, followed by drops for large cities and major cities. Drops in number of victims served were accompanied by smaller budgets in three of the four programs represented in these tables.

Conclusion

This chapter has focused on sources and levels of funding and staffing patterns. Most of the responding victim/witness assistance programs (95%) received state and/or county general-revenue funds. Although there is wide variation in the annual budgets of the 184 programs, overall funding increased during the study period (1984-1987). Obtaining stable and continual operating funds, year after year, has been one of the most significant problems facing social service and criminal justice agencies. Despite the scarcity of funds, the established prosecutor- and police-based victim assistance programs have not only survived during the 1980s, a decade of social welfare cutbacks, but in many instances they have increased staff and services. Nevertheless, the overwhelming majority of the programs operate with relatively small full-time staffs of five or fewer professionals. Paid staffs are often augmented by corps of volunteers; more than half (52%) of the respondents stated that they rely on volunteers.

TABLE 4.12: Prosecutor-Based Programs: Distribution by Size of City (N = 52)

| Size of City (population) | Prosecutor-Based Witness Assistance Programs | | Average Number of Full-Time Staff | Average 1984 Budget ($) | Average Number of Victims Served in 1984 |
	Number	Percentage			
Small town (60,000 and under)	13	25	1.4	33,672	745
Small city (61,000-275,000)	22	42	2.6	51,001	3,979
Medium-sized city (276,000-499,000)	4	8	2.8	81,278	5,990
Large city (500,000-1,999,000)	12	23	10.6	301,359	4,795
Major city (2,000,000+)	1	2	24	612,000	15,000

TABLE 4.13: State's Attorney-Based Witness Assistance Programs: Distribution by Size of City (N = 5)

| Size of City (population) | State's Attorney-Based Witness Assistance Programs | | Average Number of Full-Time Staff | Average 1984 Budget ($) | Average Number of Victims Served in 1984 |
	Number	Percentage			
Small town (60,000 and under)	0	—	—	—	—
Small city (61,000-275,000)	2	40	1.5	23,500	1,660
Medium-sized city (276,000-499,000)	1	20	7	110,500	1,448
Large city (500,000-1,999,000)	2	40	7	140,000	980
Major city (2,000,000+)	0	—	—	—	—

TABLE 4.14: Police-Based Victim Service Programs: Distribution by Size of City (N = 7)

Size of City (population)	Police-Based Victim Service Programs		Average Number of Full-Time Staff	Average 1984 Budget ($)	Average Number of Victims Served in 1984
	Number	Percentage			
Small town (60,000 and under)	1	14	1	50,000	300
Small city (61,000-275,000)	2	29	6.5	188,500	1,093
Medium-sized city (276,000-499,000)	1	14	2	45,000	2,893
Large city (500,000-1,999,000)	2	29	5	114,322	2,892
Major city (2,000,000+)	1	14	12	219,250	1,902

TABLE 4.15: Nonprofit Social Service or Criminal Justice Agency Programs: Distribution by Size of City (N = 18)

Size of City (population)	Nonprofit Social Service or Criminal Justice Agency Programs		Average Number of Full-Time Staff	Average 1984 Budget ($)	Average Number of Victims Served in 1984
	Number	Percentage			
Small town (60,000 and under)	6	33	2.7	76,528	232
Small city (61,000-275,000)	3	16	3	42,000	329
Medium-sized city (276,000-499,000)	1	6	7	95,000	1,188
Large city (500,000-1,999,000)	7	39	9.9	190,278	3,125
Major city (2,000,000+)	1	6	337	7,000,000	100,000

TABLE 4.16: County Probation Department Programs: Distribution by Size of City (N = 5)

Size of City (population)	County Probation Department Programs		Average Number of Full-Time Staff	Average 1984 Budget ($)	Average Number of Victims Served in 1984
	Number	Percentage			
Small town (60,000 and under)	1	20	1	42,110	607
Small city (61,000-275,000)	1	20	4	170,000	1,218
Medium-sized city (276,000-499,000)	1	20	4	56,000	932
Large city (500,000-1,999,000)	2	40	2.5	114,266	1,053
Major city (2,000,000 +)	—	—	—	—	—

TABLE 4.17: County Social Service or Criminal Justice Agency Programs: Distribution by Size of City (N = 3)

Size of City (population)	County Social Service or Criminal Justice Agency Programs		Average Number of Full-Time Staff	Average 1984 Budget ($)	Average Number of Victims Served in 1984
	Number	Percentage			
Small town (60,000 and under)	0	—	—	—	—
Small city (61,000-275,000)	0	—	—	—	—
Medium-sized city (276,000-499,000)	1	33	9	210,171	6,930
Large city (500,000-1,999,000)	1	33	21	525,000	4,500 +
Major city (2,000,000 +)	1	33	1	22,718	548

Notes

1. These figures were based on the following estimates: A total of 111 respondents provided budget information indicating that they had received $19.1 million in 1984, or an average of $172,813 per program. An extrapolation of the total 1984 budget for all 184 programs can be made by multiplying that $172,813 by 184. The result is an estimate of $31.8 million allocated in 1984 for the 184 program respondents. For 1985, 124 programs provided budget information that indicated they had received $24.9 million, or an average of $200,832 per program. An extrapolation of the total 1985 budget for all 184 respondents can be made by multiplying the average by 184. The result is an estimate of $37 million allocated in 1985.

2. One responding victims' center in New York City has 337 full-time staff members. However, since this program is completely unique—having a large headquarters office, eight neighborhood satellite offices, three court-based programs, three battered women's shelters, and one school-based program—it is not included in these figures.

Reference

U.S. Department of Commerce, Bureau of the Census. (1982). *State and metropolitan area data book.* Washington, DC: Government Printing Office.

5

Victim/Witness Programs: Self-Evaluation of Strengths, Problems, and Needed Changes

In order to determine the strengths and major problems of the victim/witness programs, as well as ways in which they could be improved, the following three questions were asked:

(1) Please identify the three biggest problem areas by ranking them from most severe problem (number 1) to least severe problem (number 3).

    (a) funding ____

    (b) staff turnover ____

    (c) lack of space ____

    (d) liaison with police ____

    (e) relationship with court ____

    (f) attrition of volunteers ____

    (g) other (please specify) _____

    _____

(2) What do you consider to be the strongest or best feature of your victim services program as it is now constituted?

(3) If money were no object, what changes would you make in your program/unit?

The above questions provided an opportunity for the programs to assess their strengths and weaknesses, particularly as they addressed the open-ended questions.

Three Biggest Problems

Respondents were asked to identify their three biggest problem areas, ranking them from most severe to least severe. As shown above, problem areas provided on the questionnaire were funding, staff turnover, lack of space, liaison with police, relationship with court, attrition of volunteers, and other. As shown in Table 5.1, funding was the most significant problem (140 total responses ranked 1, 2, or 3) and received the most responses (98) as the problem ranked first. Lack of space was the second biggest overall problem (118 total responses), receiving the highest number of responses (53) as the problem ranked second. Attrition of volunteers was ranked third, with 50 total responses. Relationship with the court, liaison with the police, and staff turnover were named with similar frequency (27 to 30 total responses). Most of these responses were in the second- or third-ranked position.

A total of 55 programs provided insight into their unique problems by filling in the open-ended "other" response on the questionnaire. Of these, 20 cited lack of adequate staff, with seven ranking it first. Other problems named by two programs each included the following:

- lack of an adequate waiting area in the courthouse for victims and witnesses
- lack of equipment
- expansion of program
- lack of training of professionals (physicians, D.A.s, police)
- turf problems
- a serious need to automate data-gathering and tracking functions of the program
- current legislation in need of revision
- poor relationships with probation officers

Additional problem areas, mentioned by one respondent each, were as follows:

- completing annual state reports and budgets
- D.A. was removed from office, causing turmoil
- lack of understanding of program outside of the D.A.'s office
- unrealistic monetary requests by victims
- treatment of victims in the criminal justice system
- transient population
- legal assistance for crime victims
- restitution collection assistance
- finding low-cost follow-up counseling for victims

TABLE 5.1: Three Biggest Problems

Problem Area	Rank 1	2	3	Total
Funding	98	29	13	140
Lack of space	44	53	21	118
Attrition of volunteers	4	21	25	50
Relationship with court	4	12	14	30
Liaison with police	4	10	14	28
Staff turnover	5	11	11	27
Other				55
lack of adequate staff	7	5	8	20

- educating the public
- limited supplies
- staff morale
- liaison with D.A.
- poor salaries
- need for more police referrals
- need for more volunteers
- witness reluctance due to lost wages
- referral of appropriate cases

Best Features of the Programs

Table 5.2 presents the programs' self-reported responses regarding their strongest or best features. Many respondents listed more than one feature, resulting in 252 responses. For the purposes of this book, I have grouped these responses into five main categories. The first category, *comprehensive services/ specialized services*, received the highest number of responses, with 92 out of 252, or 36.5% of the total. The remaining categories all had similar numbers of responses: *court support, advocacy, and/or court escort*, 46 responses (18.3%); *referrals and interagency linkages*, 42 responses (16.7%); *case information and status*, 39 responses (15.5%); and *use of trained and dedicated staff and/or volunteers*, 33 responses (13.1%).

Comprehensive/Specialized Services

Personal or Immediate Assistance and Availability

- Buffalo, New York: "We strive to make accessibility to the public our best feature. At this time we are only staffed 9-5, but we do flex our schedule and do a lot of fieldwork, escorts, home visits, and precinct visits."

- Littleton, Colorado: "That we are housed out of a law enforcement agency, thereby providing *immediate* service to the victim after a crime has been reported. This is a relatively new concept in that most victim services operate out of a D. A.'s office, thereby only servicing victims that get to court. . . . All reported violent crime victims receive immediate attention when a program is housed out of a law enforcement agency."

- A Pacific Northwest program: "Having witnesses and victims feeling comfortable enough with me that they feel they can call or drop in at any time, knowing I will drop everything to pay attention to their needs, both during the court process of their case, and after."

24-Hour Availability and Response to Victims

- Tuscaloosa, Alabama: "The 24-hour on-call service. I feel it is *imperative* that immediate crisis counseling is available to the victim at the scene of the crime or at the hospital, etc."

- Dayton, Ohio: "24-hour supportive services with strong positive working relationship with area law enforcement."

- A California program: "Through the efforts of staff and volunteers, the program is available 24 hours a day."

Assistance with Compensation Forms and Processing

- Spokane, Washington: "Assist victim with crime compensation and restitution."

- South Lake Tahoe, California: "Rapid filing for victim compensation."

- Mangum, Oklahoma: "Assistance with victim compensation applications."

Monitoring and Collecting Restitution

- Chehalis, Washington: "Monitoring of and collecting of restitution."

- Media, Pennsylvania: "This unit as a whole provides adequate assistance to all victims and witnesses. Two computer terminals have been added to this program. One terminal has been connected to Central Collection (Restitution), and the second terminal will soon be hooked into the courts. With the accessibility of this information we will be able to provide immediate and precise information to victims."

- Eddyville, Kentucky: "The restitution which we have recovered for victims—over $12,000 in 1985."

Court Support, Advocacy, and/or Court Escort

Two of the five features listed in this category received nearly equal numbers of responses. These were "orient witness to criminal court process and court escort," which received 19 responses, and court support that was cited as the strongest feature by 18 programs. Some illustrative responses include the following:

TABLE 5.2: Strongest or Best Feature of the Program as It Is Now Constituted

Strongest or Best Feature	Number of Programs	Percentage[a]
Comprehensive/specialized services		
Personal or immediate assistance and availability	14	7.6
Assistance with victim compensation forms and processing	10	5.4
Monitoring and collecting of restitution	10	5.4
24-hour availability and response to victims	10	5.4
Crisis intervention	9	4.8
Responsiveness to child sexual assault victims	8	4.3
Provision of professional counseling	7	3.8
Provision of comprehensive service to victims	6	3.2
Responsiveness to victims of rape, incest, and domestic violence	6	3.2
Emergency services to victims (e.g., food, lock repair)	3	1.6
Provision of services during most stressful periods	2	1.0
Ability to respond to the victim in the E.R.	1	.5
Support group for survivors of violent crimes	1	.5
Extensive outreach service to crime victims	2	1.0
Mobile units and victimization education group	1	.5
Provision of transportation and language interpreters	1	.5
Responsiveness to wide variety of victims and settings	1	.5
Total	92	36.5
Court Support, advocacy, and/or court escort		
Orient witness to criminal court process and court escort	19	10.3
Provision of court support	18	9.7
Helping victims to prepare victim impact statements	6	3.2
Advocacy in the local district courts	2	1.0
Advocacy program for domestic violent victims	1	.5
Total	46	18.3
Interagency linkages and referrals		
Rapport and/or linkages with local police departments	14	7.6
Liaison with D.A.'s office and other agencies	10	5.4
Good referral linkages and systems	7	3.8
Strong network of support groups for referral	5	2.7
Referrals for anyone in crisis	3	1.6
Follow-up of victim inquiries and referrals	3	1.6
Total	42	16.7
Case information		
Provision of information on case status	25	13.5

TABLE 5.2 (Continued)

Strongest or Best Feature	Number of Programs	Percentage[a]
Case information (continued)		
Witness notification process	10	5.4
On-call service for rescheduled cases	2	1.0
Computer terminals that provide immediate and precise information to victims	2	1.0
Total	39	15.5
Use of trained and dedicated staff and/or volunteers		
Dedicated professional staff	18	9.7
Use of trained and/or dedicated volunteers	11	5.9
Funding that allows for adequate staffing	3	1.6
Social worker to assist victims of sexual assault and aggravated assault	1	.5
Total	33	13.1

a. Percentages are based on 184 respondents. There are 252 strongest program features listed, because some respondents listed more than one feature. Percentage totals show proportion of all 252 responses that fall into each category.

- San Rafael, California: "Orientation to the criminal justice system and court escort."
- Casper, Wyoming: "Preparation of witnesses for court, especially children."
- Norman, Oklahoma: "Victim support and preparation for the prosecution process."
- Wailuku, Maui, Hawaii: "Support counseling of victims and preparation of victims in violent crime cases, especially sexual assault, to testify in court."
- Indianapolis, Indiana: "Information and explanation of the court process and experience for victims as well as escort and moral support through court proceedings (particularly in the area of domestic violence)."
- Columbus, Ohio: "Aiding victims to understand the court system and providing emotional support during a very traumatic period."

Referrals and Interagency Linkages

A total of 42 of the responses regarding the best or strongest program feature were related to interagency linkages and referrals. Of these, 14 programs, primarily based in district attorneys' offices, cited "rapport and/or linkages with local police departments" as their strongest feature; ten programs regarded their liaison with D.A.s' offices and other agencies as their best feature. Other responses in this category included good referral linkages (five responses), referral for anyone in crisis (three responses), and follow-up of victim inquiries and referrals (three responses). Listed below are examples of responses concerning these features:

- Greenville, South Carolina: "Excellent interoffice cooperation between attorneys, investigators, Victim/Witness Assistance Program staff and police."

- Ventura, California: "The strongest feature of the Ventura Program is the excellent reputation we have built with these agencies: law enforcement, domestic violence prevention centers, Rape Crisis Center, Child Abuse/Neglect Center."

- New Brunswick, New Jersey: "By being part of the County Prosecutor's Office the victim/witness coordinator has excellent rapport with all police departments within the county."

- Wilmington, Delaware: "Our direct interaction with crime victims and the 'team' approach we provide during prosecution—our 'team' approach involves a very close working relationship with the police and the assigned prosecutor."

- West Chester, Pennsylvania: "Confidence of criminal justice, law enforcement and social services in the center—its staff and volunteers."

- Salem, Massachusetts: "The program enjoys strong support from the district attorney and the entire staff. We provide a wide range of services that are seen as both necessary and helpful to victims."

- Yuba City, California: "Close liaison with law enforcement. Working relationship with the courts. Cooperation with other victim/witness agencies both public and private. Networking of community resources."

- A California program: "Through attendance at local meetings (Human Resource Council, Child Abuse Council, etc.) we have established a very good basis for distributing information about our services to all agencies that assist people. We now get notified of almost all victims, even though they've not been to the police yet—productive networking with agencies."

Case Information and Status

Of the 39 responses in the category of case information, 60% consisted of generic references to providing information on case status. Of the remaining 14 responses in this category, 10 cited their programs' witness notification processes in general. Two programs stated that their on-call service for rescheduling cases was their best feature. Computer terminals that provide immediate and precise information to victims were also cited by two services. Some examples of responses in this category follow:

- Upper Marlboro, Maryland: "Ongoing communication with the victim/witness of the case status, and to ease the burden of the victim/witness in the criminal justice system."

- Madison, Wisconsin: "Case status and disposition information systems."

- Marysville, California: "Status and disposition notice to victims—victims are kept informed of the progress of their case throughout the justice system and of the disposition rendered by the courts. I feel that this service lets the victim know that the criminal justice system takes their case seriously and that they are an *important* part of the process."

- Towson, Maryland: "Complete, up-to-date, and accurate notification procedures."
- Fond du Lac, Wisconsin: "Keeping victims/witnesses apprised of court dates and case dispositions."

Use of Trained and Dedicated Staff and/or Volunteers

A total of 33 programs indicated that some component or aspect of staff was their strongest or best program feature. Of these, 18 programs cited their dedicated professional staff, while 11 cited the use of trained and/or dedicated volunteers. There were 3 programs that indicated that funding levels allowing for adequate staff constituted their best feature; 1 service cited the availability of a social worker to assist victims of sexual or aggravated assault. Some of the comments given by programs in this category are listed below:

- Ukiah, California: "A staff who work together as a team committed to helping victims of violent crime. Our caseload is basically split up by geographic location. We will go to people who need us if they are unable to come to us. We have offices in outlying areas for the convenience of our clients."
- Madison, Wisconsin: "It's staff. The staff is not only competent, but sensitive, energetic, devoted, hardworking and on and on . . . . Without them we'd be ordinary. With them we shine."
- Gold Beach, Oregon: "The absolute dedication of a group of volunteers who are determined to provide support to the victim."
- Leesburg, Virginia: "Volunteer staff, funding and support from the community."
- McMinnville, Oregon: "Wonderful volunteers who staff a 24-hour Rape Victim Advocate Program as a part of this program."
- Waukesha, Wisconsin: "The use of trained and effective volunteers who make prompt and informative phone calls to victims and the personalized and compassionate treatment for all victims."
- An East Coast program: "The professionalism of the staff and the fact that it so thoroughly attempts to meet an existing community need."

In all, 12 features were named by 10 or more programs each, and accounted for 151 responses, or 60% of all responses given. These are listed below, each followed by the number of responses in parentheses:

- provision of information on case status (25)
- orientation of witnesses to criminal process and court escort (19)
- dedicated professional staff (18)

- court support (18)
- personal or immediate assistance and availability (14)
- rapport and/or linkages with local police departments (14)
- use of trained and dedicated volunteers (11)
- witness notification process (10)
- 24-hour availability and response to victims (10)
- assistance with victim compensation forms and processing (10)
- monitoring and collecting of restitution (10)
- liaison with D.A.'s office and other agencies (10)

Changes Programs Would Make If They Had the Money

Approximately 95% of the responding programs answered the open-ended question: If money were no object, what changes would you make in your program/unit? (see Table 5.3). Many respondents indicated that they would make changes in more than one area, resulting in a total of 390 responses. Three examples follow:

- San Rafael, California: "More space, more staff, more outreach, private waiting room for victims, more community education programs, more training for police officers."
- Canton, Ohio: "Hire additional staff, begin 24-hour services, provide additional staff training, have emergency fund for victims, expand children's services."
- Clearwater, Florida: "More office space, child-care area, fund for emergency food and child-care items, more vehicles for transporting witnesses."

Clearly, the programs surveyed are experiencing success in their efforts to reach out to victims and are discovering needs for additional changes that would enable them to provide more and better services. The changes respondents would make if they had the money fall into three general categories: *staffing* (86%), *services* (70%), and *facilities and equipment* (57%).

Staffing

Staffing changes proposed revealed an overwhelming need for more staff. Over half of the programs indicated they need more professional staff. Specific staffing needs mentioned were clerical/secretarial help, coordinator, therapist, counselors, volunteer program staff, staff attorney, child advocate, and public education person. Specific illustrations that typify the respondents' need for additional staff are listed below:

- Bowling Green, Kentucky: "Would have at least one full-time, paid person working exclusively with the program."
- Hillsboro, Oregon: "I would add clerical help, so that more time could be spent actually working with people."
- Miami, Florida: "Hire more staff to do just witness notification so existing staff can work at focusing on just victim assistance issues."
- Frederick, Maryland: "Hire a second full-time coordinator or assistant so that full-time coverage could be provided in both district court and circuit court."
- West Chester, Pennsylvania: "Increase staff. Daytime volunteer availability is very low and volunteers prefer only crisis intervention nights and weekends. Staff overtime due to pressures of direct service is running 35%."
- Fort Collins, Colorado: "I would add a full-time counselor who would also have the expertise to testify as an expert witness in cases such as sexual assault on a child."
- A California program: "Increase the number of staff and locations of program centers, and increase outreach efforts."

Respondents indicated they would benefit from additional monies in the form of stipends to enable staff to attend training seminars and workshops. Increased staff salaries and/or overtime pay were also mentioned, as in the following examples:

- A California program: "[Higher pay], more staff, staff attorney, stress management training."
- Tuscaloosa, Alabama: "Paid overtime or comp time, more space, more work delegated to assistants."
- An East Coast program: "Better salaries; more personnel to reach out into the police departments and community, more communication on the program to the general public."

Services

Desired changes pertaining to services reflected a need to develop a variety of programs and to increase available community resources. Three changes mentioned with almost equal frequency were establishment of a 24-hour crisis intervention program, increase in emergency funds to assist victims, and development of a crisis intervention service. Following close behind these emergency service needs was a wish to increase media coverage and publicity efforts. Responses in the area of service changes included the following:

- Boulder, Colorado: "Extend complete services to misdemeanor and juvenile cases plus a 24-hour crisis line."
- Duluth, Minnesota: "Crisis intervention, public education, storefront center."

TABLE 5.3: Changes Programs Would Make If They Had the Money

Proposed Changes	Number of Programs	Percentage[a]
Staffing		
Hire more professional staff	80	54
Provide stipends for staff to attend training seminars and workshops	22	14
Increase salaries of staff	10	6
Add clerical/secretarial help	10	6
Hire a paid coordinator	7	4
Hire a therapist to work with the elderly or children	5	3
Hire more counselors	4	3
Start a volunteer program	4	3
Place staff in police departments	3	2
Add a staff attorney	3	2
Pay volunteers	1	1
Pay overtime to staff	1	1
Add a child advocate	1	1
Add a public education person	1	1
Total	158	40.5
Facilities and equipment		
Add more office space	29	28
Add a separate waiting room for victims and witnesses	18	17
Purchase computers and M.I.S.	14	14
Add playrooms designed for children	9	9
Increase child-care services	7	7
Establish emergency shelters for domestic violence and sexual assault victims	6	6
Purchase more office equipment	5	5
Obtain needed county or agency care	4	4
Purchase video equipment	3	3
Add additional phones	4	4
Purchase telephone beepers	1	1
Add a toll-free number	1	1
Expand library	1	1
Contract out for videotaped courtroom depositions	1	1
Install phones in vehicles	1	1
Total	104	26.6
Services		
Establish a 24-hour crisis intervention program	18	14
Increase emergency funds to assist victims	18	14
Develop a crisis intervention service	16	13
Increase media coverage and publicity efforts	12	9

TABLE 5.3: (Continued)

Proposed Changes	Number of Programs	Percentage[a]
Services (continued)		
Change program from part-time to full-time	8	6
Develop a transportation service to and from court	8	6
Increase outreach efforts	8	6
Add a restitution program	6	5
Expand services to more specific areas	5	4
Extend services after regular hours	3	2
Provide emergency funds for repair of locks, doors, and windows	3	2
Establish a witness notification system	3	2
Add an outreach desk at the hospital	2	2
Increase mobile unit coverage	2	2
Add a sexual assault unit	2	2
Provide special medical care for sexually abused children	2	2
Provide court escort service	2	2
Increase legislative lobbying	2	2
Increase services to victims of juvenile offenders	1	1
Open a long-term shelter for runaway youths	1	1
Conduct follow-up research on victims	1	1
Provide more home visits	1	1
Purchase toys, books, and other reading materials for victims	1	1
Increase funeral reimbursements from $1,000 to $3,000	1	1
Reimburse victims of property damage	1	1
Provide more counseling for victims and families	1	1
Total	128	32.9

a. Percentages are based on 184 respondents. There are 390 changes listed, because some respondents listed more than one change. Percentage totals show proportion of all 390 responses that fall into each category.

- Garden City, New York: "Ability to give emergency funds for food, rent, emergency housing, and transportation."
- Black River Falls, Wisconsin: "I would try harder for some news coverage to let the public know I am here and what I can do to help them."

Some specific services the respondents would like to offer victims/witnesses if they had the money included the following: transportation service to and from court; a restitution program; emergency funds for repair of doors, locks, and windows; a witness notification system; an outreach desk at the hospital; a sexual assault unit; court escort service; and more counseling for victims and families.

General service changes mentioned pertaining to the programs themselves include changing the program from part-time to full-time, increasing outreach efforts, expanding services to more specific areas, and extending services after regular hours. These changes are reflected in the following responses:

- Eddyville, Kentucky: "Go from part-time to full-time and more availability to reach victims."
- South Bend, Washington: "I would work full-time only on the program; expand services in the area of obtaining restitution."
- Phoenix, Arizona: "Expand program to provide more in-depth assistance or have advocates specialize in working with victims of specific crimes."
- Kenosha, Wisconsin: "Expand services to more specific areas, i.e., juvenile crime and crime prevention. Immediate service through police, more staff for direct court service and case monitoring."
- Yuba City, California: "Availability of services after normal working hours."

Facilities and Equipment

A need for more office space was the most frequent response in the category of facilities and equipment. Specific changes in facilities mentioned were a separate waiting room for victims and witnesses, added playrooms designed for children, and establishment of emergency shelters for domestic violence and sexual assault victims. The equipment wish list included computers and management information systems, more office equipment, county or agency car, video equipment, additional phones, telephone beepers, a toll-free number, phones in vehicles, and an expanded library. Following are some typical responses:

- Superior, Wisconsin: "I definitely feel that there should be a comfortable lounge or waiting area for victims and witnesses away from the defendant and his/her relatives and friends."
- Madison, Wisconsin: "Design and build a separate interview/playroom for children."
- Skowhegan, Maine: "Purchase toys, books, other reading materials for victims."
- Anderson, South Carolina: "Telephone beepers, TV for victim waiting room, coffee, soft drinks, computer, money for snacks and lunches for victims and witnesses, parking, and private restrooms."
- Kalamazoo, Michigan: "We would provide 24-hour coverage, purchase an auto, establish a training procedure for volunteers and staff, attend more NOVA seminars, purchase a computer, etc."

Conclusion

This national survey provides a state-of-the-art summary of victim service and witness assistance programs nationwide. The recent proliferation and expansion of victim service programs in communities across the country means that they are gradually becoming institutionalized into the network of established city and county human service agencies. The strength and stability of victim/witness programs has been solidified through specific state legislation and appropriations for victim services. The programs and services examined in this chapter document the heartening concern and commitment of the many leaders who have developed these programs and services for crime victims during the past few years. Despite negative publicity in the news media about the apathy that exists in most communities, national and local victim advocacy coalitions and service providers have demonstrated that many people are dedicated and caring in their efforts to alleviate the trauma and stress experienced by crime victims.

6

Model Victim Service and Witness Assistance Programs

Sponsorship by and affiliation with a host agency have a strong influence on the services a program can provide to victims of violent crimes. The three major types of sponsors of victim/witness assistance programs are law enforcement departments, prosecutors' offices, and not-for-profit criminal justice/social service agencies; there are advantages and disadvantages to each of these auspices.

The major advantage of police-based programs is their linkage with the police, who have mobility and 24-hour-a-day availability. The police are able to notify on-call victim assistance workers immediately, thus providing the victim with speedy access to services. The major drawback to this type of agency affiliation is that since some citizens and grass-roots organizations distrust and/or are frightened by the police, some victims may be reluctant to seek help from a victim advocate if the advocate's office is located within a police department.

The major advantage of prosecutor-based programs is that they can readily provide victims and witnesses with speedy access to case information, initial hearing and trial dates, and court escort services. The most serious drawback of these types of programs is the tendency of some prosecutors and deputy prosecutors to give priority to meeting their prosecutorial functions by preparing the victim/witness to testify in court, thereby increasing the likelihood of convicting the accused. Unfortunately, most prosecutor-based programs are not able to provide 24-hour crisis intervention services. In addition, a number of prosecutor-based programs restrict services to victims whose cases are being brought to trial. It should be recognized that this type of program can be very helpful for victims/witnesses who will be appearing in court. However, because of their limited provision of social services, these programs should not be relied on exclusively but should be used in conjunction with a program offering more extensive crisis intervention and social services.

Victim assistance programs that are hosted by nonprofit criminal justice or social service agencies (e.g., the Minneapolis/St. Paul Crime Victim Center) provide access to all victims including those who do not trust or are intimidated by the criminal justice system. These programs can often assist disadvantaged victims in obtaining emergency financial aid and social services from local community agencies. However, as "outsiders" who are separate from the police and prosecutors' offices, they have somewhat limited access to victims whose only agency contact has been to file police reports and/or to file charges against perpetrators with their local prosecutors' offices.

As discussed above, each of the three types of victim/witness assistance programs has certain functions that make it advantageous to victims, as well as certain limitations. In order to assure that the unique needs of each client are met, these programs need to know when and where to make referrals, so that the individual in need can receive specific services the program is not equipped to provide.

This chapter provides detailed information on four model victim/witness assistance programs: a police-based victim assistance program, a victim center sponsored by a not-for-profit criminal justice agency, an urban prosecutor-based program, and a rural prosecutor-based program. The four model programs are as follows:

- the police-based Victim Assistance Unit and the Family Crisis Intervention Team of Rochester, New York
- the Crime Victim Centers of Minneapolis and St. Paul, Minnesota
- Victim/Witness Services of Milwaukee County, Wisconsin
- the Victim/Witness Division of the Greene County Prosecutor's Office, Xenia, Ohio.

The chapter examines the organizational structure of these different programs and also discusses the sources of funding, the amount of funding, the number of victims served annually, the background and role of staff, and the types of services provided to victims and/or witnesses by these model programs.

The four programs were selected for inclusion in this chapter because they appear to be financially stable, and they provide a comprehensive array of services to victims and witnesses. The program descriptions were based on questionnaire results, annual reports, grant proposals, formal job descriptions, and interviews with staff from these programs.

Victim Assistance Unit and the Family Crisis Intervention Team

This program operates under the auspices of the Rochester, New York, Police Department. While this section focuses on this particular program in Rochester, it should be noted that the city also has a program based at the Monroe County District Attorney's Office that provides services to victims whose cases have reached the court system. The Rochester Police Department provides comprehensive services to all misdemeanor and felony victims regardless of whether they proceed through court. The two programs coordinate their mutual cases to avoid duplication of services.

The Rochester Police Department Program serves the city of Rochester. Outreach services are focused on victims of "violent felonies, misdemeanor assaults, family offenses, and crimes against children and the elderly" (Rochester Police Department, 1987a, p.3.). Because it is Monroe County's largest, most diversified police department, individuals from outside the city are referred for victim services.

Historical Perspective

The Victim Assistance Unit of the Rochester Police Department began in 1975 with an LEAA grant. When this original federal grant ended in 1979, the department demonstrated its commitment to serving crime victims by incorporating the victim unit into the police budget. In 1981, the Rochester Police Department expanded specialized services to victims by obtaining a one-year Department of Criminal Justice Services grant. This grant provided funds to hire counselors to improve the identification, investigation, and referrals of families involved in child abuse and neglect. When the grant funding ended in 1982, the New York State Crime Victims Board took over the funding for one full-time counselor, who was primarily responsible for child abuse and neglect cases. From the beginning, the Victim Assistance Unit and the Child Abuse Unit (now called the Family Crisis Intervention Team or FACIT) have fulfilled their primary objectives of providing comprehensive services to victims of robbery, assault, rape, burglary, child abuse, and spouse abuse, as well as family members of homicide victims.

During the 1986 calendar year, Rochester's comprehensive police-based victim service program served 5,431 victims. The Family and Victim Services section responded to 4,702 victims of stranger-to-stranger crimes (Victim Assistance Unit), 307 cases of crimes against children outside the family, and 422 child abuse cases (FACIT).

Location

Victim services are located in the police department's Central Investigation Division (CID). Within this division, a police sergeant heads the Family and Victims Services Section, which is divided into three units: the Victim Assistance Unit, FACIT, and the Juvenile Unit. Because of their location within the CID facility, Victim Assistance Unit and FACIT staff are readily available to crime victims and police officers.

Services Provided

The following services are provided by the unit:

- assistance in filing for crime victim compensation
- victim outreach
- case status information
- court process information
- restitution assistance
- property release
- transportation
- home/hospital visits
- accompaniment to court
- referral to community agencies
- individual and group counseling
- educational programs to community groups, criminal justice personnel, and the general public

Victim assistance staff members specialize in assisting designated populations, particularly victims needing restitution or property release assistance, the elderly, battered women, non-English-speaking victims, and homicide survivors. The unit provides services most often to victims of rape, sexual abuse, robbery, assault (felony and misdemeanor), burglary, grand larceny, and criminal mischief, and to family members of homicide victims (Rochester Police Department, 1987a, p. 4).

The office is staffed Monday through Friday, 9:00 a.m.-5:00 p.m. After hours, the senior victim service worker (supervisor) is on call for emergencies and/or consultations.

Victim Assistance Unit Job Descriptions

The Victim Assistance Unit staff consists of one senior victim worker (supervisor), two full-time victim service workers, four part-time victim service workers, one full-time clerk, and one part-time volunteer (20 hours per week). Responsibilities of staff positions include the following:

- *Senior victim service worker*: Select, hire, and train personnel; supervise staff; assign cases; maintain statistical information; maintain community and media liaison on victimization issues; provide community education regarding victimization (Rochester Police Department, 1987a, p. 4).
- *Clerk III*: Greet clients and make appropriate referrals within the police department; interview clients and assess client problems, assign and coordinate work flow; create and maintain client files; create up-to-date client list and maintain all statistics; participate in all correspondence (Rochester Police Department, 1987a, p. 5).
- *Victim service workers*: Provide case status information to victims/witnesses through outreach phone calls; provide information about New York State Crime Victims Compensation and restitution, assist in the filing process, monitor claims progress; make home and hospital visits; monitor cases and assist individuals through the court process, notify victims/witnesses of changes; serve as liaison with social service agencies for appropriate referrals; assist with property release; provide community education (Rochester Police Department, 1987a, Attachment 92).

Each victim service worker has an area of specialization in addition to providing direct client services. One of the full-time workers is responsible for restitution investigation for city court and prewarrant hearings; the second worker specializes in elderly services.

Four part-time victim service workers provide the same comprehensive direct services to crime victims, including children, and their families. However, because each works only 20 hours a week, they are not responsible for recording reports, monitoring restitution, monitoring court activities, or attending community meetings. Approximately 75% of their time is spent in direct service to clients.

In addition to direct service to crime victims, each part-time victim service worker has a special assignment. One specializes in legislation and informs the staff and community of new crime victims bills being proposed. This worker also started a support group for all victims of crime. Misdemeanor crimes, especially third-degree assault, are the sole responsibility of one worker, who frequently makes referrals to Alternatives for Battered Women, the Center for Dispute Settlement, the Domestic Violence Bureau, and other community service agencies, because such assault cases often involve a constant state of disruption among family members and acquaintances. This worker also interfaces with the staff member from the Monroe County Victim Witness Bureau, based in city court, in an effort to avoid duplication of services. A bilingual part-time worker handles most of the cases involving Hispanic victims and serves as liaison to the Hispanic community. This worker also acts as an interpreter in city court and for police officers when called on (Rochester Police Department, 1987a, p. 3-5).

FACIT

This unit provides "crisis intervention, short-term counseling, follow-up support services on cases of child victims (both child abuse and neglect and serious crimes against children), domestic trouble, and juvenile delinquency" (Rochester Police Department, 1987a, p.5). In 1986 FACIT was involved in 422 child abuse cases and 307 cases of crimes against children. Services provided by FACIT include crisis intervention, child abuse intervention and education, liaison with Child Protective Services, liaison with community agencies, and diversion to those agencies, and juvenile diversion programs (e.g., Youth Baseball Program).

FACIT is directed toward providing a program utilizing community human service agencies and law enforcement personnel. FACIT counseling specialists "provide voluntary in-house crisis counseling and add in-depth expertise in the areas of domestic violence, child abuse/neglect, juvenile delinquency and victim services" (Rochester Police Department, 1987a). Whenever appropriate, individuals are diverted from the criminal justice system to treatment facilities within the community.

FACIT is staffed from 8:00 a.m. to 10:00 p.m., seven days a week, holidays included. An on-call staff person is available for consultations and emergency call-backs after 10:00 p.m.

FACIT Job Descriptions

The FACIT staff consists of one full-time police program coordinator and eight counseling specialists. Duties of staff members are as follows:

- *Police program coordinator*: Receives and logs in police reports of child abuse and neglect, distributes necessary copies to the Child Protective Service and the Monroe County District Attorney's Family Violence and Child Abuse Bureau, and refers each case to a counseling specialist; provides for community education programs; is a primary trainer in the areas of child abuse, neglect, and molestation for police recruits at the Regional Training Academy.
- *Counseling specialists*: Assist police officers and Child Protective Service workers in the areas of child abuse/neglect and child sexual abuse by providing crisis intervention assistance in response to police calls on a 24-hour on-call basis; assist clients

in their homes, providing crisis counseling, assessments, information about available community resources, initial agency contact for the client; identify by interviewing clients and others (police officers, schools, neighbors, and so on) and gathering other necessary data; work with the family and individual to resolve the problem and prevent another crisis situation; refer clients to other criminal justice or independent social service agencies for treatment or services; coordinate cases between the Department of Social Services and the Rochester Police Department; provide follow-up to cases to ensure the problem-solving plan is working; prepare and maintain case records and appropriate statistical data.

The FACIT unit becomes involved in cases of child abuse and neglect in two ways. First, police officers may directly request the assistance of a child abuse specialist, who goes to the scene of a crime, meets the victim and the officer at the hospital, or assists with an interview at one of the seven police sections. Second, the police officer completes the necessary paperwork and forwards it to the CARE Unit, where it is logged in and assigned by the coordinator to a child abuse specialist.

Intervention procedures followed by the child abuse specialist are as follows:

(1) Review the case and set up a plan, based on available information, for intervention with the family.

(2) Contact all other professionals who may be involved with the family in order to obtain a more complete picture of the family, avoid duplication of services, reinforce already existing services plans, and inform the other professionals that the problem has escalated to the level of police intervention.

(3) Make an initial follow-up call. This home visit is unannounced in order to minimize chances that the family will rehearse actions or coach the children not to talk. The specialist speaks with the children apart from the adults to determine their needs, how they are feeling, and if the abuse/neglect is continuing.

(4) Coordinate the case with the assigned child protective worker, who may request a criminal history of the family. The FACIT staff member may be asked to accompany the child protective worker on a home visit or to continue to make spontaneous visits to the home. It has been found that the authoritative presence of police personnel may be the impetus that stimulates the family to cooperate with Child Protective Services.

Most child abuse and neglect cases remain open and active for two to three months, and are closed with no prosecution. In some cases a decision is made to arrest the perpetrator. This action is taken only after the counselor, police investigator, district attorney, and child protective worker have determined that there is a substantial risk of continued abuse/neglect.

If a child has been a victim of other crimes (e.g., a sexual assault or endangerment by someone other than a parent or guardian), the victim and/or family is interviewed and provided with services. Services may include crisis counseling, short-term counseling, court information, accompaniment to court, emergency assistance, and/or referral to a social agency. Rape crisis centers, Family Services, Catholic Family Center, Department of Social Services, Legal Aid, and Parents Anonymous are examples of services to which the victim and/or family members may be referred. The counselor assigned to the case works with the family in an effort to prevent further victimization. Suggestions are made for better supervision of children, improving babysitting arrangements, establishment of communication between parents and teenagers, and utilization of community resources for assistance. If there are other agencies involved, information is shared with them. The Child Protective Service becomes involved only through referral for preventive service in cases where families do not follow through on recommended referrals and make no further effort to protect their children.

FACIT provides a community education program focusing on child abuse and neglect and child molestation. The presentation employs a lecture and discussion format. It is anticipated that this program will result in more children reporting child abuse and neglect and sexual abuse at an earlier age.

Crime Victim Centers of
Minneapolis and St. Paul, Minnesota

In the seven counties that make up the metropolitan Twin Cities area of Minneapolis/St. Paul, Minnesota, all victims of crime have access to a full-service program that offers crisis intervention and practical help 24 hours a day, seven days a week.

The Crime Victim Centers (CVC) program began offering victim services in 1977. It is operated by the Minnesota Citizens Council on Crime and Justice, a non profit organization formed in 1959 to provide a vehicle for citizen involvement in the criminal justice system. The primary policymakers for the agency are 32 elected volunteer members of the board of directors. The council, using a holistic approach to issues of crime and justice, engages in research, education, and direct service on behalf of the needs of crime victims, offenders, and their families. The CVC is the largest direct service project operated by the Citizens Council.

Funding for the CVC comes primarily from the Department of Corrections. In 1985 the following sources provided funds for the $225,910.00 budget:

- Department of Corrections, $112,380 (50% of the budget)
- United Way, $104,756 (46% of the budget)
- private foundations, $2,236 (1% of the budget)
- general & individual contributions, $6,538 (3% of the budget)

In 1985 the CVC responded to over 4,000 victim-related calls and opened 1,826 new victim cases. CVC staff prepare individualized coordinated service packages for victims. They provide direct services and cooperate with more than 350 other community resources and agencies as referral sources to provide a continuum of services for victims with multiple needs.

Victims may call the CVC 24-hour hot line or visit any one of the four metropolitan-area centers. Two centers are located in Minneapolis (West Metro area) and two in St. Paul (East Metro area). In addition, a mobile unit responds to victims of personal and household crimes during the evening hours. The van for this unit was donated to the CVC in 1985 by the 3M Company. Midwest Patrol, a security firm, provided funds for outfitting the van and for the first year's operating expenses.

Services

The CVC provides a place where victims of violent and property crime may call or come for help beyond the usual police appearance. Services provided include 24-hour crisis phone service provided by professional staff and trained volunteers under staff supervision, mobile unit coverage from 6:00 p.m. to 10:00 p.m. daily, and emergency transportation.

When appropriate, CVC staff provide transportation for victims, either in their own cars or in the mobile unit, to shelters, to court, to welfare offices, to police stations to press charges, and so on. No medical transportation is provided. If CVC transportation is not immediately available, appropriate transportation is located for the victim.

Elderly and handicapped services. Emergency repairs or board-ups after break-ins are provided to elderly and handicapped victims by teams of trained volunteers and staff members, often on referral from local law enforcement agencies. The CVC is the only agency authorized to issue temporary bus cards when a senior citizen's social security card has been stolen.

Information and referral for community resources. Referrals are made to more than 350 community agencies for legal aid, reparations, financial aid, counseling services, and the like.

Court-related services. Professional staff accompany victims to court appearances, educate victims on their rights and on methods of crime prevention, make sure victims' rights and needs are recognized and met, and update victims on the status of their cases (Crime Victim Centers, 1985).

Staffing

In 1985, CVC was staffed by 7 full-time and 4 part-time employees, 30 volunteers, and 3 student interns. The professional staff included one M.S.W. coordinator, five B.A.s, one M.S., one Ph.D. candidate, one A.A., one advanced specialist degree, and one nondegreed staff person. Staff titles and job descriptions follow. (All job description information is from Minnesota Citizens Council on Crime and Justice, 1985, Attachment 14.)

Title: Crime Victim Centers supervisor
Supervisor: Minnesota Citizens Council president
Responsibilities:

   staff supervision—Responsible for hiring, training, supervision, deployment of staff.

   coordination/administration—Oversee daily operation of the Crime Victim Center offices; develop quarterly objectives in conjunction with staff.

   program development—Participate in overall and long-range program planning, development of proposals and other fund-raising efforts.

   victim witness assistance—Oversee provision of all services.

   public education—Serve as a resource for organizations and speak publicly on the needs of victims, crime prevention, and the availability of victim services.

   community development—Build referral relationships with and provide training for community law enforcement and social service agencies; build helping relationships with adjunct organizations interested in and involved with victim advocacy and services.

   volunteers/interns—Assist with recruitment, training, supervision.

Title: Director of Public Affairs and Volunteer Services
Supervisor: Minnesota Citizens Council president
Responsibilities:

   public affairs and community development—Provide outreach to other agencies and media representatives for public education and media campaigns.

   volunteers/interns—Manage all aspects of these programs, including develop and implement recruitment designs, develop and update Volunteer Handbook, supervise special project volunteer/interns, supervise Volunteer Service documentation, develop and maintain a Volunteer/Intern Job Bank, develop and manage Volunteer Speakers Bureau, design and coordinate Volunteer Training Program and Volunteer Supervisor Training Program, coordinate Volunteer and Supervision Evaluations.

   program planning and implementation of program objectives

Title: Crime Victim Center specialist

Supervisor: Crime Victim Center supervisor

Responsibilities:

   victim/witness assistance—Provide crisis intervention, emergency transportation, referrals, provision of information on the criminal justice system and on crime prevention, court escort, assistance in filing reparations insurance claims, temporary home repairs, and so on.

   assist directors with community development, volunteers/interns, public education.

Title: intake secretary

Supervisor: administration assistant

Responsibilities:

   reception duties—Answer incoming victim calls and refer to appropriate specialists; provide basic information on CVC services.

   organization—Maintain and organize files, records, manuals, forms, correspondence.

   interoffice communication—Maintain staff schedule, distribute mail, assist personnel as needed.

   clerical support

Title: volunteer—crime victim assistance worker

Supervisor: volunteer coordinator and Crime Victim Center supervisor

Responsibilities:

   victim rights advocate—Interview victims; provide crisis intervention, determination of victim needs; provide counseling and other direct services; maintain accurate records for each victim served; provide emergency services, e.g., assist staff with transporting victims or boarding up homes.

   serve on Speaker's Bureau (optional)—Inform community groups of crime-prevention tips, describe victimization, present services offered by CVC.

All volunteers are required to attend ten hours of training led by a trained facilitator. They learn how to handle crisis calls through presentations, discussions, and role play at four weekly sessions, held from 6:30 to 9:00 p.m., followed by an additional required ten hours spent working side by side with a CVC staff member.

Victim/Witness Services of Milwaukee County, Wisconsin

The Office of the Milwaukee County District Attorney in Milwaukee, Wisconsin, provides services through a variety of programs to victims and witnesses who are entering the judicial system.

The *Victim/Witness Services Unit*, located in the main District Attorney's Office, serves all witnesses in all cases prosecuted by the D.A. Its goals are to provide personalized liaison with the various elements of the criminal justice process, to help with problems that arise, and generally to humanize the system. The unit has a full-time staff of fourteen: a coordinator, eleven victim/witness specialists, and two clerical staff. Two of the victim/witness specialists are funded 100% by federal Victims of Crime Act (VOCA) monies. The secretaries work as a team with eight full-time clerk-typists in the district attorney's subpoena unit. The full-time staff is supplemented by three student interns and five volunteers contributing a total of 40 per week. Bachelor's degrees are held by the coordinator and all victim/witness specialists. The unit provided services to approximately 7,200 witnesses in 1985. A total of 90% of the $385,572 budget was provided by the Wisconsin Department of Justice through a combination of general tax revenue and penalty assessments—victim/witness surcharges—on all criminal convictions, and 10% came from local and county general revenue.

Victim/Witness Services—Children's Court Center provides services for victims and witnesses involved in cases prosecuted against juvenile offenders. This program, located in the Children's Court Center in office space provided by district attorney, has a full-time staff of six. Five of the full-time staff—a unit director, three victim/witness specialists, and one clerk-typist—are employees of Lutheran Social Services. The sixth staff member (a victim/witness specialist, who works specifically with habitual, serious, and violent offenders) is a Milwaukee County employee. This unit served 2,700 victims in 1984. The $89,000 budget for 1984 was funded primarily by the United Way of Greater Milwaukee; a small percentage of funds came from the Lutheran church.

Court Watch is a program of information, support, and assistance for adult victims and court witnesses who are 60 years of age or older. This program is staffed by two full-time coordinators, Milwaukee County employees, and thirteen volunteers. The coordinator's office is located in the main district attorney's office; the assistant coordinator's office is located in the Children's Court Center. Together they monitor all criminal cases involving older adults. The volunteers, who are older adults themselves, are trained to provide information, support, and assistance at all stages of the court process. This program, begun in 1980, was first funded by United Way, then by monies from the Older Americans Act. It is now funded as a part of the Victim/Witness Services Unit.

The programs described below work cooperatively with other programs that provide services for victims and witnesses with special needs.

The *Sexual Assault Counseling Unit* of the District Attorney's Office counsels victims of sexual assault and provides support during court appearances. The program provided services to 3,036 sexual assault victims in 1985. The five full-time staff members—a director, three counselors, and one clerk-typist— work with the assistant district attorneys assigned to the Sensitive Crimes Unit.

All full-time staff are Milwaukee County employees except for one counselor who is funded 100% by VOCA funds. This counselor provides specialized services for very young child sexual assault victims. Milwaukee County Social Services provides funding from Title XX funds.

The *Witness Protection Unit* of the Sheriff's Department provides services to victims and witnesses who have been threatened or harassed. The four full-time staff members (one sergeant and three deputy sheriffs) are sworn Sheriff's Department personnel. The program is funded 90% by state funds through the Wisconsin Department of Justice and 10% by local and county tax dollars.

The following lists services provided by the staff of the Victim/Witness Services Unit (Milwaukee County Victim/Witness Assistance Program, 1985, pp. A2-A4):

(1) telephone communication with all citizen witnesses who receive subpoenas, providing case status orientation, trial date, determination and resolution of any problems relating to court appearance

(2) services to families of homicide victims: case status calls, liaison and advocate within the system for property return and victim compensation referral

(3) state Victim Compensation Program orientation and referral when appropriate

(4) property return

(5) gathering of victim loss information for possible restitution

(6) employer advocacy for wages to be paid during time of court testimony

(7) advocacy with victims' creditors

(8) court escort for elderly, juvenile, or extremely anxious witnesses and for families of homicide victims

(9) transportation arranged for elderly or juvenile witnesses and for handicapped witnesses with a professional carrier

(10) emergency child care

(11) arrangement for interpreters for nonspeaking witnesses

(12) referral to an appropriate community agency for witnesses who have problems or needs that cannot be handled directly by unit staff

(13) waiting room for witnesses staffed by volunteers

(14) witness notification: monitoring of subpoenas and court calendars to determine which cases will not proceed as scheduled; utilization of on-call system when there is some doubt as to whether a case will go on as scheduled; notification of cancellation of court appearance by telephone or by recorded message, available after office hours, listing all cases that will *not* go on as scheduled the next day

(15) attempt to locate witnesses who cannot be found for service of subpoena

(16) service to out-of-town witnesses, including travel and hotel arrangements, notification of trial trade date status and cancellations

(17) coordination of date and time of appearance of multiple witnesses in cases

Program Report: July 1, 1984-June 30, 1985

Citizen Contacts		*Law Enforcement Contacts*	
phone/written	21,051	phone/written	
in person	842	in person	
total	21,893	total	1,306

Total All Contacts

Service	*Citizens*	*Law Enforcement*
case status—10,687	not counted separately	

case disposition—2,358
witness recall—5,377
witness on-call—4,754
appearance information problems—2,804
witness fee assistance—1,373
transportation—219
employer intercession—108
court escort support—273
early property return—533
restitution information—3,295
victim impact statements—92
witness protection referrals—146
child-care assistance—26
crime victim compensation—1,001
referral to community support agency—212
notice of defendant's release from custody—482
victim/witness reception
out-of-town witnesses—268
location of not-found witnesses—575
other

If known
services to families of homicide victims—included in above figures
services to children who are victims—included in above figures
restitution assistance—3,295

Savings to Milwaukee County
subpoenas cancelled

5,377 citizen @ $17 each	savings:	$ 91,409
311 law enforcement @ $30 each	savings:	$ 9,930
subpoenas mailed, 12,304 @ $10 each	savings:	$123,040
other: City of Milwaukee 6,230 @ $30 each	savings:	$186,900
Milwaukee suburbs 1,150 @ $30 each	savings:	$ 34,500
	Total savings:	$445,779

Victim/Witness Division of the
Greene County Prosecutor's Office, Xenia, Ohio

The Victim/Witness Division of the Greene County Prosecutor's Office was created in January 1982 to serve victims of sexual crime involved in the criminal justice system. A portion of the prosecuting attorney's budget, allocated by the Board of County Commissioners, was the original source of funding. The division soon expanded its services to victims of other crimes due to numerous referrals. In December 1982, the Victim/Witness Division received a grant from the Ohio Department of Public Welfare, Bureau of Children Services, to add Project PAAR (Prevent Abuse/Assist Recovery), "a comprehensive program designed to help prevent sexual abuse of children and to assist in the recovery of the child in cases where abuse has occurred."

Today a full range of support services is provided to all victims of violent crime. The division specializes in sexual assault, child sexual abuse, and domestic violence. Sources of funding are the Prosecutor's Office and a series of grants from the State of Ohio. The division's 1985 budget was $92,500, 40% of which came from county general revenue and 60% from grants of which came from the Ohio Department of Human Services and the Ohio Department of Health.

A total of 261 new clients were served in 1985. Of these clients, 208 received information and referral services, and 53 became long-term clients. The following list shows the grouping of clients by type of victimization.

information/referral clients
sexual assault, 31
child sexual abuse, 71
felonious assault, 0
domestic violence, 93
general assault, 10
indecent exposure, 1
chemical dependency, 1
robbery, 1

long-term clients
sexual assault, 16
child sexual abuse, 32
felonious assault, 4
felony domestic violence, 0
murder, 1

Services

The Victim/Witness Division provides services to all victims of crime from the time the crime is reported through the entire investigation and prosecution process. Division staff and trained volunteers provide 24-hour crisis intervention assistance to all victims. Response to a request for assistance is made within one hour. The Victim/Witness Division representative's primary roles are as advocate and source of information for the victim. In addition, the worker acts as liaison between the victim (and the victim's family) and the hospital, law enforcement personnel, and the prosecutor.

Witness assistance services are provided to those who pursue prosecution. Any time a victim is required to participate in a segment of the criminal justice process, a Victim/Witness Division worker is available to assist the victim and the victim's family. Court-related services offered include witness notification, information about criminal justice system procedures, transportation services, employer intervention, court escort, and court support at all stages of prosecution. The division's good relationship with other county service agencies and various police departments enables it to employ a "team approach" to working with crime victims. Victims receive direct services from division staff as well as referrals to other appropriate agencies. Another important area of activity is the division's education program. Public awareness/prevention educational presentations are provided, on request, to any public or private group or organization, on a variety of topics such as sexual assault, child sexual abuse, and domestic violence.

As a result of funding for Project PAAR, Victim/Witness Division staff are able to respond on a 24-hour basis (contacting victims within one hour after the abuse is reported to the police, a hospital, or other agency) to requests for assistance in cases of child sexual abuse. All appropriate Victim/Witness Division services are provided to victims of child sexual abuse and supportive family members. Project PAAR works in close cooperation with the Greene County Bureau of Children's Services, Greene County Children's Mental Health, the Domestic Violence Project, Inc., Greene Memorial Hospital, police agencies in Greene County, and the staff of the Greene County Prosecutor's Office. Objectives of the project are to prevent child sexual abuse through a comprehensive, effective education-outreach program and to increase the likelihood of child sexual abuse reporting by making the services of the Victim/Witness Division and Project PAAR known to potential victims. To these ends, the division presents educational programs to public and private groups. Age-appropriate educational presentations concerning child sexual abuse prevention are also provided at all elementary, junior high, and high schools. Students also receive printed materials.

Staffing

Provision of Services

Staffing for the Victim/Witness Division consists of four full-time staff members and a group of fifteen volunteers. Staff positions include one project director, one victim advocate who also serves as volunteer coordinator, one victim advocate who also serves as self-help group facilitator, and one victim advocate/clerical coordinator. Each volunteer chooses one area of service: on-call assistance, witness assistance, or education assistance.

All staff and a number of volunteers provide direct services to victims and their families. During office hours (Monday-Friday, 8:00 a.m.-5:00 p.m.), staff take incoming calls for information or telephone assistance and respond to emergency requests for assistance. Requests may come from Greene Memorial Hospital, police agencies, Greene County Children's Services, and/or the staff of the prosecutor's office. Victim/Witness-Project PAAR assistance may be delivered at the hospital, at a police department, at the prosecutor's office, or in a victim's home. Court-related duties are carried out with the help of witness assistance volunteers who serve as victim advocates. These volunteers perform a variety of services, such as providing information about court procedures and requirements for court appearances and being available as needed for court escort duties.

During non-office hours, calls to the division are routed through the Sheriff's Department. An on-call assistance volunteer is available, on a scheduled basis, to respond to after-hours calls for assistance to crime victims. When a police agency or medical facility requests assistance, the scheduled volunteer is notified by a staff member on call. This staff member is available to assist the volunteer if necessary. The volunteer may be called to any hospital or police agency in the county or to a victim's home (accompanied by a representative of the agency that requested assistance). The volunteer also serves as a victim advocate, providing Victim/Witness Division services such as crisis intervention support/counseling and the relaying of information regarding justice system procedures and division services.

Job Descriptions

The *project director* holds an M.S. in education (counseling) and a B.A. in sociology, and is an Ohio peace officer with 320 hours of police training. The job description for this position includes the following responsibilities:

(1) Provide direct services to victims of violent crime and their families.

(2) Plan, develop, and implement a comprehensive program of services for victims of violent crime and their families; prepare a program description outlining goals, objectives, and services of the program; specify methods of accomplishing these goals and objectives.

(3) Serve as liaison between the Victim/Witness Division and community service agencies with which the division cooperates.

(4) Remain available, on-call, 24 hours a day to assess referrals, delegate responsibilities, answer questions, and approve actions of the volunteers and other staff when problems arise.

(5) Develop and coordinate in-service training of staff, volunteers, police, and other professionals.

(6) Participate in educational and cooperative programs made available to Victim/Witness Division professionals.

(7) Supervise all activities of division staff and supervise case management.

(8) Advocate for, assist, and support victims of violent crime and their families.

The program employs two *victim advocates*; one has a B.A. in psychology/sociology, and the other has a B.A. in psychology. Their job description entails the responsibilities listed below:

(1) Provide direct services to rape victims and their families.

(2) Remain on call 24 hours on a rotating basis to provide staff backup for volunteers as necessary.

(3) Maintain case management records, data, and follow-up of assigned clients.

(4) Participate in community education and prevention programs.

(5) Participate in the development and delivery of acquaintance rape awareness and prevention programs for adolescents and their parents and community organization to increase sensitivity and awareness of rape victims and their families.

(6) Participate in educational and cooperative programs made available to professionals in the area of rape.

(7) Assist in developing an appropriate annual volunteer training program and in recruiting, training, coordination, and supervision of volunteers.

(8) Write and distribute a monthly volunteer newsletter to inform volunteers of division activities and their contributions to those activities.

(9) Advocate for, assist, and support victims of rape and their families.

The program's *clerical coordinator* has begun work toward a B.A. in psychology and has taken Victim/Witness Division volunteer training, along with numerous related workshops and seminars. Duties of the position include the following:

(1) Provide direct services to victims of violent crime.

(2) Take incoming phone calls and refer them to the appropriate on-call staff person.

(3) Prepare correspondence and reports; maintain case files, correspondence files, and informational files.

(4) Schedule in-school and community educational programs and maintain a calendar of such events.

(5) Serve as liaison between the Victim/Witness Division and the fiscal officer of the Prosecutor's Office.

(6) Serve as receptionist for the Victim/Witness Division.

As of the time of the study, the Victim/Witness Division had 15 *volunteers* on staff. The volunteer program is considered one of the division's three main areas of activity. Once training is completed, volunteers are permitted to assist the professional staff in providing services to crime victims and witnesses and to the public as on-call assistance volunteers, witness assistance volunteers, or education assistance volunteers.

Volunteer training consists of a 21-hour program—seven 3-hour evening sessions spread over a four-week period. This classroom training takes place primarily at the Greene County Courthouse. Participants receive a training manual, are given an overview of the Victim/Witness Division and the volunteer program, and learn division procedures and responsibilities. In addition, they receive extensive instruction on specific topics, through lectures with titles such as the following:

- Rape: The Crime (definition, offender), the Crisis (rape trauma syndrome), and Prevention Concepts
- Domestic Violence: Victim/Witness Role, Court and Prosecution Procedures
- Counseling Techniques: Crisis Intervention, Peer Counseling, Values, Termination, Burnout, Role-Play Counseling Situations
- Child Sexual Abuse: Extent of the Problem/Definitions, Methods of Discovery, Offenders, Interviewing Techniques (anatomically correct dolls), CSA Prevention Materials

One session is held at Greene Memorial Hospital, where volunteers tour the emergency room and learn about medical and police procedures for victims of sexual crimes and domestic violence. On-the-job training is provided until volunteers are experienced and confident enough to respond alone to requests for assistance. In-service training and newsletters are provided to keep volunteers informed of changes in the division's program or services.

The Division accepts new volunteers once a year. Volunteers serve in three areas: on-call assistance, witness assistance, and education assistance. General requirements, in addition to completion of training, are as follows:

(1) Have a phone and an automobile.

(2) Attend bimonthly meetings.

(3) Make a commitment to cover a minimum of three shifts monthly (on-call assistance and witness assistance) or make one presentation per month (education assistance) for one year.

(4) Provide a replacement from among the other volunteers if unable to meet a commitment; notify appropriate staff member of any changes prior to the beginning of the shift.

(5) Participate in annual evaluations with the volunteer coordinator.

(6) Follow all rules and regulations of the division.

(7) Relay information regarding client contact, interaction, or educational presentation to division staff; submit a written account to the volunteer coordinator.

(8) Have good communication skills and project a professional appearance.

(9) Respect confidentiality.

(10) Be at least 18 years old.

The job description for an on-call assistance volunteer includes these duties:

(1) Serve as a victim advocate, providing division services through on-call responses to any hospital or police agency in Greene County where assistance has been requested.

(2) Follow division operating procedures, using prepared kit, including client contact forms, sexual assault handbooks, and Victim/Witness Division cards.

(3) Determine victim's needs and desires; provide information (explain hospital and medical procedures, answer victim's questions), assistance (make calls or talk with family members, locate replacements for clothing confiscated for evidence), and support (be present during procedures at victim's request, act as crisis intervention counselor if necessary) as needed.

(4) For each client contact, submit a written account to the volunteer coordinator, including (if available) offender's name, age, sex, and race; victim's name, age, sex, and race; address and phone number where the victim can be reached; date of contact and a brief description of contact.

Job duties of a witness assistance volunteer are as follows:

(1) Assist the victim/witness through the different stages of the prosecution process, beginning with the interview with detectives and continuing through the trial.

(2) Inform the victim/witness of the services provided by the division, such as witness fee, witness notification/transportation, telephone alert system, information on criminal court cancellations, continuances, property loss/property return, intimidation control, employer intervention, victim compensation; be available to answer any questions about these services.

(3) Answer questions concerning the criminal justice system and help prepare witnesses for court.

(4) Be present to provide court escort by attending interviews with detectives, polygraph exams, arraignments, pretrial hearings, preliminary hearings, trial preparation, and trials with the victim; be able to provide information about procedures and requirements for all court appearances.

(5) Submit to the volunteer coordinator a written account of each client contact, including victim's name, date of contact, type of court appearance, and a brief description of the contact.

Education assistance volunteers have the following responsibilities:

(1) Be available, as needed, to participate in presentations on sexual assault, child sexual abuse, and domestic violence to any group or organization requesting assistance.

(2) Report to the division prior to the presentation to collect all printed and/or audiovisual materials to be used; return all materials and equipment after the presentation.

(3) Submit in writing to the volunteer coordinator an account of the presentation, including name of school, group, or organization; date of presentation; number of persons present; topic of presentation; and any audiovisual media used.

Conclusion

This chapter has described the three primary auspices for victim/witness assistance programs: law enforcement departments, prosecutors' offices, and not-for-profit criminal justice/social service agencies. Each type of program has been illustrated.

The national survey of victim/witness assistance programs found that the programs affiliated with police departments or community agencies were more likely to provide crisis intervention and home visits to victims in need than were prosecutor-based programs. Preparation of victims/witnesses for appearing in court and testifying against assailants can be extremely traumatic and should not be underestimated. Prosecutor-affiliated witness assistance programs often provide important services to victims such as notification of case status, court advocacy, child care, court escort, and protection against intimidation. However, victims often have several additional needs, including crisis intervention services, emergency financial assistance, repair or replacement of broken locks and doors, help in relocating, and/or cognitive therapy to deal with phobias arising from the victimization. Therefore, it is imperative that all victim assistance programs strengthen their referral linkages so that the victims can receive needed services even when a program is unable to provide those services directly.

The National District Attorneys Association, in its report *A Prosecutor's Guide to Victim Witness Assistance* (n.d., p. 8), has underscored the importance of referral and follow-up by specifying that the following types of agencies be included in a victim/witness assistance referral network:

- community groups
- day-care centers
- domestic violence programs
- food stamps distribution centers
- job counseling/training programs
- mental health care programs
- physical health care programs
- private sector alliances
- public and community emergency organizations
- rape crisis centers
- senior citizens' groups
- unemployment services
- victim assistance or advocacy organizations
- victim compensation boards
- volunteer groups
- welfare agencies

References

Ahern, J. H., Stein, J. H., & Young, M. A. (n. d.). *Law enforcement and victim services*. Washington, DC: Aurora Associates and the National Organization for Victim Assistance.

Anderson, J. R., & Woodard, P. L. (1985). Victim and witness assistance: New state laws and the system's response. *Judicature, 68*(6), 223, 226.

Beaudry, J. K. (1985). *Annual report: Victim/witness assistance program*. Milwaukee: Office of the District Attorney of Milwaukee County.

Bolin, D. C. (1980). The Pima County Victim/Witness Program: Analyzing its success. *Evaluation and Change* [Special issue], pp. 123, 124.

Bard, M., & Sangrey, D. (1986). *The crime victim's book* (2nd ed.). New York: Brunner/Mazel.

California State Board of Control. (1985). *Victims of Crime Program 1985 annual report*. Sacramento: Author.

City of Rochester Comprehensive Victim Services. (1987). *New York State Crime Victims Board grant application*. Rochester, NY: Author.

Crime Victims Centers. (1985). *Description of services*. Minneapolis: Author. (mimeo)

Cronin, R. C., & Bourque, B. B. (1981). *National Evaluation Program phase I report: Assessment of victim/witness assistance projects*. Washington, DC: U.S. Department of Justice.

Elias, R. (1986). *The politics of victimization*. New York: Oxford University Press.

Erie County Victim/Witness Assistance Program. (1985) *1983-84 annual report*. Buffalo, NY: County of Erie District Attorney's Office. (mimeo)

Kahn, A. S. (Ed.). (1984). *Final report of the American Psychological Association Task Force on the Victims of Crime and Violence*. Washington, DC: American Psychological Association.

Lee, J. A. B., & Rosenthal, S. J. (1983, December). Working with victims of violent assault. *Social Casework*, pp. 593-601.

Milwaukee County Executive Office on Aging. (n. d.). *Court watch*. Milwaukee: Milwaukee County Executive Office on Aging. (pamphlet)

Milwaukee County Victim/Witness Assistance Program. (1985). *1985 annual report*. Milwaukee: Author.

Minnesota Citizens Council on Crime and Justice. (1985), October 1). *A proposal to continue the eight year contract for partial funding of the Metro Crime Victim Centers from the Minnesota State Department of Corrections*. Minneapolis: Author.

Minnesota Citizens Council on Crime and Justice. (1986). *Crime Victims Center procedures manual*. Minneapolis: Author.

Miron, H. J., Goin, L. J., Keegan, S., & Archer, E. (1984). *The National Sheriffs' Association guidelines for victim assistance*. Alexandria, VA: National Sheriffs' Association.

National District Attorneys Association, Victim Witness Coordination Program. (1987). *The directory of prosecutor-based victim assistance programs* (2nd ed.). Alexandria, VA: Author.

National District Attorneys Association. (n.d.). *A prosecutor's guide to victim witness assistance*. Alexandria, VA: Author.

National Organization for Victim Assistance. (1983). *The victim service system: A guide to action*. Washington, DC: Author.

National Organization for Victim Assistance. (1986, 1987). *Victim rights and services: A legislative directory*. Washington, DC: Author.

Office of Crime Victim Services. (1984). *Annual reports, 1982-1983, 1983-1984*. Madison: Wisconsin Department of Justice.

Pepper, C. (1985, May 10). *Elder abuse: A national disgrace* (Opening statement at the hearings before the U.S. House of Representatives Select Committee on Aging, Subcommittee on Health and Long-Term Care). Washington, DC: Government Printing Office.

Pillemer, K. A., & Finkelhor D. (1987 June). *Domestic violence against the elderly*. Paper presented at the Third Conference on Family Violence, Durham, NH.

Roberts, A. R. (1984). *Battered women and their families: Intervention strategies and treatment approaches*. New York: Springer.

Roberts, A. R. (1986). Policies, programs, and services for victims of violent crimes. *Emotional First-Aid, 3*(3).

Rochester Police Department. (1987a). *Crime Victims Board grant award*. Rochester NY: Author. (mimeo)

Rochester Police Department. (1987b). *New York State Crime Victims Board grant application*. Rochester, NY: Author. (mimeo)

Rochester Police Department. (n. d.) *Counseling specialist: Job description*. Rochester, NY: Author. (mimeo)

Sacramento County District Attorney's Office Victim/Witness Program. (1982). *Third year final evaluation report, Region D Criminal Justice Evaluation Unit*. Sacramento, CA: Author.

San Francisco Victim Witness Assistance Program. (1985) *Project activities outline for existing victim witness assistance centers*. San Francisco: Author. (mimeo)

Schaie, K. W. (1982). America's elderly in the coming decade. In K. W. Schaie & J. Gerwitz (Eds.), *Adult development and aging*. Boston: Little, Brown.

Singer, A. (n. d.). The Victim Witness Service Bureau: An introduction. *Law Enforcement Newsletter*. (Middlesex County District Attorney's Office, Cambridge, MA.)

Stein, J. H. (1977). *Better services for crime victims: A prescriptive package*. Washington, DC: Blackstone Institute.

Steinmetz, S. K. (1988). *Duty bound: Elder abuse and family care*. Newbury Park, CA: Sage.

Victims Assistance Services of Westchester, Inc. (n. d.) *Project S.E.A.R.C.H.—Seek Out Elderly Abused Reaching Out for Care and Help*. White Plains, NY: Westchester County Office for the Aging. (pamphlet)

Wisconsin Victim/Witness Assistance Program. (1983). *Program guidelines*. Madison: Wisconsin Department of Justice.

PART III

Programs, Recovery Services, and
Remedies for Crime Victims

7

The University and the Development of Victim Services in Orange County, California

Arnold Binder
Harriet Bemus

It would seem important at the outset to clarify the distinction between *victim services*, the topic of this chapter, and *victimology*, a term that refers to a field of social scientific study. The goal of victim services is the amelioration of the effects of criminal victimization through the operation of victim-oriented programs and agencies. The goal of victimology, on the other hand, is the formulation of theories that express understanding of the phenomena of victimization, including the special characteristics of victims and their relationships to offenders.

The field of victimology is generally assumed to have started in 1941 with the publication of an article by Hans von Hentig. In that article, von Hentig described various conditions—psychological, biochemical, and social—that made certain people more vulnerable to becoming victims of crimes. But above all, he stressed the interactional nature of criminal-victim encounters. Since that start, victimology has blossomed into a field of active research with its own journal (*Victimology*), an international association with annual meetings (World Congress of Victimology), and appropriate college courses and seminars. For a detailed discussion of the emergence and development of victimology, see Chapter 1, this volume.

It is not as easy to select a starting year for the current emphasis on victim services, but surely a reasonable choice is 1957 when Margery Fry published her initial plea for the adequate reimbursement of crime victims. She pointed out in the article that the mode of restitution was so inadequate in England at the time that one victim blinded in an assault would have had to wait 442 years to get the full amount awarded to him at the rate of payment decreed. Her efforts led to the introduction in England of victim compensation, where the government assumes the responsibility of paying victims directly for losses resulting from criminal acts.

The first victim compensation program in the United States was created in California in 1965; that was followed by similar programs in New York, Hawaii, and Massachusetts. In all these program enactments, cash compensation was allowed only for the victims of violent crimes because it was considered too costly and too cumbersome to compensate for property crimes. Interestingly, Aynes (1984) has argued that victim compensation should be considered a right rather than a mere act of benevolence on the part of the government:

> While the government cannot do the impossible and should not be considered an "insurer," it should be held responsible for acting reasonably in attempting to fulfill its duties of protection and prosecution. In the event of its failure to meet tort standards of conduct, it should be held responsible to victims, both in the form of damages for injury and through equitable relief in requiring investigation and prosecution. (pp. 115-116)

The establishment and operation of compensation programs made it abundantly clear that crime victims had needs extending far beyond those satisfied by cash payments. The anguish, anxiety, fear, hatred, and uncertainty following criminal victimization remained to make life difficult (see, e.g., Fogelman, 1971). That sort of awareness interacted effectively with the efforts of the women's movement to bring public attention to the special needs of the victims of rape and of domestic violence (see Geis, 1978). Further synergism came from such other sources as the law-and-order movement, which argued for fewer rights and privileges for offenders and greater concern for victims, and special emphasis movements such as those for children's rights and for the rights of older people. The result was the launching of rape crisis facilities, centers for the victims of wife abuse, and, more generally, programs for victim assistance. Many programs were started by dedicated volunteers, often victims themselves or the relatives of victims. Although these pioneers had considerable effect on the attitudes of people in the criminal justice system and public generally, their initial efforts led to failures all too frequently because of limited availability of funding and lack of expertise in management and organization. The proliferation and expansion of approaches that did succeed came about as a result of political processes, institutional initiatives, and individual efforts such as those described below that were associated with a unique program at the University of California, Irvine: the Program in Social Ecology.

The Program in Social Ecology

The Program in Social Ecology was founded on the basis of a set of guiding principles that were summarized as follows:

> The Program [in Social Ecology] at Irvine was started in January, 1970 for the explicit purpose of providing direct interaction between the intellectual life of the university and the recurring problems of the social and physical environment. And since it was founded on the conception of man as biological organism in a cultural-physical environment, the orientation is necessarily multidisciplinary . . . .
>
> It is axiomatic in the Program that learning must be applicable to the community and the community must serve as an auxiliary source of educational enrichment . . . . The curricula are oriented toward producing a coordination between on- and off-campus experience, theoretical and applied learning, so that each enhances and enlarges the other. The Program thereby enables students to work effectively on community problems in a variety of contexts while simultaneously meeting the central goals of a university education. (Binder, Stokols, & Catalano, 1975, p. 41)

That orientation toward direct interaction between the university and the community not only produced an extensive pattern of field placements for students in the Program in Social Ecology, but became the basis for cooperative efforts that led to the creation of innovative community programs. For example, the program and several police departments jointly started a youth diversion program that developed over the years from an unfunded project with two (unpaid) field study students to a very large nonprofit agency with a staff of full-time employees (See Binder, 1989; Binder, Monahan, & Newkirk, 1976; Binder & Newkirk, 1977; Binder, Schumacher, Kurz, & Moulson, 1985).

It is important to note, too, that the Program in Social Ecology was a leader in introducing various new approaches to education on the Irvine campus of the University of California. One of these approaches was called the Extended University; through this program, nontraditional, most frequently older, students were admitted in curricula that led to degrees. These were students who had special qualifications but did not meet the requirements for regular university admission or may have had jobs that did not allow attendance of classes during the usual hours. Prior to the introduction of the Extended University, such students could take courses through university extension, but could not pursue a curriculum leading to a degree.

The Setting

The southern part of Los Angeles County was given jurisdictional autonomy in 1889, and it became officially the County of Orange. (The name came not from the abundant array of orange groves that existed throughout the area, but from the family name of King William III of England, who established Protestant supremacy over Catholicism in his defeat of King James II at the Boyne in 1690.) According to the census of 1890, there were 13,589 people then resident in the new county. By 1978, the population had increased to 1,814,700, a density rate of 2,309 people per square mile.

According to the Orange County Administrative Office (1979-1980), "Overall, 1978 was a year of growth and prosperity for Orange County. . . . the County continues to be one of California's and the Nation's area growth leaders" (p. 4). There were 26 cities in the Orange County of 1978, ranging in size from Anaheim, with a population of 205,600, to Villa Park, with a population of 7,275. Anaheim is the city that contains Disneyland, while Villa Park is a purely residential community that did not and does not have its own police department. Even Anaheim, with a density rate of 5,064 people per square mile, could not be considered a congested metropolis.

In terms of race-ethnicity distribution, 88% of household heads were nonminority Whites, according to the special census of 1976. Corresponding proportions for other groups were as follows: Latinos, 7.2%; Blacks, 1.2%; Asians, 1.6%; and "other races," 2.0% (see Orange County Administrative Office, 1979-1980, p. 21). In addition to being heavily nonminority White in cultural heritage, Orange County was relatively affluent. While the median family income in 1978 was estimated to be $17,250 for the United States and $19,830 for California, it was estimated at $20,525 for Orange County (Orange County Administrative Office, 1979-1980, p. 4).

Despite the usual expectations in a WASPish affluent setting, there was a good deal of crime in the Orange County of 1978. There were, for example, 117,699 reports of serious crimes (that is, those that compose the FBI Crime Index) and 69,868 reports of several major offenses: willful homicide, forcible rape, robbery, aggravated assault, burglary, theft of $200 or more, and motor vehicle theft (see California Department of Justice, 1979). The rate of the seven major offenses was 3,813 per 100,000 population for the year, which may be compared with a rate of 5,140 per 100,000 for these offenses in the United States as a whole (U.S. Department of Justice, Federal Bureau of Investigation, 1987). There were 14,915 arrests for felonies in 1978, or 814 per 100,000 people. Complaints were filed against 12,119 of those arrested for felonies, leading to 6,491 convictions (in superior court and the several municipal courts). Clearly, then, there were many victims of relatively serious crimes in the Orange County of 1978, despite its low population density (for a metropolitan area) and its relative affluence.

Starting Victim/Witness Services
in Orange County

One of the two authors of this chapter, Arnold Binder, was the founder of the Program in Social Ecology and the person who worked with local police departments in developing the juvenile diversion program mentioned above. The youth program was launched in 1971 with two field study students working with young offenders in one police department; each student devoted ten unpaid hours per week to the effort. The success of the program is indicated by the fact that by 1978, the Youth Service Program, as it was called initially, had an annual budget of over one-half million dollars and a staff of about 30.

Harriet Bemus, the other author of this chapter, became an Extended University student at the university in 1972. She had taken much of the course work toward a degree in England several years earlier, but had never put the package together for completion. Marriage brought her to the United States, and to Orange County, where she took on the traditional role of housewife and mother. When the Extended University program became available for the nontraditional student, she matriculated. One of the courses in which she enrolled had as a requirement the preparation of a proposal for funding from a federal or state agency. A natural choice for her in that assignment was a proposal to fund a victim/witness assistance program because of her earlier experiences as a member of the grand jury of Orange County and as a director of a local center for volunteers. In the latter capacity, she had attended a conference sponsored by the National Conference of Christians and Jews that was aimed at encouraging the establishment of victim/witness programs.

Bemus's general background in community affairs, particularly as a member of the grand jury and director of the volunteer center, led to wide familiarity with personnel in the District Attorney's Office and in other criminal justice agencies throughout the county. Even before she wrote the proposal as a class project, she had been involved in discussions of establishing a victim/witness program staffed entirely by volunteers, but even that was not possible without some funding—which was not available.

Shortly after completing the class project, Bemus learned that funding might be available through the local agency responsible for distributing federal funds for the support of programs throughout the criminal justice system.[1] She contacted an assistant district attorney who was most receptive to the idea of a formal proposal, and that led to the formation of a countywide ad hoc committee to raise consciousness about the issue, mobilize support, and provide a forum for planning. Invited to become members of the committee were prosecutors, police officers, and representatives of such government agencies as health, mental health, social services, and senior services. Almost all of those invited accepted.

The ad hoc committee, after due deliberation, decided that it was highly desirable to proceed with preparation of a formal grant application for federal funds to start a victim/witness assistance program, and Bemus's class project was to be its prototype. It also decided that the use of volunteers would be central to operations and that a nonprofit agency would be approached for sponsorship and administration of the program when (and if) it was funded.

Since the youth diversion program referred to above was a nonprofit agency directed by Arnold Binder, it was natural enough for Bemus to ask Binder if he would support submitting a proposal for a victim/witness assistance program that would become a component of that nonprofit agency if funded. He agreed, and the proposal prepared by Bemus as a student project for her course in social ecology and developed by the ad hoc committee was modified and expanded, then submitted as a request for funding from a federal source.[2] The application proposed a program of services for victims and witnesses in one of the county's municipal courts and in an adjacent police department. Letters of endorsement came from all the agencies that had representatives on the ad hoc committee and from many others; these letters were used as attachments to the proposal, making it clear that there was solid support from various levels of the criminal justice system and from the broad array of human service agencies. Of particular help was the support that the proposal received from the local chapter of the National Conference of Christians and Jews, since that organization was so influential with political figures.

The result was an award of $70,000 in 1978 for a one-year project, the principal goal of which was to provide aid for crime victims and witnesses in the forms of advice and guidance, and such services as transportation, information regarding restitution and compensation, listings of referral resources, and continuing informative contact in regard to case development and disposition. The initial staff consisted of three full-time and two part-time people organized into a subprogram of the larger nonprofit agency directed by Binder, to whom Bemus reported as the operating head of the victim services unit. The first few weeks of operation of the unit were spent in such activities as the following: meeting with the personnel of agencies throughout the criminal justice system, speaking before community groups, putting together an active board of directors that included judges and senior police officers, scrounging equipment (such as a photocopying machine) that could not be purchased because of the limited first-year funds, and setting the stage for a network of volunteers so that delivery of services could be extended far beyond that possible by paid staff. Incidentally, an important source of voluntary help came from students in the Program of

Social Ecology who were in the process of completing their field study requirements.

Federal funding was later approved for a second year, extending the project to August 1980. A new direction for funding was on the horizon, however, due to the efforts in California by advocacy groups concerned about the welfare and rights of crime victims, and by various law-and-order groups who wanted offenders to pay more heavily for their crimes. In 1979, California's governor signed a bill that stipulated fines up to $10,000 against violent offenders as well as assessments of $20 against felons and $5 against misdemeanants for deposit in the Indemnity Fund of the State Treasury.[3] Proceeds of the fund were to be used to indemnify people who filed claims under the state's victim compensation program, and to provide assistance to locally established victim/witness programs. The program within each of the state's counties to receive monies from the Indemnity Fund was to be selected by the board of supervisors of that county on the basis of its recognition by the board "as the major provider of comprehensive services . . . to victims and witnesses" in the county.[4]

Our program was so selected in 1980 in Orange County, and awarded $215,886 to extend services to other courts in the county.[5] Among the services to be provided were short-term counseling; emergency transportation; child care; notice of the facts of victimization to relatives, friends, and employers, as requested by victims; help for victims of violent crimes in their application for compensation directly from the Indemnity Fund; and assistance in recovery of property and in obtaining court-ordered restitution.

The Early Development of Services

An advisory board to the program, consisting of professionals and general citizens, was established in the first few weeks of program operations in 1978 to continue where the ad hoc committee left off. One of the first tasks taken on by the advisory board was the development of methods for recruiting, training, and certifying volunteers. Moreover, members of the board were individually and collectively of central importance in making available a group of highly qualified trainers.

The training was provided only to volunteers who were selected after a process of careful screening and who agreed to work for no less than six months at 16 or more hours per month. (Social ecology students were required to spend a minimum of two quarters of field study at 10 hours per week.) The volunteers were taught basic operations of victim/witness assistance; how to deal with apprehensive victims and witnesses; to be sensitive to signs of trauma that warrant referral to professional specialists; to understand the particular personal difficulties associated with rape, child abuse, and spousal violence; to know how to use the listings of the extensive countywide referral network; and operations of criminal justice agencies and providers of ancillary services.

Since the new victim/witness assistance program was the first organization located in a court of Orange County that was independent of court administrative authority, it was necessary to establish rapport with court personnel at an early phase. Considerable help in that effort came from members of the advisory board, as did the fact of affiliation with the University of California. It was important in this regard, too, that the nonprofit agency of which the victim/witness program was a component was known and accepted by police departments throughout the county.

Although staff members were initially referred to, somewhat disparagingly, as "those federal people" by many people in the District Attorney's Office, repeated demonstration of the value of the program in encouraging participation of victims and witnesses led to full acceptance in that realm. In a short while, the program's telephone number was included with all subpoenas for witnesses. It is, perhaps, of incidental interest to point out in this context that, by the end of the second year of operations, over 15,000 victim/witnesses were contacted, and over 13,000 of them were placed on call so that they could continue their normal daily activities despite the necessity of court appearances. In addition, rapport on a broad front was gained as program personnel provided emergency child care and transportation to make possible the appearance in court of victims/witnesses, and as traumatized victims and terrified children were accompanied in their court appearances.

An early indication of the development of general rapport came when a judge requested the program to handle restitution services for misdemeanants. That involved the collection of court-ordered restitution, forwarding the collected restitution to the victim, and informing the court of the outcome.

By the end of 1980, there was a victim/witness unit in each of the courts of the county: superior, juvenile, and five municipal courts. Eventually, a separate advisory board was established in each court in conformity with the desire to provide greater responsiveness to the unique needs of each setting.

Unlike smaller, and more rural, counties where ancillary services were often not available for the referral of crime victims, Orange County had professionals in virtually every needed specialty. Therefore, developing a network of cooperation rather than attempting to establish needed services was a major goal of early efforts. An additional cooperative network was created with such organizations as Mothers Against Drunk Driving and the Coalition Against Domestic Violence because of shared concern about victimization. Interestingly, it became evident that there was indeed a shortage of therapists qualified to work with child sexual assault victims, and so program personnel (particularly Harriet Bemus) became instrumental in founding an organization, the Child Sexual Assault Network, that provided the framework for expanding the availability of relevant therapists.

Expansion of Services

Over subsequent years, the program extended and expanded its services considerably, with particular emphasis on the special needs of women and children. In 1981, two ancillary programs were established: the Sexual Assault Victim Services/Prevention Program and the Child Abuse Prevention Program. The former provides assistance to victims of rape and child sexual abuse. Services are provided on a 24-hour basis, seven days a week. The latter uses a didactic approach, involving school personnel, parents, and children, to prevent child abuse. Emphasis during presentations is on the rights of children, particularly in the area of inappropriate demands by important adults in their lives, the detection of early signs indicating potential or beginning child abuse, the array of remedies available when such signs are observed, and the responsibilities of parents and teachers in protecting children. Beginning three years ago, enough funding has been provided to allow presentations in every school district of the county.

A program that was launched in 1982 is aimed at providing special assistance to victims of domestic violence. Among the services provided to such victims is help in filing temporary restraining orders so that some measure of court-ordered protection can be obtained. The program also provides legal assistance by means of a panel of lawyers available (on a pro bono basis) to victims of spousal abuse.

Up to 1984, services for victims were provided almost exclusively in the several courts. But it was recognized that victims may have their greatest need for help shortly after the crimes have occurred. Accordingly, a program was started in that year to provide crisis intervention services for crime victims and their families when requested by police officers who had been dispatched to crime scenes. This program started well but limped along in its second year due to the difficulty of getting continued financial support. Since 1987, however, it has received adequate funding to work with six police departments. Teams are available to respond to the needs of crime victims on a 24-hour basis, seven days each week.

Finally, in 1984, a crime compensation unit was established where claim specialists verify the claimed losses of crime victims that are reimbursable from the state's indemnification. Prior to that year, all claims for compensation were verified only at the state level, often creating a burdensome task for the victims of violent crime.

Net Gains

While the victim/witness program in Orange County is a component of a nonprofit agency, its intellectual progenitor was the Program in Social Ecology at the University of California, Irvine. And there has been a continuing flow of energies between university and program, on the one hand, and agency, on the other, due to the large number of undergraduates who complete their field study at the agency generally and in its victim/witness program in particular, the graduates of the Program in Social Ecology who have taken full-time jobs in those programs, the graduate students who have done evaluational studies and other research at the agency and its subprograms, and the fact that the director of the nonprofit agency was a professor in the Program in Social Ecology. From the university's perspective, the collection of agency programs provides a laboratory in the real world where the intellectual forces of academe can be used to help people and solve problems in the social environment.

The community has gained from the relationship commensurately. It would of course be foolish to argue that there would be no comparable programs for crime victims in Orange County without the impetus derived from the Program in Social Ecology, indirectly, and from Harriet Bemus, directly. But the impressive structure that did eventually develop was, to a large degree, a product of elements that could come only from the intellectual ferment of a university. That ferment included emphasis on research, evaluation, innovation, and the education of students to be responsible citizens. To highlight that unique type of contribution, one need only be reminded that an initial moving force behind the creation of victim services in Orange County was the proposal prepared by Harriet Bemus for a course in social ecology.

Notes

1. That agency was the Orange County Criminal Justice Council. Funds were provided to the council, and hundreds like it throughout the country, by the Federal Law Enforcement Assistance Administration.

2. The request for funding went to the Orange County Criminal Justice Council, which, as stated in note 1, had responsibility for allocating certain federal funds provided by LEAA (on the basis of grant proposals) and then monitoring the expenditure of those funds. LEAA had been established by the Omnibus Crime Control and Safe Streets Act of 1968 (42 U.S.C.A., 3701 et seq.). The

goal of Congress in that act was to provide a mechanism to assist state and local efforts in reducing the occurrence and impact of crime and delinquency.

3. That was Senate Bill No. 383, which amended Section 13967 of the State's Government Code.

4. Section 13967 (e) (2) of the California Government Code.

5. The shift from LEAA to state funding was fortunate from several perspectives, not the least of which was the growing disenchantment with LEAA and its operations in congressional and administrative circles. That disenchantment, showing itself most clearly toward the end of the 1970s, stemmed from perceptions of bureaucratic inefficiency and of poor judgment in the allocation of funds—a good deal of which was used for the purchase of armored vehicles by police departments. The inevitable demise of LEAA was accomplished by Public Law 98-423, enacted in October 1984 (42 U.S.C.A. 3711 et seq.), which amended the Omnibus Crime Control and Safe Streets Act of 1968—the act, that is, that established LEAA. A new Bureau of Justice Assistance was created to handle disbursement of more limited funds in block grants to the states for the improvement of their criminal justice systems. But the termination of LEAA did mark the end of an era when it was thought that massive federal support of local programs in criminal justice would produce significant reduction of crime and the reduction of suffering by victims.

References

Aynes, R. L. (1984). Constitutional considerations: Government responsibility and the right not to be a victim. *Pepperdine Law Review*, *11*, 63-116.

Binder, A. (1989). Juvenile diversion: History and current status. In A. R. Roberts (Ed.), *Juvenile justice policies, programs, and services*. Belmont, CA: Wadsworth.

Binder, A., Monahan, J., & Newkirk, M. (1976). Diversion from the juvenile justice system and the prevention of delinquency. In J. Monahan (Ed.), *Community mental health and the criminal justice system*. New York: Pergamon.

Binder, A., & Newkirk, M. (1977). A program to extend police service capability. *Crime Prevention Review*, *4*(3), 26-32.

Binder, A., Schumacher, M., Kurz, G., & Moulson, L. (1985). A diversionary approach for the 1980s. *Federal Probation*, *49*(1), 4-12.

Binder, A., Stokols, D., & Catalano, R. (1975). Social ecology: An emerging multidiscipline. *Journal of Environmental Education*, *7*(2), 32-43.

California Department of Justice. (1979). *Criminal justice profile—1979*. Sacramento: Bureau of Criminal Statistics and Special Services, Division of Law Enforcement.

Fogelman, S. (1971). *Compensation to victims of crimes of violence: The forgotten problem*. Unpublished master's thesis, University of Southern California.

Fry, M. (1957, July 7). Justice for victims. *Observer* (London), p. 8. Reprinted in *Journal of Public Law*, 1959, *8*, 191-194.

Geis, G. (1978). Rape in marriage: Law and law reform in England, the United States, and Sweden. *Adelaide Law Review*, *6*, 284-302.

Karmen, A. (1984). *Crime victims. An introduction to victimology*. Pacific Grove, CA: Brooks/Cole.

Orange County Administrative Office. (1979-1980). *Orange County progress report* (Vol. 16). Santa Ana, CA: Author.

U.S. Department of Justice, Federal Bureau of Investigation. (1987). *Crime in the United States*. Washington, DC: Government Printing Office.

von Hentig, H. (1941). Remarks on the interaction of perpetrator and victim. *Journal of Criminal Law, Criminology and Police Science*, *31*, 303-309.

8

Responding to Missing and Murdered Children in America

Eric Hickey

Homicide in the United States generates among its citizens degrees of horror, concern, curiosity, and fascination. The taking of human life has always received differential attention and treatment. In particular, the abduction and murder of children elicits terror, dread, and anger among the general public. The aftermath of such killings leave many with feelings of helplessness and fear. The purpose of this chapter is to examine the extent of missing and murdered children in the United States and our response to these crimes. A growing fear among communities is that children have become prime targets for strangers, especially serial killers. Methods and techniques of these offenders used to lure children into their control are examined, followed by guidelines for parents to help them ensure the safety of their children.

Parents, school officials, and social service agencies must be aware of avenues for educating children about the inherent dangers of becoming involved with some strangers. Libraries and police departments can prove to be valuable resources in educating children about strangers. Parents of murdered children experience tremendous grief and anguish, which often turns into anger toward the offender and a criminal justice system that has been slow to respond to these atrocities. During the past several years, victim coalition groups have emerged to take up the plight of the victim and those who are the survivors. To date, victim rights/advocacy groups and groups catering especially to those involved with missing or murdered children have formed a grass-roots movement.

Types of Child Abduction and Murder

- In 1979, six-year-old Etan Patz walked along a busy New York street to meet his school bus. He had walked that one block to the bus before, but that day was the first time his mother felt he was capable of going alone. Etan never arrived at the bus stop and has never been seen or heard of since his disappearance eleven years ago.
- In 1981, six-year-old Adam Walsh was abducted from a shopping mall when he was momentarily left unattended. Part of his corpse was eventually recovered by investigators.

These two cases attracted extensive media coverage, and the latter resulted in the creation of the Adam Walsh Child Resource Center in Ft. Lauderdale, Florida. In many other cases the offenders, rather than the victim, have received the national media attention. For example, in 1981-1982, eleven children disappeared in the area of Vancouver, British Columbia, Canada. Eventually, Clifford Robert Olson was arrested in the murder of the eleventh missing child. Although Olson was a suspect in the other disappearances, no one was sure what had become of the children and teenagers, ages 9-18. Olson, a man with an extensive history of criminal behavior, offered to take investigators to the graves of several victims in return for money. Unless Olson was paid, there would be no names determined or bodies returned, and parents might never know if their children had been his victims or had disappeared for some other reason. If Olson did kill their children, the families wanted to know, and they desperately wanted the bodies returned for proper burial. After some deliberation, the Canadian government agreed to pay Olson $10,000 for each body returned. The killer responded by leading them to ten grave sites. Olson's wife was given the $100,000; she has since divorced him and, with the money and her son, relocated. Olson now resides in a prison in Kingston, Ontario, where he must serve a minimum of 25 years before he will be eligible for a parole hearing.[1]

Such abductions, murders, and serial killings of children generally precipitate alarm and fear in any community. The true extent of the problem of missing and murdered children is often subject to more speculation than fact. In 1983, the U.S. Department of Health and Human Services stated that 1.5 million children are reported missing every year. The executive director of the National Center for Missing and Exploited Children, a nonprofit clearinghouse set up by the government in 1984, indicated that strangers were responsible for abductions of 4,000 to 20,000 children each year. In addition, the center reported that 25,000 to 500,000 are victims of parental kidnapping (Newsweek, October 7, 1985). Other organizations, such as the Federal Bureau of Investigation, strongly disagree with such figures and report much smaller numbers of victims.

Part of the problem with current data can be traced to (a) methodological issues in data collection and (b) operationalizing definitions of categories of missing children. Only in recent years has national attention been focused on the plight of missing children. Much more is needed in the area of national surveys that can be compared to regional and statewide data. A need is also apparent for consistency in defining the types of missing children. Most missing children can be classified as runaways, many leaving home several times in one year. Each time a child runs away, however, he or she can be counted again as a missing child. Most runaways eventually return home, while others can be classified as parental kidnappings (Abrahams, 1984).

The following categories suggest ways to expand definitions of missing and murdered children if we are to understand the depth of the problem.

- *runaways*: children who voluntarily leave home without parental/guardian permission
- *parental abductions*: children abducted by noncustodial parents or parents who do not have legal guardianship
- *relative abductions*: children abducted from parents or legal guardians by relatives, such as uncles, aunts, or in-laws
- *discarded children*: children forced to leave their homes by rejecting parents or guardians
- *disposable children*: children who are murdered by their parents or legal guardians
- *stranger abductions*: children abducted by people who are strangers to them and their families
- *abbreviated abductions*: children abducted for short periods of time (minutes or hours) and then released (many may never be reported to police)
- *aborted abductions*: children who manage to escape attempted kidnapping

The National Center for Missing and Exploited Children recently released the number of children reported to that agency as missing between June 1984 and January 1988. As expected, runaways represented the greatest percentage of children found alive, while stranger abductions constituted the greatest percentage of those children found dead.

Abrahams (1984) found that only three out of every ten children kidnapped by a parent will ever see the other parent again, and that physical and sexual abuse of the abducted child are common. Table 8.1 indicates that nearly one-fourth of children abducted by parents or relatives and later found had been murdered. These findings also challenge the generally accepted notion that 95% of missing children are runaways. According to the National Center, parental and relative abductions constituted nearly half of all missing children reported to their agency. In contrast to their earlier findings of several thousands of children

TABLE 8.1: Missing and Murdered Children Reported to the National Center for Missing and Exploited Children Between June 13, 1984 and January 7, 1988 (in percentages)

	Found Alive (N = 8,562)	Found Dead (N = 117)	Still Missing (N = 7,832)	Total (N = 17,511)
Runaways	65	13	28	50
Parental abductions	28	3	54	38
Relative abductions	5	20	15	9
Stranger abductions	2	64	3	3
Total	100	100	100	100

SOURCE: U.S. Department of Justice (1989).

being abducted by strangers each year, their data indicated approximately 150 stranger abductions per year during the 3½-year study (U.S. Department of Justice, FBI, 1988).

In 1987, the FBI found that 2,398 children were murdered. These deaths included those reported to the National Center for Missing and Exploited Children as well as children who were killed by their parents or legal guardians and those categorized as discarded children. Death tolls could be much higher if we were able to account for all of the still-missing children.

According to the FBI, approximately one-fourth of all male children murdered in 1987 were 14 years of age or younger. By comparison, over half of all female children murdered that year were 14 years of age or younger (see Table 8.2). When controlling for all age categories, male children were more than twice as likely to be murdered. When the 15-19 age group is excluded, the ratio near-ly evens out between males and females. In other words, the percentages of male children being murdered in all age categories, with the exception of the 15-19 group, are similar to those of female children in respective age groupings. The dramatic difference between male and female murders at ages 15-19 may be explained in part due to drug- and gang-related violence. Yet these data also reveal that nearly one-fourth of all children reported murdered in 1987 were 4 years of age or younger (U.S. Department of Justice, FBI, 1988). This, of course, involves mothers or fathers who kill their own children as well as ab-ducted and murdered child victims.

Racially, Blacks constituted less than 13% of the U.S. population, yet they represented half of all the murdered children reported to the FBI in 1987 (see Table 8.3). While males were more likely than females to be murdered between the ages of 15 and 19, Blacks were more likely than Whites to be murdered in the same age group (U.S. Department of Justice, FBI, 1988). Again, this can

TABLE 8.2: Murdered Children in the United States in 1987 Reported to the Federal Bureau of Investigation, by Sex (in percentages)

Age	Males (N = 1,662)	Females (N = 735)	Unknown (N = 1)	Total (N = 2,398)
Less than 1 year	8	13	—	10
1-4	9	21	—	13
5-9	4	8	100	5
10-14	7	12	—	8
15-19	72	46	—	64
Total	100	100	100	100

SOURCE: U.S. Department of Justice, FBI (1988).

be explained in part by the socioeconomic conditions under which the majority of Blacks are forced to live. When we exclude the 15-19 age group, however, Black children represented 41% of all children murdered aged 14 and younger. It appears that even young Black children are at significantly higher risk of being murdered than are their White counterparts.

In January 1989, the Office of Juvenile Justice and Delinquency Prevention published a bulletin of the preliminary estimates of stranger abduction homicides of children. The data were gathered from the FBI's Supplemental Homicide file and represent the first findings from the National Studies of the Incidence of Missing Children. In this bulletin, the Office of Juvenile Justice estimates between one and two stranger abductions per million per year, with teenagers between the ages of 14 and 17 with the highest rates. Such figures indicate that the risk of a child being abducted and murdered by a stranger is much lower than previously believed (U.S. Department of Justice, 1989b). The Office of Juvenile Justice notes that child murders by strangers, which may have involved abduction, ranged from a low of 110 in 1980 to a high of 212 in 1982, and that there is no evidence to suggest that these types of homicides are on the rise. Where strangers are concerned, the preliminary data suggest that girls are at greater risk than boys and that the rates for Black children are three times higher than those for White children. This report, along with five other major studies cited, dispels the myths that thousands of children are being abducted and murdered each year and that such cases are on the rise (U.S. Department of Justice, 1989b). As the report also observes, most of these data originate from police statistics, and the conclusions, therefore, are tentative. Nonetheless, the preliminary report is encouraging. Studies currently being conducted will continue to shed light upon this phenomenon. The fact remains, however, that some children do fall prey to strangers, some of whom are serial offenders. The

TABLE 8.3: Murdered Children in the United States in 1987 Reported to the Federal Bureau of Investigation, by Race (in percentages)

Age	White (N = 1,140)	Black (N = 1,193)	Other (N = 47)	Unknown (N = 18)	Total (N = 2,398)
Less than 1 year	12	7	17	22	10
1-4	15	10	15	5	13
5-9	6	4	13	17	5
10-14	10	8	4	17	8
15-19	57	71	51	39	64
Total	100	100	100	100	100

SOURCE: U.S. Department of Justice, FBI (1988).

following section explores factors involving children who were victims of serial killers.

Children as Victims of Serial Murderers

Due to an increase in stranger-to-stranger homicides, it is now the case that as many as one-third of all murders are perpetrated by strangers (Eitzen & Timmer, 1985, pp. 130-131). Increasing numbers of serial murders are believed by some experts to constitute many of these unsolved cases (Holmes & DeBurger, 1988, pp. 19-20).

While the recent emergence of serial murders has attracted considerable attention by researchers, relatively little attention has been accorded their victims. In essence, the category of serial murderers should include any offenders, male or female, who select their own victims and kill over time. This includes offenders who, on a repeated basis, kill within the confines of their own homes—for example, a woman who poisons several husbands, children, or elderly boarders to collect their insurance. Recently, Mary Beth Tinning of New York was arrested and charged with murdering seven of her children over a 14-year period in order to collect the insurance (Associated Press, 1987). Thus some victims of serial murderers will have personal relationships with their assailants and others will not; some victims are killed for pleasure and some merely for gain.

If we are to protect children from adults who would kill them, we must be willing to look beyond traditional notions of victim-offender relationships. Although researchers are still attempting to measure the extent of the serial murder phenomenon, the evidence is clear that young women and children are the prime targets of such attacks. Based on the case files of 201 known serial killers in the United States, 62 (31%) had killed at least one child. This child-killer group is 73% male and 27% female; only 7% of the offenders were Black (author's files).

Although there has yet to be consensus in explaining the low numbers of Black offenders among serial killers, there has been a surge of Black serial murderers in the past ten years. It is possible that Blacks have been overlooked during the emergence of the serial murder phenomenon. Most serial offenders are White and lower-middle or middle class, and their homicides—both domestic and serial—tend to be intraracial. In 1981, Wayne Williams, who is Black, was arrested in the killings of 25-30 Black youths in Atlanta, Georgia. The fact that some major urban centers are now predominantly Black and are politically controlled by Black citizens may in part explain why increasing attention is being focused upon the plight of Black missing and murdered children. In recent years a few Blacks have also been involved in interracial serial killings, and have received considerable publicity for their crimes. In 1980, the "Stocking Strangler" of Columbus, Georgia, killed several elderly White females, and in 1985, Alton Coleman and his companion Debra Brown, both Black offenders, went on a killing spree in the Midwest, murdering several victims, including young children both Black and White.

Of serial offenders who killed one or more children, 73% had murdered at least one female child, while 68% had targeted at least one male child. A few of the 62 offenders (19%) targeted children only. Nearly half (45%) of the child killers were parents of one or more children. Some 81% of the female offenders were mothers of one or more children, while only 29% of male offenders were fathers.

As expected, female child killers from this group were more likely to murder victims in their own families or other relatives, while males were more likely to be total strangers to their victims (see Table 8.4). Similarly, female offenders were much more prone to use poisons to kill their victims, while males who killed children frequently mutilated, strangled, shot, or bludgeoned their victims.

Children become prime targets because they can be easily controlled and manipulated. Given a conducive environment for child killers, abductors, and molesters, children have little resistance to their persuasive powers. Parents need to be just as concerned about where their children go during their unsupervised time as they about teaching their children not to "take candy from strangers."

On January 24, 1989, Robert Theodore Bundy was executed in the state of Florida for the murder of 12-year-old Kimberly Leach, whom he kidnapped from the grounds of her junior high school in 1978. Another 15-year-old girl was lured into Bundy's car while attending a youth conference at Brigham Young University in Provo, Utah, in June 1975. Bundy's charisma and ability to per-

TABLE 8.4: Relationship of Serial Murderers to Their Child Victims in the United States (in percentages)

Relationship	Male Offenders (N = 45)	Female Offenders (N = 17)	Total (N = 62)
Stranger	49	18	40
Stranger/acquaintance	29	18	26
Family member	7	29	13
Family/acquaintance	—	35	10
Family/stranger	9	—	6
Acquaintance	4	—	3
All	2	—	2
Total	100	100	100

suade his victims to ignore precautions with total strangers allowed him to abduct, sexually torture, and murder several dozen young women. His usually fail-safe method involved approaching potential victims in the daytime and in places where the victims felt no danger. He often feigned an arm or leg injury and simply asked an intended victim to help him carry something to his car. He was also known to have posed as a police officer and to have talked victims into entering his vehicle. By the time his victims may have sensed danger, they were already under his control.

Luring Children

We all hear the horror stories about abducted children. Many who have never experienced such a crime or have never been a family member or friend of a victim may want to discount tales of abduction as distortions of reality. Unfortunately, child abductors can be particularly creative in their methods of finding suitable victims. One 16-year-old offender being evaluated for a sex-offender program in a western U.S. psychiatric facility noted how simple it was for him to find child victims to molest. His favorite hunting grounds were shopping malls because he always found parents who were willing to leave their children, sometimes even young children, alone for a few minutes around the toy counters. The children whom he approached, escorted to the washroom, and molested inevitably seemed to trust him. Some of his victims were so young he was sure they would not understand what had occurred once he allowed them to leave. On a "good" night he claimed he could lure three or four children to the washroom.

In another case, a 15-year-old offender who had been arrested in Hawaii for sexual molestation of children was never prosecuted because his family relocated. A few months later the offender abducted a two-year-old child while she played inside her fenced front yard. After raping and strangling the child, he left her body in a vacant building.

In 1977, Operation Police Lure was organized in Oakland County, Michigan, by a law enforcement task force in response to a series of seven unsolved child homicides. Some believed at the time that a serial killer was responsible for several of the abductions. A survey was administered to 54 elementary and junior high school students in grades four through nine in efforts to gather more data on child molestation and abduction. The children reported 782 incidents of attempted or actual cases of molestation that had never been reported to authorities. They also found that children ages 10-12 were the most likely targets and that males and females were victimized at about the same rates. Although victims were approached at varying times of the day, 3:00-6:00 p.m. was the period most frequently reported. Children profiled the offenders as White males, usually in their 20s or 30s, who often attempted to lure them by asking for help, such as looking for a lost puppy. When vehicles were used the abductors and molesters also seemed to prefer two-door models and cars that were blue in color (Wooden, 1984).

Child abductors, of course, do not come in only one mold and generally do not fit the stereotype of the peculiar-looking "dirty old man." Some individuals of very benign appearance are arrested for child abductions/molestations. Creating a new stereotype of such offenders becomes problematic, as it excludes many variations of that stereotype. There are, however, some important concepts that should be noted about the nature of child abductions. While coercion, bribery, and other methods of luring victims are frequently employed, the ploy of asking for help from a child is not only effective—from an offender's perspective—but also creates difficulty for parents in protecting their children. The thought of helping find a lost puppy or kitten can easily preclude attention by the child to the person seeking the assistance. Similarly, an offender may use a badge or a blue vehicle to appear as an authority figure to intended victims. Most children are taught or have learned by experience a degree of respect for authority figures and will automatically respond to their commands.

Wooden (1984) outlines a variety of child lures used by offenders, including an appeal to a child's ego, by telling the child he or she is to be in a beauty contest or television commercial. Some offenders tell the child an emergency has occurred and they have come to escort the child home immediately. Wayne Williams, involved in the Atlanta child murders, was known to have posted employment advertisements for young men throughout the area in which he resided. In the case of Ted Bundy and others like him, similar themes are used but in a more sophisticated manner. For offenders, wearing a cast to evoke sympathy or displaying fictitious business cards can initially alleviate a child's fears of dealing with a stranger. Offenders who have become adept at manipulation can exert complete control over others, especially children.

There are many ways in which child abductions can be avoided if parents, school officials, and community leaders are prepared to carry out intervention strategies. Parents or guardians must ensure the safety of their children. The most important tool ever used in preventing abductions is that of educating children. The following list of strategies has been compiled and adapted from recommendations made by the National Center for Missing and Exploited Children, the Indiana Missing Children Clearinghouse in Indianapolis, and the National Finger Print Center for Child Identification in Kirksville, Missouri:

(1) Never leave children unattended while in a public place. This includes being left alone in a car, store, or shopping cart. Telling children, especially younger children, not to unlock the car door until mom or dad returns places the child at a distinct disadvantage in attempting to make quick decisions when being confronted by an adult stranger. Some parents find using expanding cords to tether their small children to them useful in keeping toddlers from wandering off. Tethering lines are available that can be attached to the wrist of the parent and the clothing of the child. More elaborate and expensive beeper devices can be purchased by parents who wish to allow their children more movement. With these, a beeper alarm automatically is triggered when the child crosses over a preset radius.

(2) If children do become separated for any reason from their parents, they should know to go to the nearest store employee, checkout counter, or police or security officer and ask for assistance. Children must understand that wandering around often makes it more difficult for parents to locate them. Having children go to a prearranged location if they are separated from their parents is a good idea.

(3) Children should be taught that strangers are all persons they do not know, or persons they do not know very well. Consequently, children must learn to avoid going anywhere with strangers—such as entering cars—without the prior verbal approval of the parents.

(4) Children must know they are not to get close to strangers who may be following them or calling them to their cars.

(5) Children must understand that adults who need assistance should be asking other adults for help, not children. Many children easily succumb to the lure of helping a stranger "look for the lost puppy."

(6) Children should be taught that if they feel they are being followed or if they become afraid of an adult, the best course of action is to yell out for assistance rather than to hide.

(7) Parents should inform their children which homes in the area are designated as "block watchers" or that otherwise participate in community programs designed to assist and protect children.

(8) Children should be taught that if they are being forced to go somewhere, they need to protest loudly, screaming and yelling that this person is not their parent or guardian.

(9) Children should be taught how to reach the telephone operator in an emergency.

(10) Children should learn as young as possible their own names, full addresses, telephone numbers—including area codes—and full names of both parents.

(11) Children should avoid going places alone.

(12) When children are alone at home, they should never open the door to strangers. They should also be taught to tell unfamiliar phone callers that neither parent can come to the phone at that moment (rather than saying the parents are out) but will return the call later.

(13) Children should always ask permission of parents when leaving their homes or play areas, or when entering other people's homes.

(14) Children should never hitchhike, and should accept rides only with those who have been approved by the parents.

(15) When in public, children should not wear clothing emblazoned with their names, because they are more likely to respond if strangers call them by name.

(16) Children should be taught that if strangers want to photograph them, they should immediately inform their parents and/or school officials.

(17) Children must be taught that others do not have the right to touch them inappropriately and that any occurrence of such touching should be reported immediately to parents or teachers.

(18) Divorced parents should understand their legal rights if they fear noncustodial parental abduction. School officials should be aware of children's custody status.

(19) Babysitters, day-care centers, and schools should release children only to those specifically designated by the parents.

(20) Children should be fingerprinted by properly trained personnel.

If a child does disappear, the parents should contact authorities immediately and be prepared to give a complete description of what the child was last seen wearing, unique physical characteristics (such as braces or glasses) and the child's height, weight, hair color, eye color, and date of birth. A recent close-up color photograph of the child should be provided to the police. Recent dental charts and medical records of the child should be obtained from the family doctor and dentist.

Educational Resources

As parents, school administrators, and law enforcement officials have become more cognizant of the potential dangers children may encounter, we have begun to see more resources available for educating our children. Parents should consult their local libraries for books addressing the protection of children. Some books are designed and written especially for children and can be augmented through discussion of the meanings of these stories with parents or teachers. For example, Vogel and Goldner (1983), in their book *The Dangers of Strangers*, deal with advances made by strangers toward children. Illustrated and written especially for children, the text is endorsed by the American School and Community Safety Association and is designed to help children understand why they must be wary of strangers. Parents should consult their public libraries for this and other books written for children.

Parents should be cautious, however, in their efforts to educate children about strangers. Children should be taught only to follow the recommended safety guidelines. Estrella and Forst (1981) note that scaring children into compliance can be dangerous in itself. Making children suspicious and fearful of strangers can make them fearful of all adults, even as they mature (p. 166). Indeed, a measured response by parents toward their children when educating them about potential dangers involving strangers is usually the best course of action. Most strangers have no designs to harm anyone, and they often prove to be valuable resources in times of need. Children, like parents, must know what to do when approached by strangers. Simple strategies of knowing how to use a pay phone, locking doors, and practicing street safety can prove invaluable to children.

Police departments are usually prepared to send representatives to schools or community action groups to discuss ways in which to protect children. Police will stress the importance of children's carrying some form of identification and maintaining regular check-in times with parents, and parents' knowing where their children are supposed to be at all times. Older children usually express an interest in why some strangers are dangerous, while younger children are not prepared to understand such motivations. Therefore, parents must be sensitive to how much information they should try to convey to their children. Children's questions should be answered if they are raised, and they should be allowed to raise them. Police representatives usually are prepared to answer such questions during their visits to schools and often will provide students and parents with literature discussing the inherent dangers of some strangers.

Parents can organize themselves and operate block parent programs in which volunteers who are at home during the day open their homes to children who may encounter problems. Such homes are usually designated by a sign in a window. Dixon (1985) points out that it is important for parents to introduce children to block parents before an emergency or crisis occurs. Block parents often are parents or grandparents themselves, and they usually are registered with and investigated by police when they first volunteer for a block parent program (p. 120). Usually such programs can be implemented with the assistance of local law enforcement agencies.

Protection and Prevention:
Getting Parents Involved

Many people today feel a sense of impending doom, believing that they will inevitably fall prey to criminal victimization. A great deal of this fear is created by constant news media reports focusing on the most heinous crimes that individuals in our society can produce. However, we must never forget there are many factors that play a role in the dynamics of victimization. Age, race, sex, socioeconomic status, place of residence, employment, education, and life-style— all of which can affect the types of crimes occurring in particular areas—must be considered when one is weighing risk factors. Even so, crimes do occur that appear to have little or no correlation to most risk factors. It becomes disconcerting for people to feel they may be at risk and yet powerless to respond effectively to such concerns. Regardless of their utility, most strategies embraced by adults to protect themselves—such as enrolling in self-defense courses, carrying weapons, or increasing home security—are not viable for children. More important, we may delude ourselves into believing that law enforcement can provide sufficient protection for our children and that school officials can always provide adequate supervision.

The increasing perceived randomness of child victimization outside the home has initiated awareness and action on the part of concerned parents and community activists. The impact of victimization often serves as a catalyst for involvement in victim rights and victim advocacy groups. Some organizations function primarily as support groups, while others focus on introducing legislation aimed at addressing the rights of victims, including the handling of criminals in our judicial system. The impact of a murdered child extends far beyond the loss of life, as is evidenced by parents of child victims. While some may seek vengeance on offenders, others become involved with groups that work to prevent future victimizations, assist other victims who are being processed through the criminal justice system, and provide counseling. We may quickly forget a child murder after the headlines subside, but the agony is only beginning for many of those related to the victim. The following statement, provided by Ruth

Kuzmaak and her husband Dr. John Kuzmaak of Portland, Oregon, describes the impact of their daughter's homicide on the Kuzmaak family and the frustrations they continue to face eleven years later.

The Kuzmaak Story

I write the following not to enlist the reader's sympathy. I do not want sympathy. I write instead hoping that others will have a better understanding for those persons who have endured criminal victimizations.

I keep searching for the right descriptive words to convey the emotional impact our daughter's murder made on us. "Devastating" just doesn't make it—"ravaged" is closer, engulfed, overwhelmed, drowning in sadness, numb, oblivious to *everything* else, totally immersed in the horror, the why, the who, what she had to go through in her closing minutes of her short life, how terrified she had to have been, did she scream for help and no one came, did she fight, the pain, how it felt to be strangled, what her dying thoughts were, how she must have held out hope until the last that she would be rescued, her shock and disbelief that this was happening, and as the information unfolded itself to us in bits and pieces that first day, the anguish of hearing how badly she was beaten, then a couple of hours later crying out when I heard that she had been repeatedly stabbed. Then, the ultimate horror to learn that the cause of death was strangulation. To be deprived of breath—lungs bursting—"Oh, God, oh God," I would wail, tears streaming, hands clenched and imploring.

That is how I remember that day, March 21, 1979. A decade has passed, but the emotions go on, the anger, the sorrow, and the loss.

I wanted to go to the funeral home to see her, but everyone told me that I should remember her the way she was in life, not in death, so I didn't. I have regretted it over and over—that I didn't have the courage to look at her after she had suffered through so much. It was something I should have done.

A big, black Cadillac picked us up in the morning she was to be buried. We drove slowly to the funeral home, parking in the rear. Shortly, the back door opened and men in dark suits started carrying out her casket to the hearse.

"There she is," said our son. She had been so vibrant, so much fun to be with, so bright, and so loving, and here she was being carried out in a coffin. Gone from life. Gone from us.

I counted 75 cars winding up the hill behind us at the cemetary. Many more had mistakenly gone to the funeral home. Plainclothes police photographed the cars and people. I asked that the poem, "Thanatopsis" be read. The minister asked if she had been baptized, and I said she had.

Within six weeks I had lost 22 pounds, going from 141 to 119. My husband and I kept working at his dental office, which helped considerably during the day, but the nights were a horror. I would wake up two and three times an hour, and each time I had to face, once more, the reality. I had always been an avid reader, and so I would grab a book and start reading until I once more fell asleep. Books became my narcotic.

Relatives, friends, and our dental patients were extremely kind to us during this time. They say that sorrow needs a good support system and we had one. But, within a few months all but Ken, Janet, Aunt Lois, and Donna's girlfriend, Chris, had dropped away and out of our lives. When I did have occasion to talk to people they avoided the subject. It was as though Donna had never existed. One night we went out with a couple we had known for years. I was describing a court hearing we had gone to. We had heard that the defendant might be a suspect in Donna's murder, and he was being tried on another charge. Our friend, a dentist, interrupted with, "Ruth, could we talk about something else? This is so depressing."

Increasingly, we became more isolated.

We could get so little information from the police that we would think up ruses in order to try to get them to say more. "Was she raped? Sodomized? No?" Then, we would wrack our brains trying to figure out why they called it a "sex crime." Ken and I had long conversations, filled with theories and speculations.

An enormous boulder had been dropped in our river of life and we all struggled to stay afloat. Within 18 months I had breast cancer. Grandma Kuzmaak developed a giant stomach ulcer from which she never recovered. I was glad that my mother had died, for she just couldn't have stood it. Janet had lost her best friend, for she and Donna had been very close in both ages and affection. The 12-year-old neighbor girl had to have psychiatric help.

Nightmares were constant for me. They were filled with vicious, evil, predatory men, and in some of them I was trying to shelter Donna from them. But, I had good dreams, too. In them, Donna was again a small little girl in pigtails. She had always been such a gentle child.

About 1982, Janet talked me into going on a local television talk show. The audience was to be made up of parents of murdered children. During the program, I complained about the inaccessibility of information from the police about what had happened to her. Afterwards, Dr. Larry Lewman came over to me and said that he had done Donna's autopsy, and that this information was open to us. No one had told us this.

We went down to his office two days later and he went over the autopsy with us. I learned that her nose had been shattered, that she had received a violent blow on the back of her head, that she had been stabbed nine times in the chest and also in the vagina, and strangled with her pantyhose. The vaginal sexual mutilation was why the police considered it a sex crime. Now, we knew.

I started reading everything I could get my hands on about the mentality of these sexually sadistic killers. It was an ugly education. I added new words to my vocabulary, such as necrophilia. Although Donna's autopsy showed no semen, I learned that these killers frequently masturbated on or near the body.

We met with other victims and formed a group called Crime Victims United. This, then, became the focus of my life. I could channel my energies, my rage, and Donna's murder into something really worth while.

It took us two attempts to pass a statewide victims' rights measure. No longer would surviving family members be forced to sit in the hall during the trial. We got equal peremptory challenges (before, the defendant had twice as many as the state), victims could make victim impact statements in court, prior convictions could be raised to the jury, and many other important changes.

My husband, Jack, showed gritty determination in these efforts, getting thousands of signers in order to get it on the ballot in each of the elections. Having accomplished this goal, however, I believe he feels now that "enough is enough." But, I go on. We have had several arguments about it recently.

Our children have been quite supportive of our efforts, though one day Janet said to me, "Mom, we're here, too." And . . . that really hurt!

Recently [11/25/88], I watched Dr. Martha Gluckman of Patuxent Institute being interviewed on *Nightline*.

She was being questioned about the paroles given to convicted murderers and rapists at Patuxent and also the unsupervised weekend passes.

One inmate had been convicted of murdering his girlfriend and her parents. He had been sentenced to three life sentences to be served consecutively starting in the early 1980s. Already he had been given 12 weekend unsupervised passes.

Another inmate, Charles Wantland, murdered a 12-year-old boy three weeks after being paroled. He had served only 6 years of a 30-year sentence for murder.

Yet another sex offender convicted in 1972 was serving a life sentence for rape, perverted practices, assault, and kidnapping. He was paroled in 1980, and within a year convicted of three more rapes.

Dr. Gluckman vigorously defended the passes and furloughs, saying, "George Bush said he wants a kinder and gentler nation, and I think it should start with corrections."

The remark left me totally outraged.

On Memorial Day and Donna's birthday we go to the cemetery. I can't keep the tears from flowing each time I stoop to arrange the flowers.

I can talk about Donna's murder with the kind of detachment I use when discussing the weather. But, I still can't really *think* about it.

This statement had made me think about it, and it has been difficult. But, I truly hope that it will be of benefit in helping people understand.

Our daughter's murder is unsolved. (author's files, 1989)

The Kuzmaak story stands proxy for many families affected by the murder of a loved one. In this case the murder is believed to have been the work of a serial killer.

Both Mr. and Mrs. Kuzmaak have been active members of Citizens for Justice and Crime Victims United. The latter, a politically active support group for crime victims, holds monthly general meetings in the Portland, Oregon, area. Each meeting is highlighted by a keynote speaker who has worked or is currently involved in criminal justice policymaking, corrections, law enforcement, victim advocacy, or some other crime-victim-related profession.

During meetings reports are given regarding the states of various pieces of victims' rights legislation generated by Citizens for Justice. A newsletter, *Victim's Voice*, is published monthly by this victims' group. Bob and Dee Dee Kouns, parents of a murdered child, are both very active in contributing their resources to this newsletter. Mr. Kouns serves as the legislative liaison and Mrs. Kouns as the editor. Recently they reported on the committee's 1989 legislative campaign to seek further rights for victims of crime as well as increased sentencing for offenders. One goal for 1989 was to alter Oregon's rape law by changing second-degree rape to first-degree rape when the victim is incapable of consent by reason of mental defect, mental incapacitation, or physical helplessness. The bill was generated as the result of a case in which a hospital therapist raped an incapacitated female patient on three consecutive nights. The newsletter also contains editorials discussing recent advances or regressions in the criminal justice system. Members and nonmembers alike contribute personal stories of victimization, poems, and other notes that keep the focus upon the plight of crime victims and their survivors. One member expressed her concerns about the lack of confinement for convicted criminals in Oregon:

> The National Institute of Justice puts the average cost of crime at about $2,300 per crime. However, this places a value on petty larceny and underestimates the cost incurred in rapes, homicides, and serious assaults. The Justice Report goes on to say that a typical inmate reported committing an average of 18 crimes per year, making him responsible for yearly crime costs of $143,000. Even if we were to double the annual cost of confinement, cut in half the estimated crimes committed per offender and also cut in half the average cost per crime, we would still save over twice as much in societal costs by using confinement. (*Victim's Voice*, June 1988)

Contributors also write about the injustices meted out to survivors of crime. In one case a woman admonished the governor of Oregon:

The Oregon voters and taxpayers voted in the death penalty four years ago; however, young, innocent children continue to be brutally murdered and the death penalty is yet to be implemented! When will the punishment for the criminal match the crime against the innocent victim? Governor, the people in this state made a very strong statement in voting for the death penalty in 1984. We don't want murderers to be protected, given free room and board at great cost to the taxpayers. We asked for a change to the system. Those who murder innocent children should be the first to receive the justice we voted into law. (*Victim's Voice*, February 1989)

Anyone interested in knowing more about Citizens for Justice and Crime Victims United may write or call:

CJ/CVU
P.O. Box 19480
Portland, OR 97219
Ph. (503) 246-5368

Victim Coalitions

Parents who have missing or murdered children now have the opportunity to become involved in a variety of action groups dedicated to assisting victims and/or survivors. For some survivors, the lack of concern for the victim's plight has motivated individuals to organize their own action groups. In 1982, in Maryland, Stephanie Roper was abducted by two men and during the next five hours was brutally and repeatedly raped, tortured, beaten, shot to death, dismembered, and set ablaze. Both men were captured and convicted in Stephanie's murder. They were each given two life sentences plus 20 years, but under Maryland law they would have been eligible for parole in less than 12 years. Outraged and shocked at the injustice and insensitivity of the legal mechanisms of the state toward victims/survivors, Stephanie's parents decided to initiate their own victims' coalition to fight for more rights. Their efforts are becoming nationally recognized and have sparked others to begin similar groups. The following is a brief summary of their accomplishments to date.

The Stephanie Roper Committee (SRC) was formed in response to the criminal justice system and how it interacts with victims and families of crime victims. The ultimate goal of SRC is to persuade the Maryland legislature to enact laws that will ensure courtesy, dignity, compassion, and justice toward all those who become victims of crime. The Stephanie Roper Foundation provides direct services to victims and their families as they are funneled through the criminal justice system. This includes comfort and assistance to victims/families, including a court watch program that monitors the system in its legal application of victims' rights. The foundation also provides referrals to other agencies, including civil litigation, criminal injury compensation, and education programs for the public.

> Stephanie Roper Committee, Inc.
> Stephanie Roper Foundation, Inc.
> 14753 Main Street, No. 4
> Upper Marlboro, MD 20772
> Ph. (301) 952-0063

These two organizations are strictly nonprofit, staffed by volunteers who are willing to share their experiences, history, research, goals, and achievements with anyone interested in organizing similar groups in their areas. Although anyone in the United States may join, individuals and groups are urged to examine the laws of their own states and begin immediately to press for more laws that will treat crime victims and their families favorably. The SRC is also a member of the National Organization for Victim assistance (NOVA).

Since 1983, the Stephanie Roper Committee has been very active in lobbying for victims' rights legislation in Maryland. Prior to the formation of SRC, victims' rights advocacy did not exist in Maryland. Thanks to this grass-roots organization, victims are beginning to be heard. In 1983 Maryland increased life sentences in a capital case to 25 years before parole eligibility compared to 15 years in 1982. The use of alcohol and drugs by an offender was eliminated as a mitigating circumstance in a capital case. Since 1983, the Maryland courts must consider the impact of a crime on the victim and survivors through the use of a written victim impact statement as part of the presentencing investigation. In 1984, the Maryland General Assembly established the Governor's Task Force for Victims' Services.

In 1985, Maryland passed a bill to protect victims and witnesses from intimidation by not requiring them to declare their addresses and phone numbers aloud as part of their courtroom testimony. Also in 1985, the legislature agreed that an offender's victims must be notified when he or she is about to receive a parole release. The legislature also concurred that victim impact statements can be updated for the benefit of the parole board when early release of offenders is considered. Also, victims or their representatives now have the right to remain in the courtroom following their testimony, subject to the discretion of the court.

In 1986 a Victims' Bill of Rights was passed in Maryland that requires all criminal justice agencies, such as the arresting officer through the Parole Commission, to inform victims and witnesses of certain rights, protections, and services to which they are entitled by law. This includes the right to make a victim impact statement, the right to notification concerning parole hearings, and postsentencing reviews, and the right to employer intervention and crisis assistance. Also passed in 1986 was the Truth in Sentencing Law, which requires judges to instruct jurors at the sentencing phase of a capital trial that a life sentence does not mean the duration of an offender's natural life, but carries the eligibility for parole. Victims now also have the right to address the judge and/or jury at the sentencing phase of a trial concerning the physical, financial, and psychological impact of the crime on their lives.

In 1987, Maryland passed a bill to allow life imprisonment without the possibility of parole for any capital crime or first-degree murder. Contracts for compensation, or "Son of Sam laws," were enacted, disallowing offenders from profiting from their notorious crimes. Money earned from crime dramatization must now go into a fund to which victims/survivors may apply for compensation.

In 1988, Maryland created the position of coordinator to enforce and implement the 1984 Victims' Rights Bill. Another bill now allows, but does not require, a judge's recommendation at sentencing in granting the possibility of parole. Also in 1988, a bill was passed requiring imprisonment for life without possibility of parole for first-degree murder by a minor.

In 1989, bills were passed in Maryland that strengthened a victim's right to be present during a criminal trial, that mandated that restitution become a condition of parole, and that extended the statute of limitations for civil action in cases of battery from the original one year to three years.

The impact of SRC and SRF are becoming immeasurable as more and more victims/survivors become active members. Persons who wish to become involved in victim support groups and organizations such as the Stephanie Roper Committee should contact those now operating within their states. Such persons can contact NOVA for information:

National Organization for Victim Assistance
P.O. Box 11000
Washington, DC 20008
Ph. (202) 232-NOVA

The next section contains a partial list of support groups compiled by the National Center for Missing and Exploited Children. Some of these groups operate primarily to assist victims/survivors, while others are involved in legislative action. Addresses are given for some groups that focus particularly on missing, murdered, and exploited children. Just in the past five years, several dozen victims' groups have emerged to take up the issue of the victims' plight. As Stephanie once wrote in her diary, "One person can make a difference and every person should try."

Agencies Concerned with Missing, Murdered, or Exploited Children

At the national level, a multitude of agencies are now beginning to organize themselves specifically to address the issues of missing, exploited, and murdered children. One of these is the National Center for Missing and Exploited Children:

> National Center for Missing and Exploited Children
> 1835 K Street, N.W., Suite 700
> Washington, DC 20006
> Ph. (202) 634-9821, Hotline (800)-843-5678

Established in 1984 by the U.S. Department of Justice, this agency operates as a national clearinghouse for information about missing and murdered children and child sexual exploitation, including child pornography and prostitution. A hotline is available to anyone with information about missing children ([800] 843-5678). The TDD hot line number (for the deaf) is (800) 826-7653. The agency offers a variety of brochures addressing parental kidnapping, child protection, runaways, sexually abused or exploited children, who to contact if a child is missing, and a host of other topics regarding children. Anyone interested in the safety and welfare of children is well advised to contact this agency.

The parent agency that directly coordinates with many federal agencies pertaining to children is the U.S. Department of Justice's Office and Juvenile Justice and Delinquency Prevention:

> U.S. Department of Justice
> Office of Juvenile Justice and Delinquency Prevention
> Washington, DC 20531

The U.S. Department of Justice, utilizing the Coordinating Council on Juvenile Justice and Delinquency Prevention, also includes representatives from the Department of Health and Human Services and Department of Education. This council works in conjunction with the Attorney General's Advisory Board on Missing Children and coordinates with the Federal Bureau of Investigation, the National Obscenity Enforcement Unit (both agencies of the Department of Justice), U.S. Department of State, U.S. Postal Service, U.S. Customs Service, Interstate "I SEARCH," Advisory Council on Missing and Exploited Children, as well as the National Center for Missing and Exploited Children, also an arm of the U.S. Department of Justice. The U.S. Department of Justice is very active in collecting and disseminating information about missing and exploited children and has recently published a report summarizing the progress made in the 1980s. This report, *Missing and Exploited Children: Progress in the 80's* (U.S. Department of Justice, 1989a), is available to the public and is an excellent resource for a better understanding of the extent to which the federal government has begun to address the issue of exploited children.

Another agency that has achieved national recognition in addressing the issues of missing, abused, and neglected children is the Adam Walsh Child Resource Center:

> Adam Walsh Child Resource Center
> Executive Office
> 1876 N. University Dr., Suite 306
> Fort Lauderdale, FL 33322
> Ph. (305) 475-4847

This agency provides information for callers who wish to report missing children or have information regarding the disappearance of a child. The center has close ties with law enforcement agencies and other social service agencies. The center has literature available to the public addressing the issues of missing and murdered children, and representatives from the center are available to address public forums and community action groups.

Several states have now created clearinghouses for information on missing and exploited children and usually can be contacted through the state police. These agencies are coordinated with the National Center for Missing and Exploited Children. In the state of Indiana, for example, extensive information packets are available upon request from the Missing Children Clearinghouse:

> Missing Children Clearinghouse
> Indiana State Police
> State Office Building
> 100 N. Senate
> Indianapolis, IN 46204
> Ph. (800) 831-8953 (Indiana only)
> (317) 232-8248

Parents or groups needing additional information about the functions and roles of various victims' coalitions throughout the United States should contact NOVA (address and phone given above), a national agency that serves as an umbrella organization to coordinate and facilitate the functioning of hundreds of victims' groups throughout the country.

Appendix: Major Local and National Support Groups

* Alabama
  Portraits International Corporation
  2503 Old Shell Road
  Mobile, AL 36607
  Ph. (205) 479-6050

- Alaska
  Missing Children of America
  P.O. Box 10-1938
  Anchorage, AK 99510
  Ph. (907) 272-8484

- California
  Child Save
  P.O. Box 27136
  Concord, CA 94527-1356
  Ph. (415) 676-SAVE

  Find the Children
  1811 W. Olympic Boulevard
  Los Angeles, CA 90064
  Ph. (213) 477-6721

  Home Run: A National Search for Missing Children
  4575 Ruffner Street
  San Diego, CA 92111
  Ph. (619) 292-5683

- District of Columbia
  Missing Children of Greater Washington
  4200 Wisconsin Avenue, N.W., Suite 201
  Washington, DC 20016
  Ph. (202) 686-1791

- Florida
  Missing Children Help Center
  410 Ware Boulevard, Suite 303
  Tampa, FL 33619
  Ph. (813) 623-KIDS (in Florida)
  (800) USA-KIDS (outside Florida)

  Missing Children Information Clearinghouse
  P.O. Box 1489
  Tallahassee, FL 32302
  Ph. (904) 488-5221
  (800) 342-0821 (Florida only)

- Georgia
  Find Me
  P.O. Box 1612
  LaGrange, GA 30241
  Ph. (404) 884-7419

- Illinois
  I-SEARCH (missing children)

Illinois Department of Law Enforcement
200 Armory Building
Springfield, IL 62706
Ph. (217) 782-6429
(800) 843-5763 (hot line for sightings)

• Kansas
Lost Child Network
P.O. Box 6442
Shawnee Mission, KS 66206
Ph. (800) 843-5678 (hotline for sightings)

• Kentucky
Kentucky Alliance for Exploited and Missing Children
400 South Sixth Street, 3rd Floor
Louisville, KY 40202
Ph. (502) 587-3621

• Maryland
Society's League Against Molestation
P.O. Box 833
Beltsville, MD 20705
Ph. (301) 953-3237

• Massachusetts
New England K.ID.S.
516 Grafton Street
Worcester, MA 01604
Ph. (617) 791-1130
(800) 392-6090

• Michigan
National Child Safety Council
4065 Page Avenue
Jackson, MI 49204
Ph. (517) 764-6070

• Missouri
Child Find-Missouri
P.O. Box 19823
St. Louis, MO 63144
Ph. (314) 781-8226

• Nebraska
Project: Missing Children
5804 Ames Avenue
Omaha, NE 68104
Ph. (402) 347-6674

- Nevada
  Community Runaway and Youth Services
  190 East Liberty
  Reno, NV 89501
  Ph. (702) 323-6296

- New Jersey
  Foundation to Find and Protect America's Children
  P.O. Box 436
  Oak Ridge, NJ 07438
  Ph. (201) 697-4088

- New York
  Child Find
  P.O. Box 277
  New Paltz, NY 12501
  Ph. (914) 255-1848

  Child W.A.T.C.H.
  606 Mt. Zoar
  Elmira, NY 14904
  Ph. (607) 732-0562

- North Carolina
  Reach Out Center for Missing Children
  1003 Stadium Drive
  Durham, NC 27704
  Ph. (919) 471-3112

- Ohio
  Parents of Murdered Children
  1739 Bella Vista
  Cincinnati, OH 45237
  Ph. (513) 721-5683
  (513) 242-8025

- Oklahoma
  National Child Search
  P.O. Box 800038
  Oklahoma City, OK 73180
  Ph. (405) 685-5621
  (405) 685-5761

- Oregon
  Friends of Child Find of Oregon
  P.O. Box 756
  Springfield, OR 97477-0131
  Ph. (503) 341-3822

- Pennsylvania
  Friends of Child Find
  P.O. Box 10682
  Pittsburgh, PA 15235
  Ph. (412) 244-0729

- Rhode Island
  Society for Young Victims
  29 Thurston Avenue
  Newport, RI 02840
  Ph. (401) 847-5083

- Tennessee
  Commission on Missing and Exploited Children
  P.O. Box 310
  Memphis, TN 38101
  Ph. (901) 528-2005

- Texas
  Missing Persons' Center of Nueces County
  P.O. Box 1940
  Corpus Christi, TX 78403
  Ph. (512) 888-0265 (24 hours)

  Parents of Murdered Children
  8227 Roebourne Lane
  Houston, TX 70770
  Ph. (713) 469-0678

- Utah
  Child Find of Utah
  5755 Hansen Circle
  Murray, UT 84107
  Ph. (801) 261-4134
  (801) 262-8056

- Vermont
  Childseekers
  P.O. Box 6065
  Rutland, VT 05701-6065
  Ph. (802) 773-5988

- Virginia
  Child Watch
  P.O. Box 2381
  Richmond, VA 23218
  Ph. (804) 346-0191

- Washington
  Family and Friends of Missing Children
  Jane Adams Building
  11051 34th, N.E.
  Seattle, WA 98125
  Ph. (206) 362-1081

- West Virginia
  Friends of Child Find
  P.O. Box 85
  Weirton, WV 26062-0085
  Ph. (304) 748-8163

- Wisconsin
  Friends of Missing Children
  P.O. Box 8848
  Madison, WI 53708
  Ph. (608) 846-9111

- Canada
  Victims of Violence: Victims' Rights Advocates
  Postal Station, South Edmonton
  10465 80th Avenue
  Edmonton, Alberta, Canada T6E 4S7
  Ph. (403) 481-5073

  Windsor Missing Children
  P.O. Box 3243
  Tecumseh P.O.
  Windsor, Ontario, Canada N8W 2M4
  Ph. (519) 735-2712

Note

1. The author is particularly familiar with the Olson murders, and has interviewed the offender regarding his crimes and his victims.

References

Abrahams, S. (1984). *Children in the cross fire: The tragedy of parental kidnapping.* New York: Atheneum.
Agopian, M. W. (1981). *Parental child-stealing.* Lexington, MA: D. C. Heath.
Associated Press. (1987, June 7). Mother faces trial in child's death. *Atlanta Journal and Constitution.*
Dixon, J. R. (1985). *Personal protection security: A practical guide.* Chicago: Nelson-Hall.

Egger, S. A. (1985). *Serial murder and the law enforcement response*. Unpublished doctoral dissertation, Sam Houston State University, College of Criminal Justice.

Eitzen, D. S., & Timmer, D. A. (1985). *Criminology*. New York: John Wiley.

Estrella, M. M., & Forst, M. L. (1981). *The family guide to crime prevention*. New York: Beaufort.

Hickey, E. W. (1986). The female serial murderer. *Journal of Police and Criminal Psychology, 2*(2).

Holmes, R. M., & DeBurger, J. (1988). *Serial murder*. Newbury Park, CA: Sage.

U.S. Department of Justice, Federal Bureau of Investigation. (1988). *Crime in the U.S.* (adapted from *Uniform crime reports*). Washington, DC: Government Printing Office.

U.S. Department of Justice, Office of Juvenile Justice and Delinquency Prevention. (1989a). *Missing and exploited children: Progress in the 80's*. Washington, DC: Government Printing Office.

U.S. Department of Justice, Office of Juvenile Justice and Delinquency Prevention. (1989b). *Stranger abduction homicides of children*. Washington, DC: Government Printing Office.

Vogel, C. G., & Goldner, K.A. (1983). *The dangers of strangers*. Minneapolis, MN: Dillon.

Wooden, K. (1984). *Child lures*. Shelburne, VT: National Coalition for Children's Justice.

9

A Model for Crisis Intervention
with Battered Women and Their Children

Albert R. Roberts
Beverly Schenkman Roberts

Do you know what some women get for their birthdays? A black eye; a punch
in the ribs; or a few teeth knocked out. It's so frightening because it doesn't just
happen on their birthday. It may be every month, every week, or even every day.
It's so frightening because sometimes he abuses the kids, too. Or maybe she's pregnant and he kicks her in the stomach in the same spot where, just a few minutes
ago, she felt the baby moving. It's so frightening because the woman doesn't know
what to do. She feels so helpless. He's in control. She prays he'll come to his senses
and stop. He never does. She prays he won't hurt their kids. He threatens to. She
prays he won't kill her. He promises he will. (Haag, n.d.)

The above description of the fear and anguish to which battered women are
repeatedly subjected comes from a training manual for crisis counselors prepared
by the Domestic Violence Intervention Program of Brown County, Wisconsin. It is included in the manual to acquaint staff and volunteers with the pain-
ful history of the women they will be counseling. Increasingly, battered women
are turning to emergency shelters and telephone crisis intervention services for
help.

Authors' Note: This chapter is reprinted with permission of the authors from Albert R. Roberts
(Ed.), *Crisis Intervention Handbook: Assessment, Treatment and Research*. Belmont, CA: Wadsworth
Publishing Company, 1990, pp. 105-123.

Recognition of the need for and actual establishment of crisis intervention for victims of the battering syndrome has increased dramatically since the mid-1970s. While there were only seven emergency shelters for battered women in 1974 (Roberts, 1981), by 1987, there were more than 1,200 shelters and crisis intervention services coast to coast for battered women and their children (National Coalition Against Domestic Violence, 1987). Through crisis intervention, many women are able to regain control of their lives by identifying current options and goals and by working to attain those goals. The children of battered women may also be in crisis, but their plight has often been overlooked as the domestic violence programs focused their efforts on emergency intervention for the women. Progressive programs now incorporate crisis intervention for children (as well as for the mothers) in the treatment plan.

Battered women are usually subjected to a prolonged pattern of abuse coupled with a recent severe attack, so that by the time the victim makes contact with a shelter, she is generally in need of crisis intervention. Abused women are subjected to an extended period of stress and trauma, which results in a continual loss of energy. A battered woman is in a vulnerable position, and when a particularly severe beating takes place, or when other factors occur (e.g., the abuser starts to hurt the children), she may be thrust into a state of crisis (NOVA Newsletter, 1980).

Effective treatment for battered women and their children in crisis requires an understanding of crisis theory and the techniques of crisis intervention. According to Caplan (1964) and Aguilera and Messick (1984), a crisis state can occur rapidly when the following four things happen:

(1) The victim experiences a precipitating or hazardous incident.
(2) The incident is perceived by the woman as threatening to her or her children's safety and, as a result, tension and distress intensify.
(3) The battered woman attempts to resolve the situation by using customary coping methods and fails to resolve the situation.
(4) The emotional discomfort and turmoil worsens and the victim feel that the pain and anguish are unbearable.

At this point of maximum discomfort, when the woman perceives the pain and torment as unbearable, she is in an active crisis state. During this time there is an opportunity for change and growth, and some women are mobilized to seek help from a 24-hour telephone crisis intervention service (or hotline), the police, a hospital emergency room, or a shelter for battered women.

The emphasis in crisis assessment is on identifying the nature of the precipitating event and the woman's cognitive and affective reaction to it. The three most common precipitating events that lead battered women in crisis to seek the help of a domestic violence program are (a) an acute battering incident resulting in serious physical injury, (b) a serious abusive injury inflicted on the woman's child, and (c) a temporary impairment of hearing, sight, or thought process as a direct result of severe batterment. Often the precipitating event is perceived by the woman in crisis as being the final incident or "last straw" in a long history of violence (L. Edington, executive director, Sojourner, personal communication, February 19, 1987; R. Podhorin, director, Womanspace, Inc. personal communication, February 12, 1987; M. Schiller-Ramirez, executive director, St. Martha's Hall, personal communication, March 4,1987; see Houston, 1987).

Crisis intervention with battered women needs to be done in an orderly, structured, and humanistic manner. The process is the same for victims of other violent crimes, but it is particularly important to respond quickly to abused women because they may continue to be in danger the longer they remain in a place where the batterer can locate them. Crisis intervention activities can result in the person returning to her precrisis state or growing from the crisis intervention so that she learns new coping skills to utilize in the future.

In this chapter we will describe the following types of crisis intervention: early intervention by police-based crisis teams and victim assistance units, assessment and detection in the hospital emergency room, specific intervention techniques used by crisis hotlines and battered women's shelters, and short-term treatment for the children. We will also discuss the importance of referrals.

Intervention by Police-Based Crisis Teams and Victim Assistance Units

Surveys of police departments around the United States indicate that approximately 80-90% of police officers' time is spent on service calls, also known as order maintenance activities, such as assaults among family members, neighbor disputes, bar fights, traffic accidents, and disturbances caused by individuals who are drunk and disorderly. Police officers may have the skills to intervene and resolve a dispute among neighbors, a bar fight, or a traffic accident, but they are rarely skilled to provide crisis intervention and follow-up counseling with victims of domestic violence.

In recognition of the large amount of time police spend responding to repeat family assault calls and their lack of clinical skills, several police departments have developed crisis intervention teams that are staffed by professional social workers and trained volunteers.

Victims often turn to their local city or county police department when confronted with the life-threatening danger posed by domestic violence. As a result of the Thurman case (in which a battered woman was awarded $2.3 million in her lawsuit against the Torrington, Connecticut, Police Department for its failure to protect her from her violent husband), more police departments are responding to calls from domestic violence victims. Police can respond quickly to domestic violence calls, and can transport the victim to the local hospital emergency room or a battered women's shelter. In some cities, police receive backup from a crisis team that arrives at the home shortly after the police. The first such crisis team was established in 1975 at the Pima County District Attorney's Office in Tucson, Arizona. The acceptance of and growing reliance on this program by the Tucson Police Department is revealed by the significantly increased number of police referrals to the crisis team; there were a total of 840 police referrals in 1977, compared to 4,734 referrals in 1984. It should be noted that these figures reflect referrals for all types of crime victims, but most referrals are for domestic violence cases. Since violence in the home constitutes a considerable percentage of police calls, abused women are frequent beneficiaries of this innovative system.

The following descriptions of programs in Tucson, Arizona, and Houston, Texas, will illustrate the intervention procedures utilized by victim assistance programs.

Tucson. The Pima County Victim Witness Program has received national recognition for providing immediate crisis intervention to battered women and other crime victims. It has served as a model for similar programs in other cities. The program was initiated in 1975 with a grant from the Law Enforcement Assistance Administration (LEAA). The grant-funded program was so successful that when the grant expired, city and county officials agreed to pay for its continuation.

The crisis intervention staff use two police vehicles (unmarked and radio equipped) to travel to crime scenes. Mobile crisis teams are on patrol every night between 6:00 p.m. and 3:00 a.m. At all other times they are contacted via a beeper system (Roberts, 1987).

Domestic violence cases are potentially the most dangerous for the crisis counselors. The staff work in pairs, generally in teams of one male and one female. They are given intensive training that includes lessons in self-defense, escape driving, and the way to use a police radio as well as crisis intervention techniques.

Houston. In 1983, the Houston Police Department developed a program (modeled after the Tucson program) to provide immediate crisis counseling to victims of domestic violence as well as to victims of other violent crimes, such as rape. The Crisis Intervention Team (CIT) provides the following services: crisis counseling, advocacy, transportation to and from medical centers and shelters, and referrals to social service agencies. An estimated 40% of CIT clients are battered women (M. Hardman-Muye, director, CIT, personal communication December 1985).

The CIT staff are civilian employees of the Houston Police Department, and all of the referrals come from the police. A crisis team (always working in pairs) is notified of a crisis situation via the police radio, and the counselors meet the police at the crime scene. The police, after determining that the counselors will not be in danger, leave the home. The counselors utilize a basic crisis intervention model of assessing the situation, discussing the options, forming a plan of action, and aiding the victim in implementing the plan. The Houston program has 12 full-time staff and 2-4 graduate student interns each semester, and has recently recruited volunteer workers. The program director, Margaret Hardman-Muye, has a master's of social work degree and is an advanced clinical practitioner with specialization in treating battered women and victims of sexual assault.

The program is funded by a State Criminal Justice grant and by the city of Houston. Initially, 100% of the budget came from the state grant, but the city is expected to fund an additional 20% of the cost each year until it is totally city funded. In its first year, the program was budgeted at $159,000. This amount had increased to $351,000 by its third year of operation.

As of 1986, similar types of crisis intervention programs had been developed under the auspices of the police departments in many cities, including the following: South Phoenix, Arizona; Santa Ana, California; Stockton, California; Indianapolis, Indiana; Detroit, Michigan; Omaha, Nebraska; Las Vegas, Nevada; Rochester, New York; Houston, Texas; and Salt Lake City, Utah. However, there are still many communities that have not initiated this type of program. It is hoped that the success of the newly developed program will encourage other localities to establish similar types of services.

Assessment and Intervention in the Emergency Room

A visit to a hospital emergency room may provide the initial opportunity for some victims to recognize the life-threatening nature of the violent relationship and to begin making important plans to change their situation. At a growing number of large hospitals in urban areas, crisis intervention is being provided to battered women by emergency room staff.

A recommended way for emergency rooms to handle detection and assessment of battering is through the use of an adult abuse protocol. Two of the pioneers in the development of these protocols are Klingbeil and Boyd of Seattle, who, in 1976, initiated plans for emergency room intervention with abused women. The Social Work Department of the Harborview Medical Center in Seattle developed an adult abuse protocol that provides specific information on the assessment to be made by the involved staff: the triage nurse, the physician, and the social worker. Using a protocol serves two purposes: First, it alerts the involved hospital staff to provide the appropriate clinical care; second, it documents the violent incident so that if the woman decides to file a legal complaint, "reliable, court-admissible evidence" (including photographs) is available (Klingbeil & Boyd, 1984).

Although this protocol was developed for use by emergency room social workers, it can easily be adapted for use by other health care personnel. The following case example describes the way in which the adult abuse protocol has been used successfully:

Mrs. J was admitted to the emergency room accompanied by her sister. This was the second visit within the month for Mrs. J and the emergency room triage nurse and social worker realized that her physical injuries were much more severe on this second visit. Mrs. J was crying, appeared frightened, and in spite of the pain, she constantly glanced over her shoulder. She indicated that her husband would follow her to the emergency room and that she feared for her life. The social worker immediately notified Security. . . .

Mrs. J indicated that she just wanted to rest briefly and then leave through another entrance. She was four months pregnant and concerned about her unborn child. She reported that this had been the first time Mr. J had struck her in the abdomen. The social worker spent considerable time calming Mrs. J in order to obtain a history of the assaultive event. Consent for photography was obtained and Mrs. J indicated that she *would* press charges. "The attack on my child" seemed to be a turning point in her perception of the gravity of her situation, even though Mr. J had beaten her at least a dozen times over the previous two years.

While the social worker assisted in the history taking, a physician provided emergency medical care: several sutures over the right eye.

With Mrs. J's permission, an interview was conducted with her sister who agreed to let Mrs. J stay with her and also agreed to participate in the police reporting. When Mrs. J felt able, the social worker and sister helped her complete necessary forms for the police who had been called to the emergency room.

Although the physician had carefully explained the procedures and rationale to Mrs. J, the social worker repeated this information and also informed her of the lethality of the battering, tracing from her chart her last three emergency room visits. Mrs. J was quick to minimize the assaults but when the social worker showed her photographs from those visits, documenting bruises around her face and neck, she shook her head and said, "No more, not any more." Her sister provided excellent support and additional family members were on their way to the emergency room to be with Mrs. J. When the police arrived Mrs. J was able to give an accurate report of the day's events. . . . She realized there would be difficult decisions to make and readily accepted a follow-up counseling appointment for a Battered Women's group. (Klingbeil & Boyd, 1984, pp. 16-24)

It should be noted that all cases are not handled as easily as the one cited above. The two aspects of Mrs. J's situation that led to a positive resolution were (a) the immediate involvement of emergency room staff and their discussion with the patient of her history and injuries, and (b) the availability of supportive relatives.

Before the woman leaves the emergency room, the social worker should talk with her about whether to return home or to seek refuge with friends or family or at a shelter for abused women. The emergency room staff should be able to provide names and phone numbers of referral sources. It is helpful if the pertinent information is printed on a small, business-size card (easy to tuck away in a pocket or purse) and given to all abuse victims as well as to suspected victims (Klingbeil & Boyd, 1984). Even if a woman refuses to acknowledge that her current bruises are the result of battering, she may keep the card for use in the future.

Merely having an adult abuse protocol does not ensure that it will be used. A study conducted by Flaherty et al. (1985) at four Philadelphia hospitals found that the protocol was used selectively, mainly for victims who volunteered that they had been battered. The medical staff thus ignored the opportunity to help battering victims who were not able to volunteer the information. The researchers cited the following reasons for underutilization of the protocol:

(1) Some physicians and nurses did not regard battering as a medical problem.

(2) They believed that it would be an invasion of privacy to ask a woman questions about how she was injured.

(3) Many of the emergency room staff viewed completing the protocol as an additional burden when they were already overworked.

Of those medical personnel who did recognize battering as a legitimate problem, the intervention technique used most often consisted of giving a victim the tear-off list of referral sources that was printed at the bottom of the protocol.

There is a major difference between Flaherty et al.'s Philadelphia study and the procedures described previously by Klingbeil and Boyd (1984) in Seattle. The Philadelphia study requested the cooperation of nurses and physicians, but did not involve medical social workers. In contrast, the Harborview Medical Center protocol was created and implemented by the hospital social work department. It emphasized a multidisciplinary team approach, with the social workers taking the lead role in conducting screening and assessment, often talking to the victim while the physician provided medical treatment.

The information presented above would indicate that the involvement of medical social workers is advisable (and perhaps necessary) for the successful implementation of a system for crisis assessment intervention with battered women in the hospital emergency room.

Intervention Techniques Used
by Telephone Hotline Programs
and Battered Women's Shelters

Battered women in crisis may reach out for help in any of a number of ways. The initial contact is generally by telephone, turning the phone line into a lifeline for many women. Violence often occurs late in the evening, on weekends, or on holidays, and shelter staff are usually available 24 hours a day to respond to a crisis call. But a woman in crisis who has just been brutally beaten probably does not know the name or phone number of a local shelter. A frequent scenario is that of a woman and her children hastily escaping from home late in the evening and fleeing to a neighbor's home to make an emergency call for help. Not having the number of the local shelter, these women generally contact the police or an areawide crisis hotline that aids people in all types of crises. If the woman contacts an areawide hotline, there is generally a brief delay while the worker gathers some basic information and then gives the caller the phone number of the closest shelter. An alternative is for the crisis counselor to take the caller's phone number and have the shelter worker call her back.

When a battered woman in crisis calls a hotline, it is essential that she be able to talk immediately to a trained crisis counselor—not put on hold or confronted with an answering machine. If she is not able to talk to a caring and knowledgeable crisis counselor she may just give up, and a valuable opportunity for intervening in the cycle of violence will have been lost. In these situations time is of the essence, because if the violent male is still on the rampage he is likely to go searching for her, thereby endangering not only his mate but the neighbor as well.

Hotline workers distinguish between a "crisis call"—one in which the woman is in imminent danger or has just been beaten—and other types of calls in which the individual is not in immediate danger but is anxious or distressed and is seeking information or someone to talk to. The overriding goal of crisis intervention is to ensure the safety of the woman and her children. To determine whether the call is a crisis call, the worker asks questions such as the following:

- Are you or your children in danger now?
- Is the abuser there now?
- Do you want me to call the police?
- Do you want to leave and can you do so safely?
- Do you need medical attention?

Programs have different policies regarding transporting women who need refuge but have no way to get there. While some shelters will send staff to pick up the woman at her home, it is more common for shelter policy to prohibit staff from doing so because of the possibility of the staff member being attacked by the abuser. In cities that have crisis intervention teams affiliated with the police department (such as those described earlier in this chapter), the shelter staff can contact the police, who investigate the situation and radio for the crisis workers to transport the victim and her children to the shelter. Sometimes the police themselves are prevailed upon to provide transportation.

The Marital Abuse Project of Delaware County in Pennsylvania encourages battered women to call the police themselves, but there are circumstances in which they are not able to do so. In those cases, shelter workers call the police (with the woman's permission) and then contact the woman again. If the facility has two phone lines, there may be times when it is advisable for the worker to keep the woman on the line while calling the police on the other line. Staff are advised to follow up on the woman's call to law enforcement by waiting a few minutes and then also calling the police to find out where they will be taking her (to the police station, hospital, or whatever). If it is too soon for the police to have this information, the worker asks the officer to call back when they do know. If 30 minutes elapse without a call from the police, the worker contacts the police department again (Roberts, 1981).

Once the urgent issues pertaining to the woman's physical safety have been resolved, the crisis counselor can begin to help the victim talk about her situation and discuss possible courses of action. Throughout this process it is important for the counselor to remember that she can present different alternatives, but the client must make her own decisions.

The following is a step-by-step guide to intervention with battered women (originally developed by Jones, 1968) that is included in the training manual prepared by the Abuse Counseling and Treatment, Inc. (ACT) program in Ft. Myers, Florida. It is referred to as the ABC process of crisis management: A for "achieving contact," B for "boiling down the problem," and C for "coping."

- A—*achieving contact*
  (1) Introduce yourself: name, role, and purpose.
  (2) If a phone call, ask the client if she is safe and protected now.
  (3) Ask the client how she would like to be addressed:—first name, surname, or nickname—this helps the client regain control.
  (4) Collect client data; this breaks the ice and allows the client and counselor to get to know each other and develop trust.
  (5) Ask the client if she has a counselor or if she is taking any medication.
  (6) Identify the client's feelings and ask for a perception check.
- B—*boiling down the problem*
  (1) Ask the client to describe briefly what has just happened.
  (2) Encourage the client to talk about the here and now.
  (3) Ask the client what is the most pressing problem.
  (4) Ask the client, if it were not for said problem, would she feel better right now?
  (5) Ask the client if she has been confronted with a similar type of problem before, and, if so, how did she handle it then? What worked and what didn't?
  (6) Review with the client what you heard as the primary problem.
- C—*coping with the problem*
  (1) What does the client want to happen?
  (2) What is the most important need—the bottom line?
  (3) Explore what the client feels is the best solution.
  (4) Find out what the client is willing to do to meet her needs.
  (5) Help the client formulate a plan of action: resources, activities, time.
  (6) Arrange follow-up contact with the client.

Careful recruitment and thorough training of crisis intervention staff are essential to a program's success. It is also necessary for an experienced clinician to be on call at all times for consultation in difficult cases. In addition to knowing what to say, workers need to learn about the tone of voice and attitude to be used while handling crisis calls. Crisis workers are advised to speak in a steady, calm voice; to ask open-ended questions; and to refrain from being judgmental.

A shelter's policies and procedures manual should include guidelines for crisis staff. For example, the ACT program in Ft. Myers, Florida, has developed a 45-page training manual that includes sections on shelter policies and procedures, referral procedures, and background information on domestic violence that discusses both victims and abusers (Houston, 1987). The ACT manual explains the wide variation in emotional reactions of women who call for help. The client's speaking style may be "fast, slow, hesitant, loud, barely audible, rambling, loss of words [or] normal." Her emotional reaction may be "angry, highly upset, hysterical, withdrawn, fearful, laughing, calm, icy, guilty, or a combination of these" (Houston, 1987). No matter what characteristics the caller exhibits, the crisis worker's task is to try to help the victim cope with the immediate situation. However, the guidelines also advise crisis counselors to avoid the pitfall of believing they need to provide the caller with immediate, expert solutions to her problems. Crisis workers should not subject themselves to guilt feelings if they cannot help an abused woman resolve her situation. If the worker suspects child abuse or neglect, she is required to notify the supervisor and then report the suspected abuse to the appropriate agency (Houston, 1987).

Shelter staff are confronted with a dilemma when the caller is an abused woman who is under the influence of drugs or alcohol or who has psychiatric symptoms. Although such women are victims of batterings they also have significant problems that the staff are not trained to treat. Shelter policy generally requires crisis counselors to screen out battered women who are under the influence of alcohol or drugs, but there are exceptions. At Womanspace (in central New Jersey) women with drug/alcohol problems are accepted provided they are simultaneously enrolled in a drug or alcohol treatment program (R. Podhorin, personal communication, February 12, 1987). Likewise, it is the crisis counselor's responsibility to determine whether a woman's behavior is excessively irrational or bizarre or whether she is likely to be a danger to herself or others. If a woman is suspected of having psychiatric problems, she is generally referred to the psychiatric screening unit of a local hospital or to a mental health center for an evaluation.

Another policy issue relates to battered women in crisis who have no psychiatric or drug problems but are denied admission to a shelter because they have sons aged 12 or older who need shelter also. Many programs subscribe to the belief that by the time a boy from a violent family reaches the age of 12 he will have adopted his father's violent behavior patterns, and they want to avoid the possibility of violent outbursts at the shelter. However, not all shelters have such a policy. There is a minority view that an abused woman in crisis should be helped regardless of whether or not she has a young adolescent son (D. Arbour, director, Jersey Battered Women's Shelter, personal communication, February 12, 1987).

Telephone Logs

Battered women's shelters usually maintain a written record of all phone calls, whether or not they are crisis calls. In addition to seeking such routine information as name, address, phone number, marital status, and ages of children, the recording form may also include the following questions: Are you in immediate danger? Do you want me to call the police? How did you get our number? There are often also places to record any action taken by the crisis worker and any follow-up action (R. Podhorin, personal communication, February 12, 1987). Shelters that are often overcrowded may also have a part of the form on which the counselor can indicate whether the family is able to be housed immediately, is to be referred to another shelter or safe home, or needs to be put on a waiting list.

Womanspace has developed a one-page telephone log form that asks many of the questions listed above on the front and, on the reverse side, contains further screening questions and an explanation of the shelter's policies. An example is this printed statement, which explains the program's policy on weapons:

> We do not allow weapons in the shelter. We ask that you not bring a weapon or anything that may be used as a weapon with you.
>
> Do you own a weapon? _____
>
> If yes, do you agree to let us keep it in a safe place for you? _____

The advantage of printing this and other procedural statements on every telephone form is that it helps to ensure that all crisis workers impart the same basic information.

At the bottom of the Womanspace form is a list of nine of the most frequently used telephone numbers, including those of three area police departments. The advantage of having those phone numbers on every form is that during a crisis, they are always readily available, so that valuable time will not be lost searching for them.

Group Therapy

Once the woman and her children have arrived at a shelter or other safe place and the immediate danger of further violence has passed, group counseling can be initiated. Rhodes and Zelman (1986) have developed group therapy sessions based on a crisis intervention model that are *intended for mothers as well as their children*. The sessions are provided for current and former residents of a spouse abuse shelter in White Plains, New York, and are led by staff from a local mental health clinic. The clinic staff believe that the families who come to the shelter are in crisis; therefore, group treatment focuses on crisis intervention principles. The group sessions emphasize (a) relieving feelings of isolation and alienation of persons in crisis and (b) strengthening the relationship between the mother and children, which is viewed as the "natural support group."

When a woman comes to the shelter, the group leader talks to her individually and develops a treatment plan for the woman and her children. The group sessions are one component of the treatment plan. The group leader is careful not to overlook the needs of the children during group sessions. As a result of the children's presence, special types of intervention are included, such as playing, educating parents, modeling of appropriate parent-child interactions, and encouraging the children to facilitate an exchange of ideas and feelings.

The one-hour sessions are held at the shelter two afternoons a week. During the first 45 minutes of each meeting there is discussion, while the last 15 minutes are reserved for play activities chosen by the children.

Treatment for the Children

Battered women who seek temporary shelter to escape from the violence at home generally have children who come to the shelter with them. The children often feel confused, afraid, and angry. They miss their fathers and do not know if or when they will see them again. It is not uncommon for children to be misinformed or uninformed about the reason they were suddenly uprooted from their home, leaving their personal possessions, friends, and schools to stay at a crowded shelter. Similarly, the children may not realize that all of the other children at the shelter have come for the same reason.

Moreover, large numbers of these children have, at one time or another, also been victims of physical abuse. The 1986 annual report from the Family Violence Center, Inc., in Green Bay, Wisconsin, provided data on child abuse committed by a batterer. This agency found that close to half (73) of 148 wife abusers had on one or more occasions also beaten their children (S. Prelipp, director, Family Violence Center, personal communication, February 13, 1987).

The following is a true story written by a 10-year-old girl who came to a shelter after her father's violent attack on her mother. This account appeared in the *Disabuse Newsletter*, published by the Jersey Battered Women's Shelter, in December 1986:

MY LIFE
by Lisa, a ten year old shelter resident

One day around two months ago my mom and dad got into a fight. First, my mom and I came home from the mall. We had a really nice time there. But, when we came home our nice time got to be terrible. I knew they were going to get into a fight so I went into my bedroom and did my homework. I knew he was going to talk to her about something, but I didn't know what. Then I heard my mom start screaming and I went to the door and asked what was wrong. My dad said, "Oh, nothing is wrong. Go do your homework." But I knew something was wrong so I went and prayed to God. My dad was really mean that night. I hated him so bad. My mom did not deserve to get hurt. I love her more than anything else in the entire world. Then I heard my mom scream something but I didn't understand what she said because my dad covered her mouth with his hand. Afterward she told me she said call the cops. Anyway, I went back to the door by the bedroom and told my mom I needed help on my homework, but I didn't. I just wanted my mom to come out of the bedroom because I was afraid. Then they both came out. And I hugged my mom and went to bed. Then my dad started to strangle my mom. So I went out and told my dad to stop. He told me to go back to the bedroom and go to sleep. So, I did. But I was so stupid. Then I heard my mom screaming. So I went back into the living room and he was kicking my mom. He wouldn't stop, he kept kicking her in her arm and legs. I told him to stop. He told me to go back to bed but I said, No! Then he took his guitar and was gonna hit her over the head. But I went on top of my mother. He told me to get off. But I said, No. So he put down the guitar, then he got her ice for her arm. Then I went to sleep crying. The next morning I didn't go to school and she didn't go to work. Then he called up the house and talked to her for a while. He threatened to kill her. So we left to go to the shelter. And here I am now. (p. 4)

This girl was fortunate in that her mother brought her to the Jersey Battered Women's Service, Inc. (in northern New Jersey), which has a carefully developed counseling program for battered mothers and their children. Sadly, however, the majority of shelters offer only basic child-care services; they do not provide the crisis counseling needed to help children deal with the turmoil of family violence (Alessi & Hearn, 1984).

Nevertheless, innovative techniques for helping children have been incorporated into the program of the more progressive shelters. At St. Martha's Hall (a shelter in St. Louis, Missouri), in addition to providing counseling for the children, the shelter requires mothers to participate in parenting classes and to meet with the coordinator of the Children's Program about establishing family goals and meeting children's individual needs. The program also provides opportunities for mother and child to participate jointly in relaxing recreational activities (M. Schiller-Ramirez, personal communication, March 4, 1987). Group therapy for mothers and children was discussed in the previous section. Two other types of intervention—the use of coloring books and groups for children—are described below.

Use of Coloring Books

As part of an individualized treatment approach, some shelters utilize specially designed coloring books that discuss domestic violence in terms children can understand. Laura Prato of the Jersey Battered Women's Service, Inc. (JBWS), in Morristown, New Jersey, has created two coloring books—one for children ages 3 to 5, titled *What Is a Shelter?* (26 pages), and another for 6- to 11-year-olds, called *Let's Talk It Over* (22 pages). In addition to the children's books, Prato (n.d.a, n.d.b) has also written two manuals for shelter workers that serve as a discussion guide for the counselors. The books contain realistic, sensitive illustrations that depict the confused, sad, and angry emotions that the children are feeling. They are illustrated in black and white so that the children can color the pictures if they wish. Funding for the preparation and printing of the books and manuals came from the New Jersey Division of Youth and Family Services and NORWES CAP.

The purpose of the coloring books and the way in which they are to be used is explained in the introductions to the counselors' manuals. The manuals state that the book are used as part of the "intake and orientation process" for all children who stay at the JBWS shelter. The stated objectives of the books are as follows:

- to provide assurances of the child's continued care and safety
- to encourage children to identify and express their feelings
- to provide information needed for children to understand what is happening in their families
- to provide information that will improve each child's ability to adapt to the shelter setting
- to begin to assess the individual child's needs and concerns

The counselors' manuals stress the importance of the way in which the book is presented to the child, as shown in the following passage:

> The process surrounding the use of the orientation books is extremely important. It is likely to be the initial contact between the counselor and the newly arrived family and one that will set the tone for future interactions. Consistent with the JBWS Children's Program philosophy, this initial meeting communicates respect for mother and child and acceptance of their feelings. (Prato, n.d.a, n.d.b)

Before meeting with the child, the counselor meets privately with the mother to show her the book, explain its purpose, and ask for her permission to read the book to her child. The counselors are advised to read any available intake information prior to meeting with a child so that they are better able to "anticipate the individual child's special concerns and place the child's responses in a meaningful context" (Prato, n.d.a, n.d.b).

The books have been prepared in a way that encourages the child's active participation. Throughout both books there are several places where the child is given the opportunity to write his or her thoughts on the page. For example, one of the pages in *Let's Talk It Over* focuses on a child staying at a shelter who misses her father. The caption under the picture states:

> Many children at the shelter think a lot about their fathers, and that's okay. You may not see your father for a while until everyone in your family has a chance to think about things carefully. The little girl in the picture is wondering about her father . . . . What questions do you think she is asking? (Prato, n.d.a)

There is a place on the page for the child's response to the question asked in the above quote. The response could be written by the child or dictated to the counselor, who would write it in the book. On the next page of the book is a large blank space and a caption that reads, "You may use this page to draw a picture of your father."

Books such as those developed by the Jersey Battered Women's Service are very appropriate in helping children cope with the crisis that has led to their staying at the shelter.

Group Treatment for Children

Another way to help children cope is through therapeutic groups, such as the approach developed at Haven House, a shelter for battered women and their children in Buffalo, New York. Alessi and Hearn initiated the group approach when they observed the maladaptive ways in which the children reacted to the crisis they were experiencing. The children tended to be aggressive and attempted to resolve problems through hitting. They had considerable anxiety, "biting their fingernails, pulling their hair, and somaticizing feelings as manifested by complaints of headaches and 'tight' stomachs" (Alessi & Hearn, 1984). They had ambivalent feelings toward their fathers—loving as well as hating them.

The two group leaders established a six-session treatment program for children ages 8 to 16 focusing on the following topics: "1) the identification and expression of feelings; 2) violence; 3) unhealthy ways to solve problems; 4) healthy ways to solve problems; 5) sex, love and sexuality; and 6) termination and saying goodbye" (Alessi & Hearn, 1984).

To provide an indication of the scope of the group sessions, the content of the session on violence is summarized below:

The purpose of the session on violence is to give children an opportunity to explore and express feelings about the violence in their families and how it has affected them. This helps children break down their denial and minimization of the problem. It also gives children a chance to learn that other families have similar problems and that many families do not. The following questions are presented to each of the children for reflection and discussion:

(1) Why did you come to Haven House?

(2) Do you think it's right for a man to hit a woman or a woman to hit a man, and why?

(3) Do you think it's right for a parent to hit a child, and why?

(4) How do you think you've been affected by the violence in your family?

(5) Do you think you'll grow up to be violent or accept violence in intimate relationships? (Alessi & Hearn, 1984)

The children are always given "homework" to "keep the session alive" between meetings. For example, after the discussion on violence they are asked to develop a "minidrama" on family violence to be presented the next week. Following the session on healthy problem solving, they are asked to prepare a list of healthy ways of coping with their problems.

Referral

Knowledge of referral sources is essential. It is just as important for the police, hospitals, and human service agencies to know about and refer to programs helping beaten women and their children as it is for staff at domestic violence treatment programs to refer clients to appropriate community resources.

It is frequently determined that the battered woman needs a variety of services, such as job training and placement, low-cost housing, day care, and ongoing counseling; therefore, referral should be made to the appropriate service providers. In its 1986 *Year End Report*, St. Martha's Hall in St. Louis itemized the agencies to which clients had been referred (Schiller-Ramirez, 1987). Most women were referred to three or more agencies, while several clients were given nine or more referrals, depending upon their individual needs. The most frequently used referral sources involved legal aid, medical care, Careers for Homemakers, Job Bank, day-care programs, Women in Need (WIN; an agency concerned with long-term housing for single women), Alcoholics Anonymous, Women's Self-Help Center (providing counseling and support groups), and St. Pat's (a Catholic social service agency that finds low-cost housing and provides classes in budgeting money and other life skills). Examples of other, less frequently used, referral sources included a shelter in another state, Alateen, AlAnon,

Literacy Council, Big Brothers, dental care, GED program, Crisis Nursery, victim services, and the Red Cross.

There are two ways in which programs providing crisis intervention services can facilitate the referral process: (a) by publicizing their services to the population at large and to other service providers and (b) by becoming knowledgeable about community services needed by their clients and, in some instance, accompanying them to the agency.

Programs may be publicized through the following methods:

- printing brochures that describe the program's services and having business cards that provide the program's name and phone number (should be made available in large quantity to police officers, emergency room staff, and other potential sources of referral to the program)
- participating in interdisciplinary workshops and seminars on family violence so that the program can become widely known (also enables staff to learn about appropriate programs to which their clients can be referred)
- attending in-service training programs for police officers, countywide hot line staff, emergency room staff, and others to discuss referral of abused women and to resolve any problems in the referral process that may have occurred
- alerting the public through newspaper articles and public service announcements on radio and television, with the program's phone number prominently mentioned

Information for crisis counselors on appropriate referral sources should be available in several ways:

- The phone numbers of the most urgently needed agencies—such as the police, victim assistance programs, drug/alcohol treatment programs, and psychiatric screening units—should be readily available, preferably printed on each intake sheet or telephone log form.
- The program's training manual should contain a section on the most frequently used referral sources. For example, the manual of the ACT program in Ft. Myers, Florida, contains eight pages of often-used referral sources that list the address, phone number, office hours, and services provided for each source.
- Most major metropolitan areas have comprehensive resource guides (published by the local United Way or an affiliate, such as Call for Action) that provide comprehensive listings of all area community services. All programs serving abused women and their children should have a copy of and be familiar with their community's resources handbook.

The way in which referrals are made is extremely important, since it may affect the outcome. All too often, victims in crisis do not follow through in making initial contact with the referral agency. Counselors at St. Martha's Hall and other shelters provide support by accompanying the client to the agency in order to demonstrate how to obtain services. This is viewed as a positive alternative to the often intimidating and frustrating experience encountered by women who are given referrals, but are expected to fend for themselves.

Conclusion

A number of important issues and techniques relating to crisis intervention with battered women and their children have been examined. Specific methods for crisis intervention in different settings have also been discussed. As increased numbers of women in acute crisis seek help, crisis counselors and victim advocates must be prepared to respond without delay. Crisis counseling for battered women and their children may do much to alleviate the emotional distress and anguish experienced by those exposed to the trauma of domestic violence. Because of their experience and specialized training, crisis counselors and medical social workers can play a vital role in assisting women and children in crisis.

Law enforcement officers, victim advocates, hospital emergency room staff, and counselors at areawide crisis lines and battered women's shelters often come in contact with beaten women who are experiencing crisis. Effective crisis intervention requires an understanding by these service providers of the value and methods of crisis intervention as well as of the community resources to which referrals should be made.

Battered women are often motivated to change their life-styles only during the crisis or post-crisis period. Therefore, it is important for service providers at community agencies to offer immediate assistance to battered women in crisis. With an estimated two million couples involved in battering episodes annually, policymakers and program developers should give priority to expanding urgently needed crisis-oriented and follow-up services for battered women and their children.

References

Aguilera, D. C., & Messick, J. M. (1984). *Crisis intervention: Theory and methodology*. St. Louis, MO: C. V. Mosby.

Alessi, J. J., & Hearn, K. (1984). Group treatment of children in shelters for battered women. In A. R. Roberts (Ed.), *Battered women and their families: Intervention strategies and treatment approaches* (pp. 49-61). New York: Springer.

Caplan, G. (1964). *Principles of preventive psychiatry*. New York: Basic Books.

Flaherty, E. W., et al. (1985, February). *Identification and intervention with battered women in hospital emergency departments: Final report.* Philadelphia: Philadelphia Health Management Corp.

Haag, R. (n.d.). The birthday letter. In S. A. Prelipp, *Family Violence Center training manual.* Green Bay, WI: Domestic Violence Intervention Program.

Houston, S. (1987). *Abuse Counseling and Treatment, Inc. manual.* Ft. Myers, FL: Abuse Counseling and Treatment, Inc.

Jones, W. A. (1968). The A-B-C method of crisis management. *Mental Hygiene, 52,* 87-89.

Klingbeil, K. S., & Boyd, V. D. (1984). Emergency room intervention: Detection, assessment and treatment. In A. R. Roberts (Ed.), *Battered women and their families: Intervention strategies and treatment approaches* (pp. 7-32). New York: Springer.

National Coalition Against Domestic Violence. (1987). *National directory of shelters and services for battered women.* Washington, DC: Author.

Prato, L. (n.d.a). *Let's talk it over: A shelter worker's manual.* Morristown, NJ: Jersey Battered Women's Service, Inc.

Prato, L. (n.d.b). *What is a shelter? A shelter worker's manual.* Morristown, NJ: Jersey Battered Women's Service, Inc.

Rhodes, R. M., & Zelman, A. B. (1986). An ongoing multi-family group in a women's shelter. *American Journal of Orthopsychiatry, 56,* 120-130.

Roberts, A. R. (1981). *Sheltering battered women: A national study and service guide.* New York: Springer.

Roberts, A. R. (Ed.). (1984). *Battered women and their families: Intervention strategies and treatment approaches.* New York: Springer.

Roberts, A. R. (1987). *National Survey of Victim Service and Witness Assistance Programs: Final report.* Indianapolis: Indiana University School of Social Work. (mimeo)

Schiller-Ramirez, M. (1987). *St. Martha's Hall year end report.* St. Louis, MO: St. Martha's Hall.

10

Crisis and Recovery Services
for Family Violence Survivors

Arlene Bowers Andrews

People who are intentionally hurt or threatened with harm by family members confront exceptional challenges as they cope with the aftermath of victimization. Family violence is an extraordinary stressor, one that challenges the competencies of the survivor and erodes the support that could mediate the survivor's stress. This chapter reviews a variety of effective crisis and recovery interventions developed to promote the individual's healthy recovery from family violence and reduce the risk of long-term psychosocial damage. First, a conceptual foundation is introduced that integrates stress theory and knowledge about family violence.

Conceptual Foundation:
Stress and Family Violence

Synopsis: Stress Theory

The foundation for this conceptual framework lies in general stress theory (Goldberger & Breznitz, 1982) as well as in the specialized variants of stress theory known as crisis theory (Slaikeu, 1984) and traumatic stress theory (Figley, 1985).

People of all ages confront routine stressors, external events that are part of their social and physical environments. Normally, people reduce the anxiety induced by environmental stressors and maintain emotional and functional equilibrium by coping effectively with these routine stressors. Coping involves adjusting cognitions, feelings, and behaviors in response to environmental events, including changing the environment if necessary (Moos & Billings, 1982). Each person tends to have characteristic ways of coping; family systems tend to have their coping styles, too.

Examples of adaptive coping methods are acknowledging and expressing feelings, using social help, engaging in task-focused behavior, exercising, and relaxing. Maladaptive methods include chemical substance use, denial, aggression, suicide attempts, psychosomatic complaints, and social withdrawal. Any of these methods may reduce anxiety, but they also have obvious healthy or unhealthy side effects.

If the stressor is exceptionally strong, multiple stressors are simultaneously present, or the chosen coping response is not effective, the individual may experience the subjective state of stress. Stress is manifest as an aroused physiological state and subjective feelings of tension that can lead to exhaustion. Chronic stress can have harmful, even fatal, physical and psychological effects on the individual, including coronary disease, depression, immune system deficiency, and problems in maintaining interpersonal relationships.

Stressors may be routine, extraordinary, or catastrophic. Routine stressors include such events as a child's test at school, a verbal disagreement between spouses, and a holiday celebration. Periodically all people confront extraordinary stressors, such as change in life status (e.g., marriage, divorce, retirement), loss of a loved one, or residential relocation. The cumulation of routine and/or extraordinary stressors can induce particularly intense stress. Some people will also be faced with catastrophic stressors, which include events that are "sudden, overwhelming, and often dangerous, either to one's self or significant other(s)" (Figley, 1985, p. xviii). Individuals who experience catastrophe are at risk of developing psychic trauma, "an emotional state of discomfort and stress resulting from memories of an extraordinary catastrophic experience which shattered the survivor's sense of invulnerability to harm" (p. xviii).

A person's exposure to multiple, extraordinary, or catastrophic stressors may precipitate a temporary state of psychological crisis, depending on the coping resources of the person at the time of exposure. Slaikeu (1984) defines crisis as "a temporary state of upset and disorganization, characterized chiefly by an individual's inability to cope with a particular situation using customary methods of problem solving, and by the potential for a radically positive or negative outcome" (p. 13). People in crisis may have uncontrolled emotional expressions, disorganized thoughts, anxiety, and fatigue. They may have difficulty completing routine tasks and may withdraw from or cling to social contacts. The person in crisis is highly vulnerable to influence by others, acts helpless, and may appear to be psychopathological or suffering from chronic stress. In fact, the symptoms are temporary, typically resolved within a few weeks. The return to normalcy may be misleading, as serious residual psychological damage may have occurred. Figure 10.1 summarizes the crisis process. Crisis intervention techniques are used to facilitate crisis resolution in an adaptive direction.

How a person handles stress, trauma, or crisis is influenced by personal and social factors. Personal factors that promote healthy growth include effective normal coping skills, good physical and mental health, and general self-confidence. All people have strengths and competencies; the degree to which they can master stress is apparently related to their awareness of and ability to apply their competencies. Perceived competence includes a sense of personal efficacy, freedom from self-denigration, perceived control over emotions and imagery, interpersonal trust, and a sense of wholeness and integrity. The person who acts competently will be able to communicate empathy, bond with other persons, experience pleasure, and engage in positive health and safety behaviors.

When the survivor is a child, developmental issues obviously must be considered (Mowbray, 1988; Smith, 1984; Wolfe, 1987). A child's cognitive, moral, and physical ability to master his or her environment, understand what happened, and seek help will be directly affected by maturity. The younger the child, the more social support he or she will need (Eth & Pynoos, 1985). Adolescents have particular challenges when they must cope with victimization within their families while also confronting the development of identity and sexuality. Children cope better when they have an intimate attachment to at least one adult and history of being able to trust in the reliability and support of a relationship (Zimrin, 1986). The demand of coping with trauma or extraordinary stress can interfere with a child's normal developmental tasks and thus impair the child's future development. When the child copes with maladaptive behavior, the parent's stress may be increased, leading to even higher risk for psychosocial and physical harm.

Families have competencies, too. Under routine circumstances, families can potentially provide support to members as they cope. Families can enable adaptive coping strategies, share in problem solving, encourage communication of feelings, buffer the impact of external stressors on the individual, and provide a sense of stability when other environmental factors are unstable (Dunst, Trivette, & Deal, 1988). Through its major socializing role, the family teaches coping and problem solving to its members. The strength of competence varies from one family to another, but most families play some supportive role for family members.

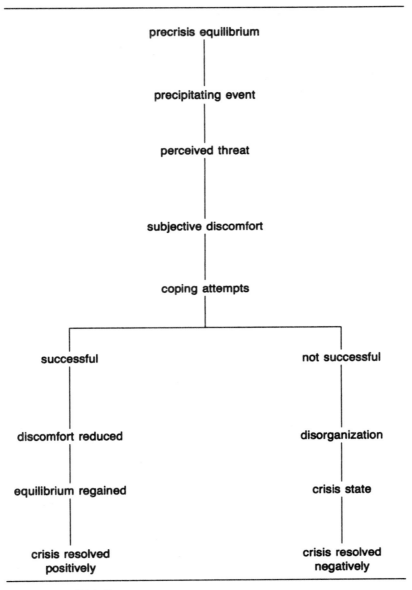

Figure 10.1. Crisis Process

Social networks and community support resources also affect an individual's ability to cope. The availability of responsive helping resources can inspire the trust that is important for a person's perceived competence as well as provide material resources necessary for control of the stressor in some cases. Trained professionals and volunteers who can render crisis intervention and recovery services are part of the formal community support system of the survivor. Some survivors will master their situations without formal help, because their personal and social resources for effective coping are adequate. Other persons will look to formal helping resources for assistance as they work to regain competencies, grow through the stressful or traumatic experience with minimal residual damage, and develop new psychosocial strengths.

Nature of Family Violence

The potency of family violence as a precipitator of psychosocial harm lies in the fact that the nature of the act is a direct affront to the competencies necessary for effective coping. That violence occurs in a family is a symptom of a family systems problem, indicating a reduced capacity for the family to function in a supportive role for the person who must cope. Thus the survivor's resources for coping are depleted by the act itself, leaving the survivor exposed and susceptible to the harmful effects of stress or the secondary effects of maladaptive coping responses.

Family violence can be broadly defined as covering a range of potentially harmful acts, including the use of physical force, sexual assault, neglect, and exploitation. The use of physical force includes direct assault, such as hitting and using a weapon on the body of the survivor, as well as indirect acts, such as restraint (e.g., locking in a closet) and destruction of pets or personal property. Sexual assault includes direct physical acts, such as rape and molestation, as well as indirect acts, such as making pornographic images, exhibitionism, and voyeurism. The threat of physical or sexual assault can induce psychosocial harm even if the act is not carried out. Neglect includes withholding food, health care, or economic resources, deprivation of rest, and failure to supervise dependent family members. Exploitation includes requiring family members to perform inappropriate roles (e.g., jobs that are illegal or unhealthy) and such acts as financial extortion. Neglect and exploitation may not be forceful acts, but the impact on the psyche and body of the survivor can be as severe as assaultive acts. A survivor is anyone who has lived through victimization by a family member or has been a vulnerable witness to another family member's victimization.

Acts of family violence may be chronic, such as chronic nutritional deprivation or repeated use of mild physical force by adults against one another or children in the family. The act may be extraordinary, as in the case of an exceptionally severe beating or near-starvation. If the act is sudden and unexpected, it may be perceived as catastrophic, particularly if it is life threatening. Any of these acts may precipitate a state of crisis or increased stress in the victim, leading to the risk of maladaptive coping responses.

The survivor's ability to cope successfully is hindered by several factors that tend to be present when victimization occurs in the family. These include the survivor's perceived isolation, violation of trust, risk of recurrence, and loss, or threat of loss, of home.

Survivors often perceive support from potential helping resources as ambivalent, leading to a pervasive feeling of isolation. The family as a whole is usually coping with the aftermath of the violence and the factors that precipitated it. Survivors often believe they cannot get help from other family members. Battered women, for example, have reported asking for help from extended family and being rejected (McEvoy, Brookings, & Brown, 1983). Abused children may perceive collusion among family members, even when only one is the perpetrator. Support through extended social networks such as friends and colleagues may be strained by family violence.

The isolation is intensified by ambivalent cultural messages from people in the family's community and formal helping resources. Family violence generally occurs within private boundaries. Cultural norms and, to some extent, legal standards in the United States dictate that a family's business is its own, that problems within the family should be resolved by the family. Survivors of all ages usually understand and accept these norms, and struggle to maintain the secrecy of the victimization. Thus disclosure of the victimization by the survivor to someone outside the family becomes a critical moment, one that can itself precipitate crisis, increased stress, or trauma. Survivors are at risk of "secondary victimization," harm that results from inappropriate responses from potential helping resources. Asking for help and not receiving it can be a crushing disappointment to someone who is already suffering intense stress related to victimization.

Disclosure may occur in many different ways. The survivor may ask for help, as when a battered woman calls the police. Someone else may recognize the indicators of family violence, as when a teacher reports child abuse or neighbors call the police about a spousal conflict. Survivors may be ill prepared for the response to the disclosure. They may feel blamed or manipulated. The type of help they want may not be the intervention that is offered, as when a sexually abused child wants her father to stop molesting her and the intervention takes her away from her home, a move she does not want. Throughout the literature on family violence, survivors' frustration with responses to requests for help and intense sense of isolation are major themes. The combination of ambivalent family and community support can be a significant deterrent to healthy coping for the family violence survivor.

Certain forms of family violence involve deception by the perpetrator. Sexual abuse of children and financial exploitation of elderly family members are two situations in which deception plays a major role. In other cases, the perpetrator may offer well-intended assurances that are subsequently violated, as when the physically abusive parent or spouse promises to stop using force but continues to does so. The violation of trust implicit in this type of interaction can have devastating consequences for the victimized family member. Asking for and accepting support are healthy coping behaviors, but when a survivor has been deceived or repeatedly disappointed, mistrust can become generalized, and the help-seeking behaviors of the survivor are restricted.

Another factor that makes family violence an extraordinary stressor is its chronicity. Neglectful families are unpredictably available as providers of physical and emotional nurturance. Violent episodes recur—sometimes with predictability, sometimes erratically. The threat of harm is ever present in the physical and social environment of the survivor, and constant vigilance is required. Survivors sometimes cope by developing extraordinary behavioral patterns as a way of exerting control over their environment, such as the child who withdraws completely, refusing ever to speak, and the battered woman who develops a ritualized schedule for herself and her children that includes cleaning house in the middle of the night to avoid irritating the perpetrator.

Stress is further accentuated in family violence by the survivor's realization that her or his attachment to home and family, the primary sanctuary despite its faults, is in jeopardy. Child and adult survivors sometimes must flee home temporarily, often against their own wills. Survivors in these situations must cope with grief as well as with the fear that the loss will become permanent. The lack of predictability and stability of the home may induce feelings of powerlessness and lack of personal control. When the loss is permanent, the survivor becomes even more vulnerable to unresolved feelings and maladaptive coping. Survivors may lose family members to death by homicide or suicide, to imprisonment, or to permanent separation.

In some unfortunate cases the loss is compounded by the phenomenon that family violence is repeated in the new family system, as when child abuse recurs in a foster home, an abused elderly person is again abused in a nursing home, or a battered woman is revictimized in a new relationship. Revictimization or adjustment problems may lead to another loss of home. Victims are at risk of developing serious attachment disorders when such loss and vulnerability are present.

As this review of selected factors unique to family violence has indicated, being victimized in one's own family not only can cause immediate physical and psychosocial harm but also drastically impedes the ability of the survivor to cope with the aftermath of victimization. Following is a summary of the damage that can result.

Consequences of Family Violence

Research to document the consequences of family violence is fragmented, organized according to the nature of the precipitating act and the target of the abuse. While one can review studies about the impact of specific forms of child or adolescent maltreatment, spousal violence, and elder abuse on the survivor, it is difficult to draw conclusions about victims of family violence in general with precision about the nature and prevalence of the impact. However, by reviewing the fragmented literature, one can identify general themes that suggest the kinds of harm done by various forms of family violence.

Survivors obviously are at risk of physical harm, including direct injury, disability, and even death. They suffer physical stress reactions such as fatigue, insomnia, and headaches. They also suffer material losses such as loss of property, economic support, and access to basic necessities (food, shelter, clothing). These physical and material needs lead victims to require assistance and sometimes even long-term service, as in the case of permanent disability.

Some of the most damaging consequences of surviving family violence are psychological and social, which is the emphasis here. Survivors may develop negative affective, cognitive, behavioral, and social symptoms (Bolton & Bolton, 1987; Figley, 1985; Lystad, 1986; Walker, 1984; Yin, 1985). Affectively, survivors may express sadness and depression, reporting limited ability to experience pleasure. They may feel chronically anxious or "numb" or vacillate between the two feelings. Anger, including anger displaced toward persons other than the perpetrator, hopelessness, and loneliness may be persistent.

Cognitively, the survivor may develop a negative view of the world that is based on the generalized appraisal that the world is a bad place. Fearful ideation about everyday phenomona is common and may escalate to become flashbacks, nightmares, and intrusive images of death and destruction. Perceived control over environmental influences is likely to be low, causing survivors to describe themselves as "powerless." Often they minimize their perceptions of threat by denying the severity of the violence and the potential for harm as well as by denying the emotional impact on themselves. The survivor may develop a negative self-concept, including attributing self-blame for the victimization. Body image may become negative. In some cases, sexual identity may become confused. The problem-solving capacity of the survivor may be restricted by confused thoughts, disorganized consideration of various options for action, and a pervasive sense that there are no feasible solutions to life's problems. These negative and disorganized cognitions are reinforced when unsuccessful attempts are made to seek help or solve the problem, leading to a cluster of symptoms known as "learned helplessness" (Walker, 1984). These cognitive messages, when combined with the cluster of negative emotions, can lead a survivor to feel exhausted and to give up trying to stop the probability of repeated family victimization or to resolve the negative aftermath.

Behaviorally, the survivor may lead a restricted life, limiting routine activities to those over which he or she perceives some degree of control. Some survivors become highly dependent on others. Those who cope with chronic threat of harm develop ways of responding to cues that the risk of assault may be escalating. Some replicate the perpetrator's behaviors; for example, the manipulated incest survivor becomes manipulative, or the controlled wife becomes controlling of her children. Some cope with their negative emotions and cognitions by using behaviors that, at least temporarily, change their perceptions and feelings, such as use of chemical substances, thrill-seeking behavior, and aggression toward others. Suicide attempts are higher in the survivor population than in the general population. As noted earlier, these maladaptive behaviors can have negative consequences of their own.

Socially, survivors may be detached and isolated. They may have difficulty forming intimate relationships, including parent-child attachments. Their trust of others tends to be low. The potential for conflict in relationships is high when one of the parties is a family violence survivor who has not positively resolved the victimization. Some resort to shallow serial sexual relationships for attachment. Survivors are susceptible to entering exploitive relationships, leading to revictimization.

In severe cases, the survivor may develop posttraumatic stress disorder, a cluster of symptoms that may include intrusive memories causing reexperience of the stressor, numb affect or social withdrawal, hyperalertness, sleep disturbances, guilt, thought disturbances, and sensitivity to events similar to the stressor (American Psychiatric Association, 1981).

Child survivors may react in ways that are analogous to the symptoms for adults noted above, only the manifestations are developmentally linked (Ammerman, Cassisi, Hersen, & Van Hasselt, 1986; Augustinos, 1987; Browne & Finkelhor, 1985; Erickson & Egeland, 1987; Mowbray, 1988; Wolfe, 1987; Wolfe, Wolfe, & Best, 1988). Preschool children are likely to be fearful and sick, showing compulsive or restitutive play and regressed behavior (e.g., separation anxiety, enuresis). School-age children may have these symptoms as well as anger, social withdrawal or aggression, guilt, depression, underachievement, and self-deprecation. Adolescents may be fearful but otherwise unlike the preschool children. They may have many of the same symptoms as school-age children but also may be apathetic and/or anxious, express rationalizations about the victimization, and act out or exhibit personality changes if the victimization began during adolescence. Children and youth may be hindered in their efforts to attain a sense of competence and mastery when their primary environment is so controlling and unpredictable.

The probability that any of these psychosocial harms will affect a particular survivor is mediated by a number of factors. One, of course, is the general coping strength of the individual, based in personal characteristics and social support. The nature of the stressor itself makes a difference, with intrusive acts such as sexual assault, use of severe physical force, and psychological torture inducing the greatest harm, as do sudden onset and severe force. The survivor's relationship to the perpetrator makes a difference, with the most severe damage related to intimate relationships in which trust is violated. The survivor's previous victimization in another family system will affect how he or she copes; if the victimization was resolved in a positive direction, the survivor will be better prepared to handle a new assault. If it was not, serious consequences can evolve.

Some survivors develop none of the symptoms described above. Others experience the feelings, cognitions, and behaviors for a period of time and then move beyond them to a new state of being. Survivors have resolved their victimization when they are able to feel relaxed, connected to others, and in control of their anger. They can experience pleasure in a variety of ways. They have positive self-esteem, perceive themselves to be whole, and are free from intrusive negative thoughts. Their belief in their ability to exert personal power in the world is adequate, as is their confidence about their problem-solving capacity. They engage in positive health and safety behaviors and are able to form and maintain social relationships, including intimate bonds. They essentially are able to express competencies that they may have had prior to the victimization or can develop as they cope with the aftermath.

Crisis and Recovery Interventions

No magical intervention can minimize the pain of the victimization itself. The survivor has no choice but to confront the reality of what happened. The goal of crisis and recovery interventions is to help the survivor grow through the pain and beyond, to avert residual damage and promote new strengths for coping with the memories and future similar challenges.

Any survivor should be able to ask for and receive help in coping with family violence, although not all survivors will need help. This section describes three levels of assistance. The first is psychological first aid, which is a basic helping skill that anyone with minimal interpersonal skills can learn. Public awareness efforts about all forms of family violence during the past three decades have emphasized that anyone should be able to recognize the indicators of family violence. The survivor's initial contact may be with a friend or colleague or someone from a formal agency, such as a law enforcement officer, teacher, or crisis telephone worker. Anyone may be the first help contact for a survivor, so training in how to respond is important.

The second level is survivor need assessment and empathic support, which all human service agencies should be prepared to do. Many agencies designate workers to assume survivor support functions, as when police departments, mental health centers, and hospitals have victim specialists. Survivors may present for help years after the victimization, with indirect presenting problems such as depression or substance abuse. Whether the victimization is recent or distant, an appraisal of how the event(s) affected the survivor's life is important for targeted recovery intervention. Survivors also need information, advocacy, and companionship, particularly when going through legal proceedings or dealing with multiple agencies.

The third level, recovery intervention, requires greater skill in psychoeducation and psychotherapy. Examples of interventions at each level are briefly reviewed here.Ideally, survivors will receive coordinated assistance from the many specialized agencies that may be involved. Many communities have formed survivor services networks and assessment/treatment teams to promote interdisciplinary and interagency collaboration for the good of the client.

Crisis Intervention

Crisis intervention is recommended for all initial contacts between helping persons and survivors, even though many survivors will not experience crisis. The strategies are effective in establishing initial rapport, gathering sufficient information for a short-term assessment, and averting a potential state of crisis.

Whether a family violence survivor enters a state of crisis depends on such factors as how threatened the survivor feels, her or his confidence in being able to emerge safely from the situation, and the degree of social support available. The following situations are particularly intense for family violence survivors, so they may be considered indicators of potential high risk for crisis:

- physical and emotional exhaustion of the survivor due to cumulative stressors
- severity of actual or threatened harm, particularly sexual assault or use of potentially lethal force

- first-time disclosure of the violence outside the family
- high probability of leaving home or family dissolution, even if temporary
- discovery or realization by the survivor that he or she has been deceived
- initiation of court proceedings involving the survivor

People in crisis can be recognized by their expressed personal discomfort and apparent disorganization (Borgman, Edmunds, & MacDicken, 1979; Halpern, 1973; Hoff, 1978; Lazarus, 1976; Roberts, 1990; Slaikeu, 1984). Figure 10.2 describes common symptoms, using a case example of a mother in crisis due to her child's abuse. Persons in crisis tend to be emotionally aroused and highly anxious; often they are weepy. Occasionally they will act extremely controlled and noncommunicative as a way of coping with high anxiety, but most often they will express despair, grief, embarrassment, and anger. Their thoughts are disorganized, leading to trouble in relating ideas, events, and actions. They may overlook important details, or may jump from one idea to another, making communication hard to follow. They may confuse fears and wishes with reality. Persons in crisis may not be able to perform routine behaviors such as basic grooming. They may avoid eye contact, and may mumble. Some persons may act impulsively. People in crisis have reported feelings of fatigue as well as appetite and sleep disruptions. They are socially vulnerable, which means that a helper can have significant influence, but so can people with exploitive motives. People in crisis act in ways similar to people with certain forms of chronic mental illness, but it must be emphasized that the crisis state is time limited, usually lasting no more than a few days to six weeks.

Depending on their developmental level, children display signs of crisis that are analogous to adult symptoms (Smith, 1984; Wolfe, Jaffe, Wilson, & Zak, 1985). They are likely to display random, manic activity, including aggressiveness. Often they have an insatiable craving for attention, and cling to caretakers. They may have sleep difficulties, including enuresis. Usually their ability to cope is directly related to the coping of the adult to whom they are primarily attached. The child who is temporarily out of home must cope with adjustment to a new environment as well as with the history of violence and the separation.

Psychological first aid is a process that anyone can learn (Slaikeu, 1984). Crisis helpers must essentially be empathic, able to listen actively, able to focus the survivor's immediate problem and to assess resources, and knowledgable about community resources. The goals of psychological first aid are to help the survivor feel supported and able to cope and to link the survivor with resources for longer-term support. A significant point is that the goal of crisis intervention is not to solve the family violence problem; rather, it is to manage the state of crisis and promote a competent approach to the challenge of solving

This case is based on a call to a crisis hot line.

Facts: Three days ago Doris discovered her husband in the act of sexually fondling their 4-year-old daughter. Doris immediately took the child and her 2-year-old sister to Doris's mother's house, where she and the children have stayed.

Affect: Doris is obviously upset when she calls. Her voice is trembling. She says she is afraid of what is going to happen; afraid of Murray and afraid of the future in general. She feels physically safe at her mother's, but she is irritated with her mother, who tends to fuss at the children. Doris has not told her mother what happened, she just says she and Murray had a fight. Doris wants to talk about her mother. Her affect fluctuates quickly between anger at her mother and sadness about what Murray has done. She avoids talking about the abuse, seems to be embarrassed, and says, "I can't believe it happened." She is irritated that the children are asking to see their father.

Sensations: Doris did not sleep last night and does not feel like eating.

Thoughts/images: Doris keeps repeating, "I don't know what to do." She believes Murray is mentally ill. Her major plan is to get bus tickets for herself and her children to flee to another state, where she will stay with her former college roommate. She does not plan to tell the roommate she is coming. She will get a job there and never see Murray again.

Behavior: Doris says she is too upset to take care of the kids. It is 1:00 p.m. and they are still in their pajamas. Her mother has been fixing their meals. Doris will not speak to her daughter about the fondling because she wants her to forget about it. Doris impulsively decides that if she calls Murray's boss, whom she has known since childhood, and tells him about what Murray has done, then maybe Murray will be shamed into getting psychiatric help.

Social/interpersonal behavior: Doris fluctuates between speaking harshly to her children and hugging them close to her. She and her mother argue whenever Doris comes out of the bedroom. Doris cannot remember the name of the agency she is calling, since she closed the phone book after she dialed the number. She repeatedly asks the crisis worker, whose name she cannot remember even though she has been told twice, "What should I do?"

Figure 10.2. Case Example: Crisis Precipitated by Child Abuse

the broader problem. Psychological first aid is a first step, to be followed by other interventions.

Psychological first aid tends to take from 20 minutes to 3 hours. When such intervention is done with a child, the child's ability to understand, feelings of solitude, and lack of personal power should be considered. The process takes place through successive stages found in any problem-solving process (adapted from Roberts, 1990; Slaikeu, 1984; Hoff, 1978):

- *Stage 1*: Establish psychological and emotional contact.

    Goal: Survivor feels heard, understood, and accepted. Intensity of emotional distress reduced. Problem-solving ability reactivated.

    The worker listens actively. Most survivors have been coping remarkably well with their situations; they need to hear spoken support for their strength and courage. The focus is on how the survivor feels, not on actions that might be taken. The worker lends calm control to an intense situation. This first stage leads to establishment of rapport, the mutual feeling that the two people are interested in and understand one another.

- *Stage 2*: Explore dimensions of the problem.

    Goal: Person in crisis can distinguish immediate needs and needs that can be addressed through later action.

    The crisis worker inquires about the nature of the problem, asking questions, if necessary, as the survivor relates the story. Useful information includes who was involved (e.g., perpetrator, other victims, witnesses, helpers), what happened, where it happened, whether the survivor is immediately safe, how the survivor is handling the problem now, how the survivor has handled it in the past.

    After gathering the information, the crisis worker ascertains what the survivor believes to be the immediate problem and then shares his or her own perception of what the immediate problem is with the survivor. In many cases, the immediate need is for safety. When the survivor minimizes the threat of harm, the worker may need to help her or him understand the danger and need for protection.

    An important issue at this stage is assessment of lethality. A survivor may feel so overwhelmed by the situation that she or he believes suicide or homicide is the only way out. Scales are available to facilitate assessment of lethality (Hoff, 1978), to aid the worker in exploring such issues as whether the survivor has considered killing her- or himself or another person, has or did have a plan to do so, has the means to do so, or has a history of having attempted to do so. The crisis worker takes a directive stance if lethality risk is high.

    This stage is complete when the crisis worker and the survivor have agreed about what problem needs to be addressed immediately and what can be handled later.

- *Stage 3:* Examine possible solutions.

  Goal: Survivor identifies and accepts one or more solutions to immediate and later needs.

  The worker begins by asking the survivor to identify alternative actions that can be taken to address the immediate needs. Prompts may help, such as "What have you considered or done thus far?" "What can you do?" "What else can you do?" "What might happen if you try to . . . ?" The worker may offer additional suggestions, using this time to educate the survivor about available resources. The worker may need to initiate a list of actions with depressed survivors who believe there are no options. The availability of social support is discussed and included in the plan for action.

  Solutions to immediate and later needs should be distinguished. During crisis is no time to initiate actions such as divorce, termination of parental rights, getting a new job, or moving to another town. These are long-term solutions that require careful deliberation.

  Advantages and disadvantages to various immediate actions should be discussed, and obstacles to action identified. The survivor's understanding of resources should be explored, since persons in crisis tend to have magical thinking about being rescued and may assume that a resource can help more than it can, leading to disillusionment.

  This stage ends when the worker and survivor have agreed on an action plan, including safety measures, that the survivor will follow. The plan is focused on the immediate problem, appropriate for the survivor's functional level, consistent with life-style and culture, inclusive of social networks, realistic, time limited, concrete, and adaptable.

- *Stage 4:* Assist in taking concrete action.

  Goal: The survivor accomplishes what is necessary to meet immediate needs.

  In a situation where lethality is not likely, the worker's role is primarily that of backup support and provider of information. The survivor is capable of acting on his or her own behalf; the worker should encourage the survivor to assume control of the action plan, avoiding the inclination to "rescue" the survivor. The worker must take care not to pass judgment on what the survivor chooses to do, even if the choice is not one the worker would have made.

  In a situation where lethality is likely, the worker assumes a more directive role. In these cases, the worker actively mobilizes resources such as the police or other emergency services.

- *Stage 5:* Prepare for follow-up.

  Goal: Feedback is secured on how adequate the support to the survivor is, whether linkages to resources were made, and whether lethality was reduced. Linkages for resources to help nonimmediate needs can begin to be made.

Before the end of the psychological first aid session, the worker secures identifying information so that the survivor can be contacted again. The possibility of making a follow-up contact should be explored. Survivors sometimes ask that a fictitious name be used and specify limited availability for recontact because they do not want the perpetrator to know that a helping resource has been contacted.

These procedures operationalize the precepts that have been summarized previously; that is, people have competent ability to cope and can master their abilities when temporarily lost due to crisis if appropriate help is offered.

Assessment

After the survivor has expressed some degree of increased personal control as a result of psychological first aid, a more comprehensive assessment of need can begin. The purpose of the assessment is to determine how the crisis is affecting all parts of the survivor's life, so that a plan for recovery intervention can be developed and the survivor can begin to face the future. Comprehensive assessment covers the survivor's physical, affective, interpersonal, cognitive, behavioral, and legal situations. One goal of assessment is to differentiate normal from pathological reactions. Figure 10.3 illustrates two alternative resolutions of crisis due to battering—one adaptive, the other maladaptive. Recovery services are most effective if they are initiated during the crisis period.

In some cases of family violence, the assessment also serves the purpose of collecting evidence for legal purposes. Legal proceedings may be of long-term benefit to the survivor by increasing protection and/or promoting perpetrator treatment, but in the short term the evidentiary demands are often intrusive and can aggravate the survivor's crisis. The comprehensive collection of information requires the potential involvement of numerous individuals from various disciplines, such as medicine, social work, nursing, and law enforcement. Many emergency service settings, such as hospital emergency rooms, child protection programs, and battered women's shelters (Bross, Krugman, Lenherr, Rosenberg, & Schmitt, 1988; Klingbeil & Boyd, 1984), have developed protocols to ease the demands on the survivor while comprehensive information is collected.

A comprehensive assessment will thoroughly cover information about the precipitating event, presenting problem(s), social environmental context of the crisis, precrisis functioning of the survivor, and current functioning of the survivor. The protocol usually provides a checklist of pertinent documents to complete at this time, such as photographs/X-rays of injuries, consent forms, and forms for filing criminal charges. The protocol identifies the roles of particular professionals and agency representatives as well as appropriate agencies to be contacted on behalf of the survivor. Ideally, the survivor will be interviewed

Sharon, a divorced teacher, is regarded by her friends as an independent person. Her daily routine involves household chores, going to work, watching TV at night. Her friends regard her as pleasant, though she seldom expresses her feelings.

Sharon's ex-husband Ted moves back to town. Within two days he comes to her apartment, starts an argument, and beats her.

Sharon drives herself to the emergency room and is treated for a fractured wrist. She is afraid Ted will kill her if she calls the police. She returns home, embarrassed to tell her friends or family. At work she says she was in an accident. Sharon begins to feel confused and afraid that Ted will return, even though he said she disgusted him and he never wanted to see her again.

Sharon feels alone. Her memories of former fear and beatings by Ted occupy her thoughts. She cannot concentrate on her work. She does not sleep well and does not feel like preparing meals.

Adaptive	Maladaptive
Sharon calls a friend. She tells her the situation and describes her past. The friend comes over and offers Sharon a place to stay for a few days.	Sharon stays home from work. She is beginning to feel paranoid, afraid Ted may come at any minute. She considers buying a gun to protect herself.
Sharon feels relieved.	Sharon feels she may be going crazy. She feels exhausted and does not want to see anyone.
Sharon feels more in control. She decides to file charges, at least having the district attorney warn Ted to stay away from her.	Sharon stays in her bedroom with the door closed. She feels like killing herself and Ted. She feels overwhelmed and alone.
Sharon has learned new skills: She can ask for and get help from friends and formal systems.	After several days, Ted does not come. Calls from the school cause Sharon to take care of herself and go back to work. She settles into a lonely routine, more withdrawn than before. She feels that her life is worthless and wonders why she bothers to live.

Figure 10.3. Case Example: Two Ways a Crisis Might Be Resolved for a Battered Woman

only once, either by a team or by a professional acting on behalf of the team. The protocol includes a list of possible persons (by relation) to contact on behalf of the survivor. The comprehensive assessment is the basis for developing a plan for recovery services.

Recovery Intervention

The goals of recovery intervention are to help survivors restabilize their lives and grow more healthy and to deter pathology. Recovery may require considerable work—that is, time and energy—on the part of some survivors and their support systems. A variety of psychotherapeutic interventions have been demonstrated to be effective in promoting healthy recovery. Several specific methods are reviewed here.

Survivors generally have multiple recover tasks. The crisis state must be resolved, if there is one. The survivor must adapt to immediate losses and changes created by the disclosure and protective response, when one occurs. The survivor must master the perceived state of victimization. And the fundamental family dysfunction that contributed to the victimization must be addressed.

Crisis therapy, which generally lasts only six weeks, involves the application of psychotherapeutic and educational interventions during the crisis period. The four tasks of crisis resolution are essentially as follows: to survive the crisis physically, to express feelings related to the crisis and any recent associated losses, to attain cognitive mastery of the experience, and to make behavioral and interpersonal adjustments necessary for future living (Slaikeu, 1984). Once the crisis is positively resolved, the survivor is likely to need longer-term, less intense recovery services to promote healthy long-term coping.

Information and support can help the survivor handle protective interventions. A support person or advocate can promote stability and security in a services system that may otherwise be unpredictable and manipulative. Clear information about all interventions can reduce uncertainty and promote accurate expectations. This is essential, particularly given the predictable disorganized thought and low trust of the highly stressed individual.

Recovery services are those that aid the survivor in resolving the long-term issues. Swift (1986) has noted the relevance of George Albee's (1982) prevention model to family violence prevention. This model, which can be conceptualized as an equation that summarizes the association of the major factors in stress and stress management with dysfunction, has relevance to recovery intervention as tertiary prevention. As adapted by Swift, the model is as follows:

$$\frac{\text{incidence of}}{\text{dysfunction}} = \frac{\text{stress} + \text{risk factors}}{\text{social supports} + \text{coping skills} + \text{self-esteem}}$$

Holistic recovery intervention targets all the variables in the equation. The goal is to minimize the strength of factors in the numerator and maximize the factors in the denominator for the lowest probability of dysfunction. A description of sample interventions, using these variables as an organizing framework, follows.

Stress reduction. Interventions to reduce stress are generally of two types: those designed to help the person prevent or manage actual stress and those aimed at eliminating or reducing the potency of the stressor.

As noted above, victimization by family violence can induce some of the most intense subjective stress known to humans. A variety of techniques to promote wellness of mind, body, and spirit have been used with survivors with demonstrated effectiveness (Mervin & Smith-Kurtz, 1988). Such techniques include *physical activity*, which should be initiated as soon as possible after the victimization. The activity can help to discharge repressed energy and promotes the survivor's perceived control over body functions and positive body image. Physically injured survivors should have their activity regimes prescribed by a health professional. *Nutrition* has important physiological effects in promoting recovery, although survivors may demonstrate initial eating disturbances, such as loss of appetite or overeating. *Spiritual support*, including religious counseling for persons who value religious beliefs and activities to promote any survivor's sense of integrity with the natural world, can help to sharpen the survivor's senses and promote a cognitive framework for understanding the stressor. Bibliotherapy, art therapy, and music therapy can help promote spiritual wellness. *Relaxation* is essential for survivors, many of whom have developed hypervigilance, and can be encouraged through a variety of cognitive and physical techniques. *Pleasure activities* that promote a perceived sense of fun and humor are critical to survivor growth. Many survivors of chronic victimization cannot initially identify any source of pleasure in their lives and report no memory of ever having felt happy. Helping them to probe their memories for what has brought pleasure is an important starting point. Education about sexuality and sexual relationships may be required before survivors can perceive their sexuality to be a source of pleasure, particularly for sexual assault survivors. *Stimulating and creative activities* help the survivor to be productive, and thus to feel competent, or to experience alternative physiological sensations to the numbness and anxiety that may pervade their existence.

Stressor abatement. Although family violence has a complex etiology, the immediate act that precipitates the survivor's stress is the violent or exploitive behavior of the perpetrator(s). Interventions to eliminate or change the behavior are thus focused on the perpetrator. Many of the interventions rely on law enforcement and *legally based protective interventions* (particularly for children, handicapped persons, and dependent elders). Unfortunately, this form of intervention is unreliable in reducing the stressor and sometimes introduces new stressors with which the survivor must cope, so the total potency of the stressor(s) is increased, at least temporarily. For example, the temporary jail detention of an assaultive family member may stop the violence, but his or her absence from the home and anticipation of long-term implications of the removal creates new stressors for the family. The external control inherent in the legal system is countertherapeutic to the needs of the survivor unless the control is carefully used to help empower the survivor. When the protective action produces long-term reduction of violent acts, then the total power of the stressor(s) is reduced. Sometimes the only resolution is permanent removal of a family member, which may occur through divorce or termination of parental rights.

A variety of *psychoeducational and therapeutic interventions* have been developed to change *perpetrator behavior*, many of which have produced an actual decrease in violent or exploitive behavior (Bolton & Bolton, 1987; Giaretto, 1982; Goldstein, Keller, & Erne, 1985; Guerney, 1986; Isaacs, 1982; Lutzker, 1984; Sonkin, Martin, & Walker, 1985; Wodarski, 1981). Interventions tend to be designed for particular forms of maltreatment, such as neglect, use of physical force, or sexual assault. Generally, interventions include components designed to increase the knowledge and skills of the perpetrator with regard to family roles, such as spouse, parent, or caregiver to an elderly parent. Support to perpetrators in fulfilling these roles and coping with associated emotions is provided through individual and group work.

Reduction of Risk Factors

Risk factors associated with the probability of family violence are imbedded in personal characteristics of the survivor and the perpetrator, the family system, and the broader social and physical environment of the family (Belsky, 1980; Mann, Lauderdale, & Iscoe, 1983). Levy, Sheldon, & Conte (1986) offer a succinct list of the numerous factors that are hypothesized to be associated with child abuse alone. Risk is often associated with poor interactions within the family or inadequate person-environment fit. Prominent among the personal characteristics of survivors that are correlated with higher incidence of family violence are special status of children (e.g., developmental disability, stepchild) and status inconsistency for battered women (i.e., the woman's social and economic status are higher than her spouse's). The perpetrator's history of violence, neglect, or exploitation in his or her family of origin and abuse of chemical substances are major correlates of using violence in the family. The family that is isolated, has poor communication skills, and is of low socioeconomic status is at greater risk. Community and societal risk factors include low availability of formal and informal support, economic depression, high workplace demands on employed family members, tolerant attitudes toward use of aggression by members of the community, and nonassertive political leadership in addressing the problem.

Interventions to reduce the prevalence and impact of these risk factors include those that change the risk factor itself and those that prepare individuals to cope adequately with the presence of the factors. Examples are *interventions that strengthen the family*, such as economic support, health and mental health care, adequate housing, and neighborhood social organizations. *Broad-scale interventions* are those that aim to change community attitudes about family violence, influence policymakers, and persuade the public and its representatives to increase allocations for formal helping agencies. Moderating the impact of risk factors is essential for promoting a supportive recovery environment for the survivor.

Risk-reduction interventions for individuals are generally educational, designed to teach how to avoid and manage high-risk situations. Training in interpersonal and family conflict resolution, personal safety practices (including physical and verbal self-defense), and preparation for life transitions such as change in family composition or loss of job are examples of these interventions.

Maximization of Social Supports

People who cope alone often develop long-term physical and psychosocial stress symptoms. Cultural norms in the United States dictate that individuals receive their primary social support from families. When the family fails or struggles with this responsibility, as in the case of family violence, efforts must be made to build social support.

Family violence has an impact on all family members, even when one member is the primary target. Sometimes family members are so occupied with their own pain that they do not or cannot assist other family members. *Family systems intervention* to help the whole family cope with its stress and support the survivor is possible in some families. In some family violence cases the family dissolves, and family systems intervention is appropriate for the new fragmented units, which may be such combinations as sibling groups without parents, isolated siblings, parents without children, and parents in different households. Even when the family structure breaks down, the family violence survivor needs to receive support from other family members.

Intervention with extended family members and social networks can increase the survivor's perceived social support. Programs that train anyone in how to be supportive to a friend or family member who experiences domestic violence or how to listen when a child discloses child abuse are significant examples of how to prepare potential natural helpers to be supportive when needed. Linking survivors with social activities such as exercise groups, church groups, and craft clubs can reduce their sense of isolation. Many survivors, when emotionally ready, have become part of volunteer services to other survivors, which has the effect of further increasing their own perceived support.

The most prevalent formal intervention is probably the *peer support group*, where family violence survivors, matched by age and nature of the violence, work together on coping with their situations and supporting one another. Most large communities in the United States now have ongoing battered women's groups, adolescent incest survivors' groups, and groups for adult survivors of childhood incest.

Many communities are also able to provide *individual support to survivors* through such programs as court-appointed child advocates, victim/witness assistants, parent aides, teen companions, and child friends. Prompt protective response by law enforcement officers who are also trained to give psychological first aid provides strong social support at some of the most critical moments. Resources to provide for individual survivor counseling by mental health professionals are increasing in some areas. Certainly the number of professionals trained to provide such assistance has increased in recent years.

Maximization of Coping Skills

Survivors must learn to reduce maladaptive coping responses and increase adaptive ones in the context of a *safe, therapeutic relationship* (Berliner & Wheeler, 1987; Figley, 1985; Gentry & Eaddy, 1980; Long, 1986; Ochberg, 1988). They may need help to master negative emotions such as guilt, fear, anger, depression, and low perceived control. Cognitive-behavior therapy is a popular approach to facilitate affective control and mastery of the victimization, although a variety of psychotherapeutic techniques are used with survivors. Some survivors may need special help, such as substance abuse treatment, systematic desensitization to overcome fears, or reality therapy to overcome denial, magical thinking, and belief in negative myths about victimization.

Behaviorally, survivors also may need to learn basic social skills and how to master neglected developmental tasks. Because of pervasive family dysfunction, some have not adequately learned basic *problem solving*, that is, how to assess a problem realistically, consider alternative solutions and their consequences, choose a feasible solution, actively pursue it, and evaluate the outcome. In such people, *decision-making skills* to facilitate gathering information from those affected by a decision and selecting the most appropriate action may be weak. *Basic communication and assertiveness skills* such as sending clear messages, actively listening, and feeding back may be needed. Skill in *nonviolent conflict resolution*, including anger management and alternatives to corporal punishment as well as other conflict management skills, is deficient in many family violence survivors. *Help-seeking skills*—that is, knowing how to identify appropriate sources of help and how to ask for help—are needed by those survivors who have low trust and a history of disappointment by others.

Survivors often get stuck at immature developmental levels because they do not have the information or skill to move ahead. Many programs offer *education about family roles* to facilitate personal growth and responsibility. For example, teaching parents to be empathic to children and to fulfill roles appropriate to the age of the child is a common treatment for child abuse or neglect. Teaching spouses to appreciate gender roles within the family and to promote role flexibility where necessary is also common. Child survivors may need guidance in how to find pleasure through play; innovative programs teach formerly maltreating parents to play with their children.

Interventions for child survivors must, of course, be developmentally appropriate. For young children, whose communication is primarily behavioral rather than verbal, play and art are often used as therapeutic media. Older children are often treated in groups to reduce their sense of isolation and scapegoating.

After the recovery from victimization has been initiated for the individual survivor, the matter of long-standing personal and family problems, some of which may have precipitated the violence, must ! e confronted. The family might be reestablished. Even if it is not, the survivor is likely to maintain attachment and at least limited interaction. Controversy exists among professionals about how soon this intervention should take the form of couples or family therapy (Neidig & Friedman, 1984). Some programs begin recovery services with such intervention, but most await the perpetrator's acceptance of responsibility for the victimization and the survivor's attainment of some degree of perceived personal control before initiating joint therapy. In cases in which family members are temporarily or permanently removed from the home, the survivor must work on redefining the family.

Maximization of Positive Self-Esteem

Although not all survivors suffer from low self-esteem, it is prevalent among abusive parents, abused children, and the survivors and perpetrators of spouse abuse. Since it may be intrinsic in the family system, it can be resistant to change and thus difficult to treat.

Self-concept is based in one's beliefs about the characteristics one possesses. Self-concept comes partially from a realistic appraisal of information about one-self communicated by others in one's environment, such as family members (Heller & Swindle, 1983). Self-esteem is the value one places on oneself. Family violence survivors may have problems with both self-concept and self-esteem. Their self-concepts are often diffuse because repeated forced intrusion into their personal space has led them to have difficulty differentiating themselves from others and developing integrated identities. They are thus often excessively dependent on people in their environment who are sending clear negative messages to them about their worth. Survivors' self-esteem may be low in part because they have been given direct family or community messages that they have done something wrong or are "bad" or "worthless." Often survivors report feeling dirty and defiled, particularly if the violation was highly intrusive, as in sexual abuse.

Self-esteem can be enhanced by feelings of competence, but the family violence survivor has seldom received affirmation of achievements from within the family. The survivor's inability to control the family violence reinforces perceptions of weak efficacy. The survivor often focuses on failures and sometimes cannot begin to identify personal achievements and strengths. The demands of coping with victimization deplete the survivor's energy, contributing to such effects as poor school achievement for children and low work performance for adults, which further depresses their self-esteem.

Recovery services to promote positive self-esteem and integrated self-concept must be handled delicately. These perceptions are based in survivors' realistic appraisals of what other people believe about them. The message that others (e.g., recovery workers) do care about and admire them must be genuine. Survivors need to hear that they are not to blame and that they are unconditionally worthy of affection from others and themselves. Recovery workers must be able to communicate such affection and to enable others to do so, such as family members and peers in support groups.

Intervention can also focus on the survivor's negative cognitions by training the survivor to recognize personal strengths and achievements. Behavioral reinforcers, such as verbal acknowledgment of minor accomplishments and celebrations of major ones, can also be effective. Simple recognition of successful survival can have a strong impact on the survivor's self-esteem.

When the survivor has achieved a satisfactory level of adjustment, recovery services can be terminated. A periodic *psychosocial needs checkup*, depending on the developmental level of the survivor, is recommended.

Conclusion

As an extraordinary or catastrophic stressor, family violence imposes excessive coping demands on survivors of any age. Recovery requires a combination of the survivor's hard work and the commitment by formal and informal helpers to promote a healthy recovery environment. The societal recognition of the responsibility to be effectively supportive to survivors and their families is a critical ingredient in the reduction of stress and prevention of serious psychosocial dysfunction. Helping professionals can provide coordinated, skilled intervention for crisis resolution, needs assessment, support, and recovery. Family violence survivors can neither change nor forget their history, but they do not have to be alone as they confront the future.

References

Albee, G. W. (1982). Preventing psychopathology and promoting human potential. *American Psychologist, 37*, 1043-1050.

American Psychiatric Association. (1981). *Diagnostic and statistical manual of mental disorders* (3rd ed.). Washington, DC: Author.

Ammerman, R. T., Cassisi, J. E., Hersen, M., & Van Hasselt, V. B. (1986). Consequences of physical abuse and neglect in children. *Clinical Psychology Review, 6*, 291-310.

Augustinos, M. (1987). Developmental effects of child abuse: Recent findings. *Child Abuse and Neglect, 11*, 15-27.

Belsky, J. (1980). Child maltreatment: An ecological integration. *American Psychologist, 35*(4), 320-335.

Berliner, L., & Wheeler, J. R. (1987). Treating the effects of sexual abuse on children. *Journal of Interpersonal Violence, 2*, 415-434.

Bolton, F. G., & Bolton, S. R. (1987). *Working with violent families: A guide for clinical and legal practitioners*. Newbury Park, CA: Sage.

Borgman, R., Edmunds, M., & MacDicken, R. A. (1979). *Crisis intervention: A manual for child protective workers*. Washington, DC: U.S. Department of Health, Education and Welfare, National Center on Child Abuse and Neglect.

Bross, D. C., Krugman, R. D., Lenherr, M. R., Rosenberg, D. A., & Schmitt, B. D. (1988). *The new child protection team handbook*. New York: Garland.

Browne, A., & Finkelhor, D. (1985). Impact of child sexual abuse: A review of the research. *Psychological Bulletin, 99*, 66-77.

Dunst, C., Trivette, C., & Deal, A. (1988). *Enabling and empowering families: Principles and guidelines for practice*. Cambridge, MA: Brookline.

Erickson, M. F., & Egeland, B. (1987). A developmental view of the psychological consequences of maltreatment. *School Psychology Review, 16*(2), 156-168.

Eth, S., & Pynoos, R. S. (1985). Developmental perspective on psychic trauma in childhood. In C. R. Figley (Ed.), *Trauma and its wake: The study and treatment of post-traumatic stress disorder* (pp. 36-52). New York: Brunner/Mazel.

Figley, C. R. (Ed.). (1985). *Trauma and its wake: The study and treatment of post-traumatic stress disorder*. New York: Brunner/Mazel.

Gentry, C. E., & Eaddy, V. B. (1980). Treatment of children in spouse abusive families. *Victimology: An International Journal*, 5(2-4), 240-250.

Giaretto, H. (1982). *Integrated treatment of child sexual abuse: A treatment and training manual*. Palo Alto, CA: Science and Behavior.

Goldberger, L., & Breznitz, S. (Eds.). (1982). *Handbook of stress*. New York: Free Press.

Goldstein, A. P., Keller, H., & Erne, D. (1985). *Changing the abusive parent*. Champaign, IL: Research Press.

Guerney, L. (1986). Prospects for intervention with troubled youth and troubled families. In J. Garbarino, C. J. Schellenbach, J. Sebes, & Associates (Eds.), *Troubled youth, troubled families: Understanding families at-risk for adolescent maltreatment* (pp. 255-291). New York: Aldine.

Halpern, H. A. (1973). Crisis theory: A definitional study. *Community Mental Health Journal*, 9(4).

Heller, K., & Swindle, R. W. (1983). Social networks, perceived social support, and coping with stress. In R. D. Felner, L. A. Jason, J. N. Moritsugu, & S. S. Farber (Eds.), *Preventive psychology: Theory, research, and practice* (pp. 87-103). New York: Pergamon.

Hoff, L. A. (1978). *People in crisis: Understanding and helping*. Menlo Park, CA: Addison-Wesley.

Isaacs, C. D. (1982). Treatment of child abuse: A review of the behavioral interventions. *Journal of Applied Behavior Analysis, 15*, 273-294.

Klingbeil, K. S., & Boyd, V. D. (1984). Emergency room intervention: Detection, assessement, and treatment. In A. R. Roberts (Ed.), *Battered women and their families: Intervention strategies and treatment programs* (pp. 7-32). New York: Springer.

Lazarus, A. A. (1976). *Multi-modal behavior therapy*. New York: Springer.

Levy, H. B., Sheldon, S. H., & Conte, J. R. (1986). Special intervention programs for child victims of violence. In M. Lystad (Ed.), *Violence in the home: Interdisciplinary perspectives* (pp. 169-192). New York: Brunner/Mazel.

Long, S. (1986). Guidelines for treating young children. In K. MacFarlane & J. Waterman, (Eds.), *Sexual abuse of young children: Evaluation and treatment* (pp. 220-243). New York: Guilford.

Lutzker, J. R. (1984). Project 12-Ways: Treating child abuse and neglect from an ecobehavioral perspective. In R. F. Dangel & R. A. Polster (Eds.), *Parent training: Foundations of research and practice* (pp. 260-297). New York: Guilford.

Lystad, M. (Ed.). (1986). *Violence in the home: Interdisciplinary perspectives*. New York: Brunner/Mazel.

Mann, P. A., Lauderdale, M., & Iscoe, I. (1983). Toward effective community-based interventions in child abuse. *Professional Psychology: Research and Practice, 14*(6), 729-742.

McEvoy, A., Brookings, J. B., & Brown, C. E. (1983, February). Responses to battered women: Problems and strategies. *Social Casework*, pp. 92-96.

Mervin, M. R., & Smith-Kurtz, B. (1988). Healing of the whole person. In F. M. Ochberg (Ed.), *Post-traumatic therapy and victims of violence* (pp. 57-82). New York: Brunner/Mazel.

Mickish, J. E. (1985). Elder abuse. In J. E. Hendricks (Ed.), *Crisis intervention: Contemporary issues for on-site interveners* (pp. 82-115). Springfield, IL: Charles C Thomas.

Moos, R. H. & Billings, A. G. (1982). Conceptualizing and measuring coping resources and processes. In L. Goldberger & S. Breznitz (Eds.), *Handbook of stress* (pp. 212-230). New York: Free Press.

Mowbray, C. T. (1988). Post-traumatic therapy for children who are victims of violence. In F. M. Ochberg (Ed.), *Post-traumatic therapy and victims of violence* (pp. 196-212). New York: Brunner/Mazel.

Neidig, P. H., & Friedman, D. H. (1984). *Spouse abuse: A treatment program for couples*. Champaign, IL: Research Press.

Ochberg, F. M. (Ed.). (1988). *Post-traumatic therapy and victims of violence*. New York: Brunner/Mazel.

Roberts, A. R. (Ed.). (1990). *Crisis intervention handbook: Assessment, treatment and research*. Belmont, CA: Wadsworth.

Slaikeu, K. (1984). *Crisis intervention.* Boston: Allyn & Bacon.

Smith, C. (1984). Children in crisis and adolescents in crisis. In E. H. Janosik (Ed.), *Crisis counseling: A contemporary approach* (pp. 63-99). Monterey, CA: Wadsworth.

Sonkin, D. J., Martin, D., & Walker, L. E. A. (1985). *The male batterer: A treatment approach.* New York: Springer.

Swift, C. (1986). Preventing family violence: Family-focused programs. In M. Lystad (Ed.), *Violence in the home: Interdisciplinary perspectives* (pp. 219-249). New York: Brunner/Mazel.

Walker, L. E. (1984). *The battered woman syndrome.* New York: Springer.

Wodarski, J. S. (1981). Comprehensive treatment of parents who abuse their children. *Adolescence, 16*(64), 959-972.

Wolfe, D. A. (1987). *Child abuse: Implications for child development and psychopathology.* Newbury Park, CA: Sage.

Wolfe, D. A., Jaffe, P., Wilson, S. K., & Zak, L. (1985). Children of battered women: The relation of child behavior to family violence and maternal stress. *Journal of Consulting and Clinical Psychology, 53*(5), 657-665.

Wolfe, D. A., Wolfe, V. V., & Best, C. L. (1988). Child victims of sexual abuse. In V. B. Van Hasselt, R. L. Morrison, A. S. Bellack, & M. Hersen (Eds.), *Handbook of family violence* (pp. 157-185). New York: Plenum.

Yin, P. (1985). *Victimization and the aged.* Springfield, IL: Charles C Thomas.

Zimrin, H. (1986). A profile of survival. *Child Abuse and Neglect, 10*, 329-349.

11

Restitution to Crime Victims as a Presumptive Requirement in Criminal Case Dispositions

Cathryn Jo Rosen
Alan T. Harland

With its focus on avenging the harm criminal offenders do to society in general, the criminal justice system for many years overlooked the more specific injuries suffered by crime victims, who were left to pursue their claims to compensation through the often illusory remedy of civil litigation. In recent decades, growing concern for victims' rights has given rise to private and publicly supported victim compensation programs that help to fill the gap caused by the inability of the civil law to reimburse crime victims adequately for their losses (Harland 1978b). Yet, these programs are not available to all victims of crime and, even when they are available, as the American Bar Association (1988) states in its *Guidelines Governing Restitution to Victims of Criminal Conduct*: "The criminal offender's responsibility for damage inflicted should not be diminished or assumed by third parties and, in the event that such third parties provide direct financial assistance to victims, they should be reimbursed by the offender, to the extent possible" (Guideline 1.1). Restitution potentially satisfies the dictates of justice by compensating victims while simultaneously requiring offenders to assume financial responsibility for the consequences of their criminal conduct. Thus, particularly during the past two decades, restitution has gained new prominence as an important means of vindicating victims' rights and, today, there is virtually universal support among international and domestic politicians, criminal justice practitioners, and academics for the proposition that offenders should be required to make restitution for the harm they cause by their criminal misconduct (Harland & Rosen, 1989).

Analysis of academic and professional literature, policy statements of diverse organizations, judicial decisions, and model and actual legislation reveals that, during the last decade, restitution has risen in popular, political, and professional perception to a presumptive norm in sentencing (Harland & Rosen, 1989). In this view, failure to require restitution in appropriate cases constitutes an egregious departure from universally recognized standards of justice (Harland & Rosen, 1989). But, despite the virtually unanimous agreement that restitution should play a central normative role in sentencing, recent commentators agree that restitution remains, as it has been for the past century (see Schafer, 1970, pp. 117-119), underutilized in actual case dispositions (Castellano, 1988; Galaway, 1988; West & Bazemore, 1988).

This chapter explores the history and development of restitution, as well as current practices, to identify and suggest solutions to some of the barriers to achievement of a presumptive restitution norm in the criminal justice system. We conclude that while broader use of restitution can and should be achieved, victims' advocates and policymakers must recognize the inherent limitations on the remedy in order for it to achieve its ultimate power as a sanction.

The History of Restitution

One explanation of the failure of restitution to achieve a more significant role in actual case dispositions, despite widespread support for victim compensation and victims' rights in general, is the inherent tension that arises when efforts are made to use the criminal law, with its primary focus on vindication of society's interests in punishing offenders, to reimburse victims for the harm done them by specific offenders. Primitive societies frequently have restitutive systems of justice (Nader & Combs-Schilling, 1975), and early precursors of modern Western codifications—such as the Code of Hammurabi, the Roman Law of Delicts, and the Mosaic Law—also made provision for restitution (Jacob, 1975; Mueller, 1965). Nonetheless, as Western legal systems developed and the interest of society in punishing offenders and suppressing private vengeance began to take preeminence over the victim's personal interest in avenging crime, restitution gave way as a social control mechanism to other sanctions designed to exact retribution for the present offense and deter future crimes. Concern with compensating the victim for losses incurred as a result of the offender's misdeeds disappeared from the criminal law and a separate body of civil tort law arose as a means of providing financial compensation for injuries incurred as a result of international wrongful conduct (Jacob, 1975, p. 37).

The concept of victim restitution as a criminal sanction, however, never really died. In the late eighteenth century, Bentham (1789) advocated inclusion of restitution in an offender's penalty whenever possible. A century later, restitution was an important topic of discussion at a series of international prison and penal congresses, although ultimately the idea was dropped in favor of reforming civil procedure to remove some of the impediments to adequate victim recovery in tort (Schafer, 1970, pp. 10-11). Ardent debate continues today about the distinction between criminal law and tort law and the respective roles that punitive and compensatory objectives should play in each (Harland, 1982b, pp. 52-55).

Early American case and statutory law indicates that restitution was used here, although infrequently, in the nineteenth century (Harland, 1982b, p. 57). As state legislatures formally adopted probation as an alternative to imprisonment in the late nineteeth and early twentieth centuries, they often authorized courts to include restitution as a condition of release (Harland, 1982b, pp. 57-58). With the rise of the victim's movement in the past quarter century and the availability of LEAA funds during the 1970s to support development of restitution programs came a significant increase in the amount and scope of legislation (Harland, 1982b, pp. 58-60). That growth continues today, fueled, in the absence of significant federal funds, by increasingly vocal victims' rights groups and the virtual industry that has developed to promote, sell, and train employees of restitution programs (Harland & Rosen, 1989).

One impediment to more extensive utilization of restitution during much of the twentieth century may be the patchwork quality of restitution legislation and programming (see, generally, Harland, 1982b). In recent years, however, legislatures have empowered courts to order restitution in ever-increasing categories of cases and, in addition, have been increasingly likely to create and fund the support services necessary to effectuate restitution (Harland, 1982b; Harland & Rosen, 1989; Comment, 1985, p. 683; Note, 1983, 1984a, 1986, 1987a, 1987b). One natural result of this activity has been the development of specialized programs in both the adult and juvenile systems to enforce restitution orders, particularly in intensive supervision probation, mediation, and victim-offender reconciliation programs (Harland & Rosen, 1987; Hudson, Galaway, & Novack, 1980; McGillis, 1986; Warner & Burke, 1987; Worth, 1987).

The federal Victim and Witness Protection Act (18 U.S.C. sec. 3579, 1983) has been particularly influential in this rapidly evolving milieu of criminal restitution legislation (Harland & Rosen, 1989). Unlike many older statutes that authorized restitution only in conjunction with particular sanctions or specific crimes, the VWPA provides a comprehensive legislative scheme in which restitution is the presumptive norm; federal district court judges who do not order full restitution in a criminal case must state their reasons for failing to do so on the record (VWPA, sec. 3579[a] [2]). Other jurisdictions, such as Maryland, have enacted similar legislation, effectively making restitution a presumptive aspect of sentencing, at least where compensation is requested on the victim's behalf (Maryland Restitution Bill, S.B. 417, April 1988, amending art. 27, sec. 640). In other cases, less comprehensive statutes make restitution mandatory in conjunction with probation (e.g., Arizona Rev. Stat. Ann., sec. 13-603[c] [1978]; Iowa Code Ann., sec. 907.12[3] [West supp. 1979]; see, generally, Harland 1982b, pp. 55-56).

The Role of Restitution
in the Criminal Justice System

Legislative authority alone will not overcome the second major obstacle to realization of restitution as a presumptive norm in sentencing. Review of the statutory and case law, model legislation and policy statements, and the academic, professional, and popular literature reveals that restitution is many things to many people. Yet, without building a working consensus on the meaning of restitution that considers the philosophical, conceptual, and practical difficulties inherent in providing restitution to victims in a punitive system, it is unlikely that the goal of complete—or even partial—restitution to victims by criminal offenders will be achieved. Should restitution be limited to restoration of stolen property or its value, or should it be broadened to include the total range of recovery available in civil litigation? Should restitution be conceptually limited to financial reimbursement of the victim, or does it include repayment to society through community service? Careful resolution of these and other, related, questions is necessary if the dialogue regarding adoption, implementation, and evaluation of restitution programs is to proceed in a useful and coherent manner.

The Philosophy of Restitution

One approach to the conceptual dilemma is to clarify the objectives that can reasonably be achieved by restitution as a criminal sanction. An understanding of the philosophical roots of criminal restitution and its standing relative to sanctions designed to further the primary retributive and utilitarian goals of the criminal process should help to clarify which components of existing restitution programs are the most desirable.

Advocacy of adoption of restitution as a presumptive norm in sentencing has come primarily from the victims' rights movement (Harland & Rosen, 1989; McGillis, 1986, p. 5). Civil litigation is expensive and, in many jurisdictions, extremely slow. The dictates of the legal marketplace effectively make the courts unavailable to many victims whose losses are not adequate to result in a recovery from which a sufficient contingent fee can be drawn. Restitution is perceived as a means of obtaining compensation for crime victims for the losses they incurred in a more convenient and accessible forum than the civil courts. The fundamental sense of justice and satisfaction that most victims derive from the knowledge that the person who harmed them is, literally, paying the financial consequences makes restitution preferable to reimbursement for their losses that emanates from other sources such as insurers or victim compensation programs. Inherent limitations on the number of crime victims who can potentially benefit from restitution orders because of low police clearance rates (Harland, 1981), considerations of offender ability to pay, and competing criminal justice system objectives—such as the need to achieve incapacitation, retribution, or deterrence through incarceration—however, dictate in favor of continued development of alternate sources of funding to compensate victims of crime. Both commentators (e.g., Hudson, 1984, p. 41; Thorvaldsen, 1987) and policymakers (e.g., American Bar Association, 1988, Guideline 1.4[a]) recognize that without revolutionary alterations in the political, social, and jurisprudential theories on which the criminal justice system is based, societal interests in crime control must of necessity override individual interests in restitution.

Although restitution has been hailed on occasion as a rehabilitative tool (see sources cited in Harland, 1982b, pp. 59-60, 73, 122-125), in an era when rehabilitation has itself assumed a subsidiary role in corrections, the potential benefits to the offender and, more indirectly, to society, are clearly secondary to compensatory concerns. The rehabilitative claim also suffers from assuming too much about the ostensible benefits of making the offender pay for the harm done; on occasion it may have the opposite result. A restitution order may teach an offender to accept responsibility for his or her conduct, but it may also instill resentment in an offender who has grounds to believe that he or she needs the money more than the victim does, increase an offender's difficulty in providing for his or her family, or even "have the perverse effect of inducing [an offender] to use illegal means to acquire funds to pay" (*Bearden v. Georgia*, 461 U.S. 660, 1983, 670-671). Indeed, these concerns are reflected, but not necessarily satisfied, by the common requirement that restitution should not be unreasonable and that judges should consider the offender's income and other financial obligations when making restitution orders (see Harland, 1982b, pp. 90-94).

Restitution has also, on occasion, been suggested as an independent sanction offering an alternative to incarceration (see Harland, 1982b, pp. 59-60, 73, 125); this claim is a weak one, however, unless the order is so onerous that it fulfills the societal demand for punishment and protection (Harland & Rosen, 1989).

Existing research provides little support for the theory that restitution either controls recidivism or is an effective general or specific deterrent (Castellano, 1988, p. 20; McGillis, 1986, p. 68; but see Schneider, 1986). Indeed, in the inevitable competition for scarce resources in intensive supervision probation, where the predominant goal is prevention of short-term recidivism, enforcement of restitution orders is very much secondary to punitive control mechanisms such as electronic surveillance and community service (Harland & Rosen, 1987).

Similar conflicts between use of the criminal justice system to pursue individual interests and societal interests arise in connection with authorizing and obtaining a restitution order as well as effectuating it and is probably the major obstacle to achieving restitution as a presumptive norm. Often the same groups and individuals who are vocal proponents of victims' rights—fueled primarily by a desire for the criminal justice system to control offenders for as long as possible in order to protect society from further victimization (Harland & Rosen, 1987)—are equally, if not more, effective advocates for increasingly punitive sanctions. Without evidence that restitution can accomplish either of these sanctioning goals and in light of the practical reality that restitution and incarceration are usually mutually exclusive sanctions (Harland, 1982b, pp. 75-77), achievement of a presumptive restitutionary norm that does not account for this endemic goal conflict is unlikely to be realized in the near future.

What Is Restitution?

There is a symbiotic relationship between the lack of conceptual clarity in the restitution literature and the fact that restitution is many different things to many different people. At its most basic, the concept of restitution involves compensation of direct victims of criminal wrongdoing by the offender for tangible economic losses they sustain as a direct result of the offender's conduct. Most frequently, restitution involves monetary compensation for the value of stolen or damaged property or for medical expenses incurred as a result of crimes involving personal injury. Occasionally, offenders may be required to reimburse their victims by providing personal services rather than money to compensate for the value of the losses. For example, a defendant who is convicted of stealing a television worth $300 may be required to return the TV, pay the victim $300, or provide the victim with $300 worth of personal services. It is generally agreed that offenders should not be required to provide restitution in an amount that is unreasonable given their financial means (Harland, 1982b, pp. 90-92).

The apparent simplicity of this basic notion of restitution masks many issues that demand consideration and resolution if the consensus favoring mandatory restitution is to develop beyond the policy level to become a reality. Issues underlying the definition above include questions such as how to value lost or damaged property—replacement/repair (e.g., American Bar Association, 1988, Guideline 1.2) or salvage value (e.g. VWPA, 18 U.S.C. sec. 3579 [b] [1] [B])—and whether or not medical expenses include costs incurred to heal mental as well as physical injuries. Ultimately, however, so long as the victim does not obtain a windfall recovery, the precise method of measuring the damages is not a concern.

More problematic is the fact that, frequently, policy proposals and model and actual legislation enlarge this basic notion of restitution to include a number of other injuries and remedies (see, generally, Harland, 1982, pp. 86-89). For example, the Victim and Witness Protection Act (18 U.S.C. sec. 3579 [b] [2]) permits restitution for other easily measurable harms such as lost earnings and funeral expenses. Whether actuarially measurable, but frequently speculative, future losses due to continuing medical expenses or inability to work may be included in a restitution order is not entirely clear, although these categories of damages should probably be treated similarly to direct and indirect intangible losses, which are generally not recoverable. The State of Washington specifically excludes recovery for mental anguish, pain and suffering, loss of consortium, or other intangible losses (American Bar Association, 1988, Standard 1.2; Washington Rev. Code sec. 9.94A.1040[1]); a result other legislative schemes achieve by more abstruse provisions allowing courts to refuse to consider restitution if to do so is overly burdensome or will unduly expand the scope of the criminal proceeding (e.g., American Bar Association, 1988, Guideline 1.4, comment to Guideline 1.5[a]; VWPA, 18 U.S.C. sec. 3579[d]). This legislatively endorsed escape hatch also permits courts to avoid the responsibility of grappling with complex issues of proximate cause where they are associated with recovery of measurable, but less direct, injuries by declining to consider the claim. Of course, the fact that courts may decline to consider restitution for injuries in cases where the issues of culpability, causation, and measurement of damages are not relatively clear-cut constitutes a considerable obstacle to achievement of presumptive restitution, especially in personal injury cases, where causation and measurement issues are frequently the most difficult. In contrast, in crimes against property, the financial consequences of the injury are often straightforward.

Part of the attraction of combining victim restitution with criminal adjudication is that the determination of guilt provides the factual and legal basis upon which to hold the offender responsible for the damages the victim incurred as a result of the criminal conduct. However, a major difference between civil and criminal law is that civil law goes beyond the question of whether a defendant is responsible for certain actions to determine also the extent of responsibility for resulting injury and to assess the value of those injuries. Depending on the crime charged, there is rarely a need to make either of these latter determinations, both of which are necessary to support a restitution order, in a criminal case.

The theory that the criminal adjudication can provide the factual and legal basis upon which to order the offender to make restitutive payments breaks down still further when, due to prosecutorial decisions not to charge certain offenses or to enter plea-bargain arrangements, there is never an adjudication of guilt for all of the offender's criminal conduct. Nonetheless, some jurisdictions allow recovery for injuries suffered in connection with unconvicted, or even acquitted, offenses (see, generally, Harland, 1982, pp. 83-86). In those jurisdictions that take the view that restitution for unconvicted crimes is inappropriate, a clear conflict arises between the prosecutor's duties to pursue societal goals while advocating the victim's interest in restitution unless the sentencing proceeding is expanded to include proof of uncharged crimes. The ABA *Guidelines* suggest that the conflict be resolved in favor of criminal justice goals other than restitution while requiring prosecutors to consult with the victim "at any stage of the criminal prosecution at which the issue of sentence or the termination of prosecution might be negotiated" (American Bar Association, 1988, Guideline 1.6[b]). Additionally, where offenses are "plea-bargained away," restitution for unconvicted crimes remains a possibility if the bargain includes an agreement by the offender (loosely analogous to settlement of a civil lawsuit) to pay restitution for injuries associated with dropped offenses in the bargain (American Bar Association, 1988, comment to Guidelines 1.2, 1.5). Other jurisdictions allow restitution for offenses the defendant admits or does not contest (Harland 1982b, p. 84).

Where there are multiple offenses or multiple offenders, additional issues make decisions about whether to prosecute jointly or singly and whether to drop some charges to enhance the likelihood of obtaining convictions for others even more complex. On the one hand, scarce offender resources must be fairly distributed among multiple victims; on the other hand, victims must not be unjustly enriched by receiving full restitution from more than one co-offender. Unless the current system of criminal sentencing is to be restructured radically, these considerations will frequently preclude victims from obtaining compensation from offenders, especially in view of the fact that a primary argument in favor of criminal restitution is the identity of parties and issues. Without macro-level policy decisions to realign the respective priorities of criminal justice system objectives, revolutionary alteration of the sentencing process to mirror civil litigation more closely is unwise.

Existing law reveals a lack of consensus on who victims of crime are (see, generally, Harland, 1982b, pp. 78-80). The basic definition offered above includes persons who suffer personal injury or property loss as a direct result of crime. In the event that the criminal act results in death, the victim's estate can also recover restitution. There is less agreement, however, over whether indirect victims can recover restitution for harm caused by the offender such as loss of support to the victim's spouse or children.

An issue of substantially broader impact is whether, and to what extent, restitution to third parties can be ordered. Legislative enactments allowing courts to order offenders to reimburse third-party payors such as private and publicly funded insurers and victim compensation funds are increasing in number (American Bar Association, 1988, Guidelines 1.5[b], 1.7; VWPA, 18 U.S.C. sec. 3579 [b][4][c], [e][1]; Maryland Restitution Bill, S.B. 417, 1989) and are extremely important if victims are to be compensated quickly without undue concern that they might be unjustly enriched by obtaining a double recovery (see American Bar Association, 1988, comment to Guidelines 1.5[b]). Otherwise, crime victim compensation boards and insurance companies might delay in assisting victims until after an offender has been captured, convicted, and sentenced—often a lengthy process and, all too frequently, one that is never completed—in order to offset an award of restitution. On the other hand, if restitution is awarded before victim compensation programs make an award, it should be offset by the amount of restitution paid, and the criminal court's order should be modified to allow reimbursement of the third party from subsequent payments (American Bar Association, 1988 Guideline 1.10 and comment). The Victim and Witness Protection Act and ABA *Guidelines* extend permission for third-party recovery to any person who has compensated the victim for losses recoverable via restitution, but the ABA *Guidelines* specifically preclude recovery for the value of services rendered, primarily because of valuation difficulties (comment to Guideline 1.5[b]).

As a practical matter, this type of provision should not bar recovery of unpaid bills by a physician or professional repairer of damaged property, in which case the value of services is easily measurable and the victim has a definitive obligation to pay; restitution to these third parties is essentially only a diversion of funds from the direct victim, who would be unjustly enriched by their receipt, to the victim's creditor. However, the view that anyone who happened to have helped the victim as a Good Samaritan should not be able to demand restitution for the value of his or her time and services is sound. Another area of concern with double payment arises in connection with the potential for recovery of compensatory or punitive damages in civil litigation against the same offender for the same conduct. Allowance of an offset against the civil judgment for restitution or vice versa, depending on which judgment came first in time, is appropriate to prevent unjust enrichment of the victim at the offender's expense (see American Bar Association, 1988, Guideline 1.10 and comment; Me. Rev. Stat. Ann. tit. 17-A, sec. 1327, pamphlet, 1982).

Some jurisdictions and commentators extend the scope of potential restitution recipients to government entities that incurred costs in connection with the offender's criminal activity other than by compensating the victim. Restitution to the criminal justice system may involve payments of the cost of criminal investigations (Harland, 1982b, p. 78) and prosecutions, court costs (La. Code Crim. Proc. Ann. art. 895.1[B] [West supp. 1982]), expenses of correctional treatment, or fees incurred in connection with recovery, storage, and return or disposal of stolen property. For example, Maryland courts can order an offender to pay restitution to appropriate government agencies in return for the costs they incur in connection with "the removal, towing, transporting, preserving, storage, sale, or destruction of an abandoned vehicle" (S.B. 417, amending art. 27, sec. 640 [b][iv]).

Other jurisdictions include "restitution fines" that require the offender to make fixed payments to relevant government or charitable entities and community service within a broad concept of "restitution to society" (West & Bazemore 1988, p. 5). This and other forms of "restitution" to the criminal justice system are appropriate only to the extent that they are intended to serve primarily as correctional devices, to make the offender responsible for all economically measurable aspects of his or her action, rather than to compensate direct victims of crime. Given the limited financial resources of many offenders, the respective priorities of restitution directly to the victim, reimbursement of third parties, and restitution to the criminal justice system must be determined. Especially for law-and-order victims' advocates, reluctant choices may have to be faced between very concrete interests in direct victim compensation and intuitively powerful but more abstract notions of restitution to the community, arguably much more a punitive than a restorative sanction (Harland & Rosen, 1987, 1989).

Effectuating Restitution

Once restitution has been defined and its role in the criminal justice system relative to other correctional goals has been clarified, presumptive restitution still will not become a reality unless due consideration is given to how the necessary victim loss and offender resources information is to be gathered, appropriate procedures for decision making are adopted, and effective collection and enforcement mechanisms are devised. Unfortunately, because there is virtually no empirical research evaluating current programs and procedures or analyzing the reasons for underutilization of restitution, it is difficult to assess the probable efficacy of various measures (see Harland & Rosen, 1989). Thus development of record-keeping procedures that will make data regarding restitutive obligations, dispositions, and outcomes more accessible is a vital step toward generating the baseline information necessary for informed decision making by policymakers interested in achieving broader use of restitution and/or developing alternative mechanisms for compensating the many victims to whom restitution will be only a partial remedy, if it is available at all.

In order for a court to consider imposing an obligation to make restitution on an offender, three factual issues must be resolved: liability, the amount of damages, and offender's ability to pay. Conviction, guilty plea, or admissions made in connection with a plea-bargain agreement establish the offender's liability to the direct victims of adjudicated crimes. In most cases, however, it is unnecessary to determination of guilt to quantify the amount of damage suffered, and facts regarding the offender's resources and financial obligations would be relevant in only the rarest of cases. This presents two problems: Loss information must be made available to the court at the sentencing stage, and procedures must be developed for fairly resolving factual disputes regarding the extent of the loss and the offender's ability to pay.

Significant increases in utilization of restitution have been demonstrated when sentencing judges are presented with reliable loss information (Harland, 1982a).[1] The rise in the number of formal restitution programs and greater use of victim impact statements and presentence reports that include statements of victim loss and, often, specific recommendations for restitution should play a substantial role in filling the information gap. Additionally, victims' rights initiatives designed to enhance opportunities for victim involvement in the criminal justice process by requiring prosecutors to keep them informed of developments, charging prosecutors with responsibility for investigating and recommending restitution, and permitting victims to present statements of loss to the court personally also increase the likelihood that loss information will be available on a timely basis.

Policy-level clarification of the role of restitution relative to traditional criminal justice objectives and statutory or judicial resolution of many of the definitional issues raised above is also essential in order to increase reliability of the information and promote consistency in both assessment of the baseline data by investigators and the resulting orders issued by judges in individual cases. Similarly, development of either statutory or administrative level guidelines for assessing offender ability to pay is essential to promote uniformity in decision making regarding issues such as the relative priority to be given restitution vis-à-vis other financial obligations, the significance of the offender's standard of living, and the percentage of prison earnings that should be directed toward meeting restitutionary obligations (see, generally, Harland, 1982b, pp. 93-94).

In most American jurisdictions, statutory and case law establishes that the amount and schedule of restitution payments must be set by the sentencing court. It appears, however, that courts frequently delegate these responsibilities—especially development of a payment schedule—to correctional authorities (Harland, 1982b, pp. 97-99). Procedures for judicial decision making on the amount and schedule for restitution vary widely, ranging from jurisdictions that imply agreement to the sentencing court's restitution order unless the offender expressly objects to its reasonableness to jurisdictions that specifically require that the defendant be given an opportunity to be heard on the issue, either informally through consultation with the individuals responsible for developing proposed sentencing plans for the court or by providing for a special hearing on the issue (see, generally, Harland, 1982b, pp. 99-108). Even when the offender is given a formal opportunity to be heard, however, the associated procedural safeguards provided fall short of those available in civil litigation. For example, the standard of proof of loss and ability to pay is often no higher than the minimal "reasonable certainty" (or similar standard) generally applicable to other aspects of sentencing decisions.

It is important that offenders be afforded due process in connection with restitution orders and that procedures be developed that provide meaningful opportunities to challenge the victim's claim of loss and to prove facts pertinent to ability to pay. Similarly, if restitution is to be permitted for unadjudicated offenses, the government should be required to prove the offender's liability. The burden of proof should be on the party with better access to the evidence; thus the government (*qua* victim) should be required to prove the loss and offenders should be required to prove inability to pay. In accord with existing sentencing practices, the rules of evidence need not be strictly applied, thus simplifying and streamlining the process of proving the necessary facts. The standard of proof should be by a preponderance of the evidence. Where the issues are complex, a separate hearing should be held, although—particularly if the narrower view of restitution is taken—the necessary proof can be established in conjunction with the regular sentencing proceeding (see, generally, American Bar Association, 1988, Guidelines 1.8-1.9 and comments; VWPA, sec. 3664).

Legislation authorizing presumptive restitution and judicial orders pursuant to the statutory mandate will be useless unless provisions are also made to enhance enforcement. Three areas of activity are important. In the first instance, effective collection and disbursement methods must be developed, authorized, and funded. As more states follow the federal lead and adopt comprehensive restitution legislation, they should include provisions establishing relative priorities of recipients of restitution with respect to one another and to other creditors of the offender (e.g., Maryland Restitution Bill). Development of procedures for modifying awards in response to either changes in the offender's economic circumstances or continuing expenses to the victim is also desirable.

Finally, consideration of default procedures is important. Current practices are for the most part dictated by the context in which restitution is ordered. Where restitution is a condition of probation or parole, nonpayment can result in revocation, leading either to modification of the conditions of release (often involving extension of the period of correctional control in order to meet the restitution obligation) or incarceration. Civil or criminal contempt of court is the usual remedy when restitution is an independent sanction.

Imposition of periods of incarceration to villify nonpayment of restitution is problematic for both practical and legal/ethical reasons. Most prison inmates do not have sufficient income to meet restitution obligations. Imprisonment of individuals who are unable to meet the financial obligation for nonpayment will violate constitutional prohibitions against imprisonment for debt and principles dictating against unequal treatment of individuals on the basis of economic status. Other default options raise problems as well. The practice of ordering community service to compensate for inability to pay raises the specter of involuntary servitude for the poor. Extension of the period of correctional control, in order to make complete payment possible, raises similar concerns of restricting liberty simply because of economic status. While these issues are not fatal to these common default remedies, policymakers should design procedures to minimize these concerns. For example, the comment to ABA Guideline 1.12, "Enforcement of Restitution Order," states that although enforcement by contempt or probation revocation is anticipated, "it is not envisioned . . . that incarceration result from nonpayment" (American Bar Association, 1988).

In some jurisdictions, use of the procedures authorized for collecting criminal fines and/or civil judgments is permitted to collect restitution (e.g., VWPA, sec. 3663 [h], [k]). While use of these collection procedures is certainly preferable to imprisonment and some other extensions of correctional control to villify the victim's interest, due consideration should be given to the respective roles of civil and criminal remedies in enforcing restitution obligations. Because civil execution mechanisms such as garnishment of wages and forced sales of property are useless against the unemployed or underemployed, here, too, it is important to consider the potential impact that only the poor will be imprisoned for failure to pay. Moreover, use of civil execution procedures should not be permitted to defeat the due consideration given to the offender's ability to pay at the sentencing stage.

Conclusion

The promise of presumptive restitution to victims of crime is a powerful one; in its broadest sense it holds the lure of restoring both the victim's tangible losses and intangible emotional injuries by making the offender acknowledge and accept responsibility for his or her misdeeds. Yet, when the impact of certain practical realities such as the low clearance rate and even lower conviction rate, the institutional structure of the criminal courts, and the multiple manifestations of conflict between victim restitution and the overriding criminal justice goal of vindicating the social harm associated with crime are considered, it becomes clear that the real potential of presumptive restitution is more limited. Nonetheless, development of comprehensive legislation that reflects consideration and, where necessary, resolution of these competing policy goals can go a long way toward achieving presumptive restitution in the narrow sense of compensating victims for their direct, tangible losses within the constraints dictated by the offender's economic means.

Presumptive restitution, like other forms of mandatory sentencing, represents an effort to guarantee a particular criminal justice outcome by restricting discretion. Yet, research has shown time and time again that the usual result is merely that discretion is displaced and ultimate outcomes are not significantly altered (Gottfredson & Gottfredson, 1980). Unless the conceptual and technical hurdles to understanding what restitution is, what it can effectively accomplish, and why it is so underutilized are overcome, so that policymakers can design comprehensive programmatic approaches that effectively surmount legislative, prosecutorial, judicial, and correctional resistance to restitution, presumptive restitution statutes are likely to be either ignored or creatively circumvented well into the twenty-first century.

Note

1. In many jurisdictions, restitution may be ordered at stages of the prosecution other than sentencing, most frequently as a condition of a pretrial diversion program (see Harland, 1982b, p. 68).

References

American Bar Association, Criminal Justice Section. (1988). *Guidelines governing restitution to victims of criminal conduct* (report to the House of Delegates). Chicago: Author.

American Law Institute. (1962). *Model penal code* (proposed official draft). Philadelphia: Author.

Bentham, J. (1789). *An introduction to the principles of morals and legislation.*

Castellano, T. C. (1988). *Assessing restitution's impact on recidivism: A review of the evaluative research.* Paper presented at the Fourth World Congress of Victimology, Italy.

Comment. (1985). Victim compensation and restitution: Legislative alternatives. *Land and Water Law Review, 20,* 681-709.

Comment. (1987). Reparation and restitution: Louisiana's response to the victims' rights movement. *Loyola Law Review, 32,* 393-418.

Council of Europe. (1985). *The position of the victim in the framework of criminal law and procedure.* Strasbourg: European Committee on Crime Problems.

Galaway, B. (1988). Restitution as innovation or unfilled promise. *Federal Probation, 52,* 3-14.

Gottfredson, M. R., & Gottfredson, D. M. (1980). *Decisionmaking in criminal justice: Toward the rational exercise of discretion.* Cambridge, MA: Ballinger.

Harland, A. T. (1978a). Compensating the victims of crime. *Criminal Law Bulletin, 14,* 203-224.

Harland, A. T. (1978b). Victim compensation: Programs and issues. In B. Galaway & J. Hudson (Eds.), *Perspectives on crime victims.* St. Louis, MO: C. V. Mosby.

Harland, A. T. (1981). *Restitution to victims of personal and household crimes* (Analytic report VAD-9). Washington, DC: U.S. Department of Justice, Bureau of Justice Statistics.

Harland, A. T. (1982a). *The decision to impose restitution in criminal court: An analysis of law and practice* (Doctoral dissertation). (University Microfilms No. 83-13, 738)

Harland, A. T. (1982b). Monetary remedies for victims of crime: Assessing the role of the criminal courts. *University of California Los Angeles Law Review, 39,* (1), 51-126.

Harland, A.T., & Rosen, C. J. (1987). Intensive supervision, probation and sentencing philosophy. *Federal Probation, 51*(4), 33-42.

Harland, A. T., & Rosen, C. J. (1989 March). *Impediments to the recovery of restitution by crime victims.* Paper presented at the annual meeting of the Academy of Criminal Justice Sciences, Washington, DC.

Hudson, J. (1984). The crime victim and the criminal justice system: Time for a change. *Pepperdine Law Review, 11,* 23-35.

Hudson, J., Galaway, B., & Novack, S. (1980). *National assessment of adult restitution programs: Final report.* Duluth: University of Minnesota, School of Social Development.

Jacob, B. (1975, November). The concept of restitution: An historical overview. In J. Hudson (Ed.), *Restitution in criminal justice* (pp. 34-35). Unpublished collection of papers presented at the First International Symposium on Restitution, Minneapolis, MN.

McGillis, D. (1986). *Crime victim restitution: An analysis of approaches.* Washington, DC: U.S. Department of Justice, National Institute of Justice.

Mueller, G. (1965). Compensation for victims of crime: Thought before action. *Minnesota Law Review, 50,* 213-221.

Nader, L., & Combs-Schilling, E. (1975, November). Restitution in cross cultural perspective. In J. Hudson (Ed.), *Restitution in criminal justice* (pp. 13-33). Unpublished collection of papers presented at the First International Symposium on Restitution, Minneapolis, MN.

National District Attorneys' Association, Victim Witness Coordination Program. (1986). *A prosecutor's guide to victim witness assistance: How to set up a program in your office.* Alexandria, VA: Author.

Note. (1983). Criminal law—power of court to impose particular kinds of punishment—trial court had power to order defendant to make restitution to survivors of auto accident to compensate them for their injuries. *North Dakota Law Review, 59*(3), 495-504.

Note. (1984a). Congress opens a Pandora's box: The restitution provisions of the Victim and Witness Protection Act of 1982. *Fordham Law Review, 52*(4), 507-573.

Note. (1984b). Restitution in the criminal process: Procedures for fixing the offender's liability. *Yale Law Journal, 93,* 505-522.

Note. (1986). Crime and punishment: The propriety and effect of South Dakota's victim restitution legislation. *South Dakota Law Review, 31,* 783-799.

Note. (1987a). Court-ordered criminal restitution in Washington. *Washington Law Review, 62,* 357-372.

Note. (1987b). Criminal restitution as a limited opportunity. *New England Journal on Criminal and Civil Confinement, 13*(2), 243-267.

Schafer, S. (1970). *Compensation and restitution to victims of crime.* Montclair, NJ: Patterson Smith.

Schneider, A. L. (1986). Restitution and recidivism rates of juvenile offenders: Results from four experimental studies. *Criminology, 24*(3), 533-552.

Stark, J. H., & Goldstein, H. W. (1985). *The rights of crime victims.* New York: American Civil Liberties Union.

Thorvaldsen, A. S. (1987). Restitution by offenders in Canada: Some legislative issues. *Canadian Journal of Criminology, 29*(1), 1-16.

U.N. General Assembly. (1985). *Declaration of basic principles of justice for victims of crime and abuse of power* (Resolution 40/34 November). New York: Author. (Reprinted in *Police Studies,* 1987, *10*[3], 105-108.)

Warner, J. S., & Burke, V. (Eds.). (1987). *National directory of juvenile restitution programs.* Washington, DC: U.S. Department of Justice, Office of Juvenile Justice and Delinquency Prevention.

West, R., & Bazemore, G. (1988, November). *Conflict and change in a state correctional system.* Paper presented at the annual meeting of the American Society of Criminology, Chicago.

Worth, D. (1987). VORP: A look at the past and future. *VORP Network News, 5*(1), 1, 8.

Appendix:

Directory of Respondents to the National Survey of Victim/Witness Assistance Programs

ALABAMA
Victim/Witness Program
Year program began: 1981
Tuscaloosa County District Attorney
410 County Courthouse
Tuscaloosa, AL 35401-1894
(205) 349-1252
Contact person: Vicki Clawson, Coordinator
Number of full-time staff: 1
Type of witness notification system: settlement cards
Year system began: 1982
Special features: Crisis intervention is done at the crime scene.

ALASKA
Advocates for Victims of Violence
Year program began: 1981
P.O. Box 132
Valdez, AK 99686
(907) 835-5168
Contact person: Carolyn Dallinger, Director
Number of full-time staff: 3
Number of volunteers: 3
No witness notification system
Special features: Crisis intervention is done in person. Child-care program served 40 children in 1984. Liability insurance is carried through NASW. Counseling and shelter are provided for these children.

ARIZONA
Victim Assistance Services
Year program began: ??
5850 W. Glendale Avenue
Glendale, AZ 85301
(602) 435-4063
Contact person: T. J. Titcomb, Assistant Director
Number of full-time staff: 11
Number of volunteers: 10
No witness notification system
Special features: Crisis intervention is done at the crime scene. Special phone and letter outreach offering counseling, home visits, case information, and advocacy is done with all elderly victims.

Maricopa County Attorney's Office
Year program began: 1978
Victim/Witness Program
101 W. Jefferson, 4th floor
Phoenix, AZ 85003
(602) 262-8522
Contact person: Carol McFaddon, Director
Number of full-time staff: 13
Number of part-time staff: 1
Number of volunteers: 3
Type of witness notification system: phone
Year system began: 1980
Special features: Crisis intervention is done in person along with short-term counseling. Child-

care program is staffed by seven advocates and served 250 children in 1984. Services for the elderly include home visits, court escorts, and more personal direct services performed by field advocates.

Pima County Victim/Witness Program
Year program began: 1975
110 W. Congress
Tucson, AZ 85701
(602) 792-8749
Contact person: Vicki Sharp, Coordinator
Number of full-time staff: 11
Number of part-time staff: 2
Number of volunteers: 65
Type of witness notification system: phone
Year system began: 1976
Special features: Crisis intervention is done at the crime scene.

CALIFORNIA
Palcer County Victim/Witness
Year program began: 1980
11562 B. Avenue, Dewitt Center
Auburn, CA 95603
(916) 823-4759
Contact person: Kim Griswold, Coordinator
Number of full-time staff: 4
Type of witness notification system: letter and phone
Year system began: 1980
Special features: Crisis intervention is done over the phone.

Butte County Victim/Witness Assistance Program
Year program began: 1979
170 E. 2nd Street, Suite 1
Chico, CA 95926
(916) 891-2812
Contact person: Janet Taylor, Director
Number of full-time staff: 4
Number of part-time staff: 1
Type of witness notification system: phone and mail
Year system began: 1979
Special features: Crisis intervention is done either in person or through an outreach letter. Extra attention is given to the elderly, including

crime-proofing their homes along with follow-up counseling.

Del Norte Victim/Witness Assistance Center
Year program began: 1984
Rural Human Services, Inc.
811 G Street
Crescent City, CA 95531
(707) 464-7441
Contact person: Dennis Conger, Program Manager
Number of full-time staff: 1
Number of part-time staff: 2
Number of volunteers: 6
Type of witness notification system: letter, in person, and phone
Year system began: 1985
Special features: Crisis intervention is done at the crime scene if invited.

Solano County Victim/Witness Program
Year program began: ??
600 Union Avenue
Fairfield, CA 94533
(707) 429-6451
Contact person: JoAnn McLevis, Program Administrator
Number of full-time staff: 3
Number of part-time staff: 1-2
Type of witness notification system: phone-in recordings for continuances only
Year system began: 1982
Special features: Crisis intervention is done in person. A child-care program is present, and transportation is provided to elderly victims.

Fresno County Victim/Witness Service Center
Year program began: 1975
P.O. Box 453
8th Floor Courthouse
1100 Van Ness
Fresno, CA 93709
(209) 488-3425
Contact person: Rose Marie Gibbs, Program Director
Number of full-time staff: 3
Number of part-time staff: 4
Number of volunteers: 3
Type of witness notification system: in person or phone

Year system began: ??
Special features: Crisis intervention is done over the phone or in person. Special services to the elderly include transportation, home visits, and referral to seniors' organizations.

San Benito Victim/Witness Program
Year program began: 1982
483 Fifth Street
Hollister, CA 95023
(408) 637-8244
Contact person: Cynthia Fahy, Director
Number of full-time staff: 3
Number of part-time staff: 1
Number of volunteers: 3
Type of witness notification system: phone or in person
Year system began: 1983
Special features: Crisis intervention done in person. Child-care program served 120 children in 1984. The children are sent to a licensed day-care provider.

Amador/Alpine/Calaveras County Victim/ Witness Assistance Program
Year program began: 1984
108 Court Street
Jackson, CA 95642
(209) 223-6474
Contact persons: Barbara Miller and Mark McCaffrey, Coordinator
Number of full-time staff: 2
Number of part-time staff: 1
Number of volunteers: 1
Type of witness notification system: phone or letter
Year system began: 1984
Special features: Crisis intervention is done in person or over the phone.

Lake County Victim/Witness Assistance Division
Year program began: 1984
c/o Lake County District Attorney
255 N. Forges Street
Lakeport, CA 95453
(707) 263-2251
Contact person: Michael R. Blakey, Coordinator
Number of full-time staff: 2

Type of witness notification system: phone
Year system began: 1984
Special features: Crisis intervention is done over the phone or in person. Additional personal contact is given to elderly victims.

L.A. City Attorney Victims of Crime Program
Year program began: 1980
1600 City Hall East
200 N. Main Street
Los Angeles, CA 90012
Contact person: Alex Vargas, Director
Number of full-time staff: 24
Number of volunteers: 5
No witness notification system
Special features: Child-care program served 2,000 victims/children in 1984. Staffed by 2 full-time people.

Contra Costa District Attorney Victim/Witness Assistance Program
Year program began: 1979
725 Court Street, Room 402
P.O. Box 670
Martinez, CA 94553-0150
Contact person: Stephanie Pete, Program Coordinator
Number of full-time staff: 5
Number of volunteers: 13
Type of witness notification system: phone and postcard
Year system began: 1979
Special features: Crisis intervention is done in person and usually within one working day of the crime. Transportation and court accompaniment are services offered to elderly victims.

Yuba County Victim/Witness Assistance Program
Year program began: 1985
215 5th Street
Marysville, CA 95901
(916) 741-6275
Contact person: Mike Barber, Coordinator
Number of full-time staff: 1
Number of part-time staff: 1
Number of volunteers: 4
Type of witness notification system: mail or phone
Year system began: 1985

Special features: Crisis intervention is done over the phone or in person.

Napa Victim/Witness Services
Year program began: 1978
1700 Second Street, Suite 308
Napa, CA 94558
(707) 252-6222
Contact person: Gayle O'Kelley, Coordinator
Number of full-time staff: 2
Number of part-time staff: 2
Number of volunteers: 2
Type of witness notification system: mail or phone
Year system began: ??
Special features: 24-hour hotline for victims of violent crimes. Services for the elderly include access to wheelchairs and making referrals to the Senior Assistance Program.

Victim Center of San Mateo County
Year program began: 1975
711 Hamilton Street
Redwood City, CA 94063
(415) 363-4010
Contact person: Robert E. Mantynen, Program Manager
Number of full-time staff: 5
Number of part-time staff: 8
Type of witness notification system: mail
Year system began: 1976
Special features: Crisis intervention is done either by phone or in person.

Sacramento County D.A.'s Victim/Witness Assistance Program
Year program began: 1977
901 G. Street
Sacramento, CA 95814
(916) 440-5701
Contact person: Veronica C. Zecchini, Coordinator
Number of full-time staff: 10
Number of part-time staff: 4
Number of volunteers: 6
Type of witness notification system: phone
Year system began: 1977
Special features: Crisis intervention is done in person. Cash is provided for elderly victims.

Victim/Witness Assistance Program

Year program began: 1977
316 N. Mt. View
San Bernardino, CA 92415
(714) 383-2942
Contact person: JoAnn Nunez, Coordinator
Number of full-time staff: 12
Number of volunteers: 10-30
Type of witness notification system: phone
Year system began: ??
Special features: None reported.

Victim/Witness Assistance Program
Year program began: 1978
850 Bryant Street, Room 322
San Francisco, CA 94103
(415) 552-6550
Contact person: Ann B. Daley, Director
Number of full-time staff: 6
Number of volunteers: 1
Type of witness notification system: subpoena
Year system began: 1982
Special features: Crisis intervention done in person on home visits. Court escort, transportation, and follow-up services are provided for elderly victims.

NCCJ Santa Clara County Victim/Witness Assistance Center
Year program began: 1977
777 N. First Street, Mezzanine
San Jose, CA 95112
(408) 295-2656
Contact person: Joe Yomtov, Director
Number of full-time staff: 9
Number of part-time staff: 4
Number of volunteers: 10
Type of witness notification system: telephone or computer
Year system began: 1984
Special features: Crisis intervention is done at the crime scene. Transportation and emergency money are also provided for the elderly and the handicapped.

San Luis Obispo County Victim/Witness Program
Year program began: 1977
County Government Center, Room 121
San Luis Obispo, CA 93408
(805) 549-5822

Contact person: Gerald O. Young, Victim/
Witness Supervisor
Number of full-time staff: 5
Number of voluneers: 1
Type of witness notification system: phone
Year system began: 1977
Special features: Child-care program served 240
children in 1984 and was staffed by vic-
tim/witness staff or through the use of Rape
Crisis Center personnel and/or interns. Ser-
vices are also provided to the elderly, 55
years or older, through victim outreach pro-
grams. Contact is made by letter, phone, or
in person.

Rape Crisis Center of West Contra Costa
Year program began: 1974
2000 Vale Road
San Pablo, CA 94806
(415) 237-0113
Contact person: Gloria Sandoval, Director
Number of full-time staff: 6
Number of part-time staff: 7
Number of volunteers: 40
Type of witness notification system: phone
Year system began: 1975
Special features: Crisis intervention is done in per-
son. Self-defense classes are offered to the
elderly and child therapy is given by 2 staff
members; 30 children were served in 1984.

Marin County Victim/Witness Assistance
Program
Year program began: mid-1970s
Room 181, Hall of Justice
San Rafael, CA 94983
(415) 499-6482
Contact person: Dyanne Bohner, Coordinator
Number of full-time staff: 3
Number of volunteers: 1
Type of witness notification system: subpoenas
Year system began: ??
Special features: Crisis intervention is done in
person.

CSP, Inc., Victim/Witness Assistance Program
Year program began: 1978
County of Orange
700 Civic Center Dr. West
Superior Court, P.O. Box 1994
Santa Ana, CA 92702

(714) 834-7103
Contact person: Kathryn A. Yarnall, Assistant
Director
Number of full-time staff: 35
Number of part-time staff: 2
Number of volunteers: 60
Type of witness notification system: telephone
Year system began: 1978
Special features: Assessment of victim's needs is
done in crisis intervention. Education pro-
grams are offered to senior citizens.

District Attorney Victim/Witness Program of
Santa Barbara County
Year program began: 1978
118 E. Figueroa
Santa Barbara, CA 93101
(805) 963-6155
Contact person: Joan M. Selman, Coordinator
Number of full-time staff: 7
Number of part-time staff: 3
Number of volunteers: 4-12
Type of witness notification system: telephone
Year system began: 1978
Special features: Crisis intervention is done in per-
son. Child care is provided by available staff
or trained volunteers.

Victim/Witness Assistance Center
Year program began: 1980
701 Ocean, Room 250
Santa Cruz, CA 95060
(408) 425-2610
Contact person: Judith A. Osborn, Coordinator
Number of full-time staff: 5
Number of part-time staff: 1
Number of volunteers: 13
Type of witness notification system: phone
Year system began: 1977
Special features: Crisis intervention is done in per-
son to calm victims and to make referrals.
Outreach services are offered to victims over
the age of 55 when their homes are
burglarized.

Rape Treatment Center—Santa Monica Hospital
Year program began: 1974
1225 15th Street
Santa Monica, CA 90404
(213) 319-4503
Contact person: Gail Abarbanel, Director

Number of full-time staff: 9
Number of part-time staff: 14
Number of volunteers: 20
No witness notification system
Special features: Crisis intervention counseling is done in the emergency room. Professional counseling is also offered to elderly victims.

Sonoma County Victim/Witness Program
Year program began: 1979
Probation Dept., P.O. Box 11719
Santa Rosa, CA 95406
(707) 527-2002
Contact person: Linda Poggi-LeStrange, Coordinator
Number of full-time staff: 4
Number of volunteers: 9
Type of witness notification system: answering machine
Year system began: 1979
Special features: Child-care program served 25 children in 1984. Liability insurance is county insurance.

District Attorney's Victim/Witness Assistance Center
Year program began: 1985
2 South Green Street
Sonora, CA 95370
(209) 533-5642
Contact person: Deborah Cooper, Coordinator
Number of full-time staff: 4
Number of part-time staff: 1
Number of volunteers: 4
Type of witness notification system: phone
Year system began: 1985
Special features: ABC model of crisis intervention is used.

Victim/Witness Center
Year program began: 1980
South Lake Tahoe Branch
Box 14506
South Lake Tahoe, CA 95702
(916) 541-0312
Contact person: Ivone Basus, Coordinator
Number of full-time staff: 1
Number of part-time staff: 1
Number of volunteers: 1

No witness notification system
Special features: Needs assessment is done at the crime scene for crisis intervention.

Mendocino County Victim/Witness Assistance
Year program began: 1981
Mendocino County Courthouse, Room 10
Ukiah, CA 95482
(707) 463-4218
Contact person: Elizabeth Anderson, Coordinator
Number of full-time staff: 4
Number of volunteers: 10
Type of witness notification system: witness call recording
Year system began: 1985
Special features: Crisis intervention is done over the phone and in person. Letters are also sent in crisis intervention.

Ventura County District Attorney's Victim/Witness Assistance Program
Year program began: 1980
800 South Victoria Avenue
Ventura, CA 93009
(805) 654-3919
Contact person: Richard Harris, Program Manager
Number of full-time staff: 20
Number of part-time staff: 1
Number of volunteers: 15
Type of witness notification system: phone and mail
Year system began: 1980
Special features: Crisis intervention is done in person.

Yolo County Victim/Witness Assistance Center
Year program began: 1981
P.O. Box 1247
Woodland, CA 95695
(916) 666-8180
Contact person: Kerry L. Martin, Program Coordinator
Number of full-time staff: 3
Number of part-time staff: 2
No witness notification system—DA's office does this.
Special features: Crisis intervention is done by phone and mail contact.

Sutter County Victim/Witness Assistance
    Program
Year program began: 1984
Sutter County Probation Dept.
446 Second Street
Yuba City, CA 95991
(916) 673-6220
Contact person: Edward F. Eden, Probation
    Officer
Number of full-time staff: 1
Number of part-time staff: 1
Number of volunteers: 1
Type of witness notification system: letter and
    phone
Year system began: 1984
Special features: Child-care program started in
    1985. Crisis intervention is done over the
    phone and in person.

COLORADO
Boulder D.A.'s Victim/Witness Assistance
    Program
Year program began: 1976
P.O. Box 471
Boulder, CO 80306
(303) 441-3730
Contact person: Barbara Kendall, Coordinator
Number of full-time staff: 2
Number of part-time staff: 2
Number of volunteers: 8
Type of witness notification: phone, mail, and
    in person
Year system began: 1976
Special features: Emergency care child-care
    program.

Victim/Witness Program
Year program began: 1981
Office of the District Attorney
326 South Tejon
Colorado Springs, CO 80903
(303) 520-6049
Contact person: Irene Kornelly, Coordinator
Number of full-time staff: 1
Number of volunteers: 7
Type of witness notification system: letter and
    phone
Year system began: ??
Special features: None reported.

Victim/Witness Assistance Division
Year program began: 1983
District Attorney's Office
P.O. Box 1489
Fort Collins, CO 80522
(303) 221-7200
Contact person: Pamela Garman, Coordinator
Number of full-time staff: 1
Number of part-time staff: 1
Type of witness notification system: telephone
    and written notice
Year system began: 1979
Special features: Phone and in-person crisis in-
    tervention. Child-care program staffed by vic-
    tim/witness staff with assistance when re-
    quired from community support groups.

1st Judicial District Attorney's Victim/Witness
    Assistance Unit
Year program began: 1983
1620 Jackson Street
Golden, CO 80401
(303) 277-8946
Contact person: Ralynee Gattmann, Director
Number of full-time staff: 5
Number of part-time staff: 2
Number of volunteers: 8
Type of witness notification system: phone and
    mail
Year system began: 1984
Special features: Crisis intervention is done over
    the phone only when a case has been filed.

Victim Assistance Program
Year program began: 1983
Arapahoe County Sheriff's Department
5686 S. Court Place
Littleton, CO 80120
(303) 795-4747
Contact person: Allison Brittsan, Coordinator
Number of full-time staff: at least 1
Number of part-time staff: at least 1
Number of volunteers: at least 1
Witness notification is handled through the
    D.A.'s office
Year system began: ??
Special features: Crisis intervention is done at the
    crime scene or wherever the victim is.

CONNECTICUT
Victim/Witness Program
Year program began: 1978
Office of the States Attorney
95 Washington Street
Hartford, CT 06106
(203) 566-3190 or 566-4787
Contact person: Charles Lexius, Victim Advocate
Number of full-time staff: 1
Type of witness notification system: mail
Year system began: 1978
Special features: None reported.

DELAWARE
Victim/Witness Assistance Program
Year program began: 1976
Department of Justice
820 N. French Street
Wilmington, DE 19801
(302) 571-2599
Contact person: Susan Baldwin, Director
Number of full-time staff: 7
Type of witness notification system: letter and subpoena
Year system began: 1976
Special features: Crisis intervention is done in person

DISTRICT OF COLUMBIA
U.S. Attorney's Office
Year program began: 1979
Victim/Witness Assistance Unit
District of Columbia Courthouse
500 Indiana Avenue, NW
Room 5201
Washington, DC 20001
(202) 724-6797
Contact person: Anita B. Boles, Chief
Number of full-time staff: 4
Type of witness notification system: letter
Year system began: 1979
Special features: Special transportation services are set up for the elderly and the handicapped.

FLORIDA
Victim/Witness Management Program
Year program began: 1982
5100 144th Avenue

P.O. Box 5028
Clearwater, FL 33520
(813) 530-6221
Contact person: Connie Mederos-Jacobs
Number of full-time staff: 7
Type of witness notification: phone and letters
Year system began: 1982
Special features: None reported.

Sexual Assault Assistance Program
Year program began: 1981
Office of the State Attorney
Post Office Drawer 4401
Ft. Pierce, FL 33450
(305) 465-1814
Contact person: Harriette Rowe, Director
Number of full-time staff: 2
Number of volunteers: 13
Type of witness notification: in person by volunteer advocates
Year system began: 1981
Special features: Respond to victims at the law enforcement office or the hospital and stay with them throughout the ordeal.

Alachua County Rape/Crime Victim Advocate Program
Year program began: 1974
730 N. Waldo Road, Suite 100
Gainesville, FL 32606
(904) 375-2068
Contact person: Elizabeth Jones, Director
Number of full-time staff: 4
Witness notification is handled through the State's Attorney's Office
Year system began: ??
Special features: Advocates respond 24 hours a day, 7 days a week to victims in local hospitals.

Victim/Witness Assistance Program
Year program began: 1981
P.O. Box 1068
Key West, FL 33040
(305) 296-2027
Contact person: Meg Bates, Director
Number of full-time staff: 3
Type of witness notification system: letter and phone

Year system began: 1981
Special features: None reported.

Victim Advocacy Program
Year program began: 1981
Pinellas County Sheriff's Department
P.O. Box 2500
Largo, FL 34294
(813) 587-6278
Contact person: Sara Sue Sopkin, Senior Victim
  Advocate
Number of full-time staff: 3
Type of witness notification system: State's Attorney's Office does this.
Year system began: 1982
Special features: Crisis intervention is done at the
  crime scene.

Dade County Advocates for Victims
Year program began: 1974
1515 N.W. 7th Street, #213
Miami, FL 33125
(305) 547-7933
Contact person: Catherine G. Lynch, Director
Number of full-time staff: 17
Number of part-time staff: 11-12
Number of volunteers: 2-10
Type of witness notification system: State's Attorney's Office does this.
Year system began: ??
Special features: Served 215 children in 1984. Program has a children's worker for the children
  in the Battered Women's Shelter.

Victim/Witness Assistance Program
Year program began: 1983
S.A.O.1351 NW 12th Street, 6th floor
Miami, FL 33125
(305) 545-3439
Contact person: Denise M. Moon, Director
Number of full-time staff: 23
Number of volunteers: 2
Type of witness notification system: phone and
  letter
Year system began: 1983
Special features: Assess victims' needs in crisis
  intervention.

Victim Advocate Program
Year program began: 1976

Orange County Sheriff's Office
3205-B W. Colonial Drive
Orlando, FL 32808
(305) 297-1117
Contact person: Denise Hassee, Advocate
Number of full-time staff: 3
Type of witness notification system: through a
  victim advocate
Year system began: 1976
Special features: Crisis intervention is done either
  in person or over the phone. Special programs are also provided to meet the needs
  of the elderly.

Seminole County Sheriff's Department
  Victim Services
Year program began: 1978
1345 28th Street
Sanford, FL 32771
(305) 322-5115
Contact person: G. Doris Hundley, Deputy Victim Services Coordinator
Number of full-time staff: 1
Number of volunteers: 10-14
Type of witness notification system: State's Attorney's Office does this
Year system began: 1984
Special features: Crisis intervention is done in person at the crime scene or over the phone.
  The child-care program served 150 children
  in 1984. Referral to senior citizens' groups,
  specialized counselors, and transportation services are all provided to elderly victims.

Palm Beach County Victim/Witness Services
Year program began: 1975
307 N. Dixie Highway, Suite 500
West Palm Beach, FL 33401
(305) 837-2418
Contact person: Robert C. Wells, Director
Number of full-time staff: 13
Number of part-time staff: 8
Number of volunteers: 15
Type of witness notification: phone and mail
Year system began: 1981
Special features: One counselor for children of
  homicide victims. Special services to the
  elderly include support groups and home
  visits.

GEORGIA
Rape Crisis Network
Year program began: 1984
1609 Newcastle Street
Brunswick, GA
(912) 267-0760, Ext. 409
Contact person: Constance Smith, Coordinator
Number of part-time staff: 1
Number of volunteers: 2
No witness notification system
Special features: Crisis intervention for rape victims is done at the crime scene or the hospital.

Victim/Witness Assistance Unit
Year program began: 1985
District Attorney's Office
Cubb Judicial Circuit
30 Waddell Street
Marietta, GA 30090-9646
(404) 429-3191
Contact person: Pamela Edds-West, Director
Number of full-time staff: 2
Number of volunteers: 30
Type of witness notification system: phone and letter
Year system began: 1985
Special features: Crisis intervention is done over the phone. Special team works with elderly victims.

Victim/Witness Assistance Program
Year program began: 1983
133 Montgomery Street
Savannah, GA 31401
(912) 944-4863
Contact person: Helen Pitts Smith, Director
Number of full-time staff: 2
Number of volunteers: 60
Type of witness notification system: letter, phone, and in person
Year system began: 1983
Special features: Crisis intervention is done over the phone or in person. Child-care program served 29 children in 1984. Try to outreach to elderly victims within 24 hours of a crime. Provide transportation services for this group.

HAWAII
Kauai Victim/Witness Program
Year program began: 1981
Office of the Prosecuting Attorney
4193 Hardy Street, Unit 6
Lihue, HI 96766
(808) 245-5388
Contact person: Michael K. Iwai, Program Coordinator
Number of full-time staff: 4
Number of volunteers: 10
Type of witness notification system: phone
Year system began: 1981
Special features: Crisis intervention is done in person. Child-care program served five children in 1984 and is staffed by volunteers and day-care centers used on a rotation basis. Moral support in the courtroom along with emergency assistance is provided to the elderly.

Victim/Witness Assistance Program
Year program began: 1982
Department of the Prosecuting Attorney
200 S. High Street
Wailuku
Maui, HI 96793
(808) 244-7799
Contact person: Brian K. Ogawa, Coordinator
Number of full-time staff: 3
Type of witness notification system: letter and phone
Year system began: 1982
Special features: Crisis intervention is done at the crime scene occasionally.

ILLINOIS
Jackson County Victim/Witness Assistance
Year program began: 1980
c/o State Attorney's Office
Murphysboro, IL 62966
(618) 684-2155
Contact person: Janet Brown, Coordinator
Number of full-time staff: 2
Type of witness notification system: mail, phone, and in person
Year system began: 1980

Special features: Crisis intervention is done in person and on home visits.

Lake County State's Attorney's Office
Year program began: 1982
Victim/Witness Assistance
18 N. County
Waukegan, IL 60085
(312) 689-6644
Contact person: Ruth Rosengarden
Number of full-time staff: 4
Number of part-time staff: 1
Type of witness notification system: letter and phone
Year system began: 1980
Special features: Crisis intervention services include emergency housing, medial attention, child protective service, and advocacy.

DuPage County State's Attorney's Center for Victim/Witness Assistance
Year program began: 1979
205 Reber Street
Wheaton, IL 60187
(312) 682-7759
Contact person: Jean A. Tuzik, Coordinator
Number of full-time staff: 1
Number of part-time staff: 1
Type of witness notification system: computer and phone
Year system began: 1979
Special features: None reported.

INDIANA
Indianapolis Police Department Victim Assistance
Year program began: 1975
50 North Alabama E142
Indianapolis, IN 46204
(317) 236-3331
Contact person: Judy Moore, Supervisor
Number of full-time staff: 4
Number of volunteers: 0
Type of witness notification system: Prosecutor's Office Witness Notification program
Year system began: 1975
Special features: On-the-scene intervention using

ABC method. Refer adult abuse victims to Adult Protective Services.

Marion County Prosecutor's Victim Assistance Program
Year program began: 1977
560 City-County Building
Indianapolis, IN 46204
(317) 236-5103
Contact person: Sallie Wills/Ruth Purcell, Coordinators
Number of full-time staff: 7
Number of volunteers: 5
Type of witness notification system: subpoena, paralegal, or victim advocate
Year system began:
Special features: Contact victims by phone after charges have been filed. Adult Protective Services Unit.

Victim Assistance
Year program began: 1979
City-County Bldg.
Ft. Wayne, IN 46802
(219) 427-1205
Contact person: Patricia Smallwood, Director
Number of full-time staff: 2
Number of volunteers: 6
Type of witness notification system: phone, letter, or personal visit
Year system began: 1982
Special features: Crisis intervention is done over the phone.

IOWA
Polk County Victim Services
Year program began: 1974
Polk County Department of Social Services
1915 Hickman
Des Moines, Iowa 50312
(515) 286-3832
Contact person: Marti Anderson, Assistant Director
Number of full-time staff: 9
Number of part-time staff: 1
Number of volunteers: 32
No witness notification system
Special features: Crisis intervention is done in person or over the phone 24 hours a day.

KANSAS

Johnson County Victim/Witness Assistance
Year program began: 1978
P.O. Box 728
Olathe, KS 66061
(913) 782-5000
Contact person: Georgia Nesselrode,
   Coordinator
Number of full-time staff: 1
Type of witness notification system: phone and
   letter
Year system began: 1978
Special features: None reported.

KENTUCKY

Victim/Witness Assistance Program
Year program began: 1975
919 College Street
Bowling Green, KY 42101
(502) 842-7581
Contact person: John Deeb, Assistant Common-
   wealth Attorney (D.A.)
No staffing numbers reported.
No witness notification system.
Special features: Conference is set up with the
   victim.

Victim/Witness Assistance Program
Year program began: prior to 1979
605 City-County Bldg.
Covington, KY 41011
(606) 292-6580
Contact person: Donald Buring, Attorney
No staffing numbers reported.
Type of witness notification: phone and letter
Year system began: prior to 1979
Special features: None reported.

Victim/Witness Assistance Program
Year program began: ??
Office of the Commonwealth's Attorney
P.O. Box 581
Eddyville, KY 42038
(502) 388-9911
Contact person: Gloria Stewart, Director, Pro-
   secutorial Services
Number of part-time staff: at least 1
Type of witness notification system: phone and
   letter

Year system began: around 1975
Special features: None reported.

Victim Advocacy/Office of Attorney General
Year program began: 1985
909 Leawood Drive
Frankfort, KY 40601
(502) 564-5904
Contact person: Leo D. Hobbs, Director
Number of full-time staff: 4
Number of volunteers: 3
Type of witness notification system: mail
Year system began: 1985
Special features: None reported.

MAINE

District Attorney's Office
Year program began: 1979
Victim/Witness Services
97 Hammond Street
Bangor, ME 04401
(207) 942-8552
Contact person: Julie Morse, Coordinator
Number of full-time staff: 1
Type of witness notification system: mail and
   phone
Year system began: 1983
Special features: None reported.

Cumberland County Victim/Witness Services
Year program began: 1985
142 Federal Street
Portland, ME 04101
(207) 772-2838
Contact person: James M. Couley, Coordinator
Number of full-time staff: 4
Type of witness notification: mail
Year system began: 1985
Special features: Child-care program served 200
   children in 1984. It is staffed by an outside
   agency and liability insurance is carried by
   the county.

Somerset County Victim/Witness Advocate
Year program began: ??
Somerset County Courthouse
Skowhegan, ME 04976
(207) 474-2423 or 474-5517
Contact person: Susan Randall, Victim/Witness

Advocate
Number of full-time staff: 1
Type of witness notification system: subpoena
Year system began: 1977
Special features: 24-hour rape victim assistance.

MARYLAND
Victim/Witness Assistance Center (V-Wac)
Year program began: 1979
101 South Street
Office of State's Attorney for Anne Arundel
County
Annapolis, MD 21401
(301) 224-1160
Contact person: Robin Davenport, Director
Number of full-time staff: 7
Type of witness notification system: phone, letters, prerecorded messages
Year system began: 1979
Special features: Crisis intervention done by phone and in person. Services to the elderly include transportation, home visits, assistance with referrals, and accommodations for handicaps.

Victim/Witness Assistance Unit
Year program began: 1977
State's Attorney's Office for Baltimore City
Room 410 Clarence Mitchel Courthouse
110 N. Clavert Street
Baltimore, MD 21202
(310) 396-1897
Contact person: Frank Perkowski, Director
Number of full-time staff: 6
Type of witness notification system: mail
Year system began: 1977
Special features: None reported.

Victim/Witness Assistance Program
Year program began: 1983
P.O. Box 210
Frederick, MD 21701
(301) 694-1523
Contact person: Shelby Hanes, Coordinator
Number of full-time staff: 1
Type of witness notification system: phone and letter
Year system began: 1985
Special features: None reported.

Baltimore County Victim/Witness Unit
Year program began: 1977
State's Attorney's Office
401 Bosley Avenue, 5th floor
Towson, MD 21204
(301) 583-6650
Contact person: Sandra B. Stolker, Director
Number of full-time staff: at least 1
Type of witness notification system: personal calls and recorded phone messages
Year system began: 1977
Special features: There is a special sex abuse unit in the State's Attorney's Office.

Victim/Witness Assistance Unit
Year program began: 1977
P.G. County State's Attorney's Office
Courthouse Room 410
Upper Marlboro, MD 20772
(301) 952-3541
Contact person: Sondra Ricks, Administrative Assistant
No staffing numbers reported.
Type of witness notification system: phone and mail
Year system began: 1977
Special features: None reported.

MASSACHUSETTS
Rape Crisis Intervention Program
Year program began: 1974
Bethesda Israel Hospital
330 Brookline Avenue
Boston, MA 02215
(617) 735-4645
Contact person: Ronnie Ryback, Director
Number of full-time staff: at least 1
No witness notification system
Special features: In-person crisis intervention.

Middlesex County District
Attorney's Office
Year program began: 1978
Victim/Witness Service Bureau
40 Thorndike Street
Cambridge, MA 02141
(617) 494-4604
Contact person: Patty McNamara
Number of full-time staff: 18

Number of part-time staff: 3
Number of volunteers: 1
Type of witness notification system: mail and
phone
Year system began: ??
Special features: Crisis contact made, but no
method mentioned.

Essex County Victim/Witness Assistance
Year program began: 1979
70 Washington Street
Salem, MA 10971
(617) 745-6610
Contact person: Michealene O'Neill McCann,
Director
Number of full-time staff: 20
Number of volunteers: 4
Type of witness notification system: phone and
letter
Year system began: 1979
Special features: Crisis intervention is done over
the phone or in person. Home visits are also
done. Elderly victims receive service prior-
ity regardless of the type of crime involved.

Hampden County District Attorney
Victim/Witness Program
Year program began: 1980
50 State Street
Springfield, MA 01103
(413) 781-8100, Ext. 2026
Contact person: Eleanor Cress, Director
Number of full-time staff: 8
Type of witness notification system: mail and
phone
Year system began: 1980
Special features: Crisis intervention is done at the
crime scene or in person. Child-care program
served 50 children in 1984. Protective services are offered to the elderly along with
transportation and other services as
requested.

MICHIGAN
Washtenaw County Prosecuting Attorney
Victim/Witness Unit
Year program began: 1980
P.O. Box 8645
Ann Arbor, MI 48107

(313) 996-3026 or 994-2380
Contact person: Colleen E. Turek, Coordinator
Number of full-time staff: 1
Type of witness notification system: phone
Year system began: 1980
Special features: None reported.

Calhoun County Victim/Witness Assistance
Unit
Year program began: 1976
109 E. Michigan
Battle Creek, MI 49107
(616) 966-1265
Contact person: Steven Barver, Director
Number of full-time staff: 2
Number of volunteers: 10
Type of witness notification system: phone
Year system began: 1976
Special features: None reported.

Victim/Witness Services Unit
Year program began: 1980
Room 307, Hall of Justice
Kent County Prosecutor's Office
333 Monroe Avenue, NW
Grand Rapids, MI 49503
(616) 774-6822
Contact person: Mark Gleason, Director
Number of full-time staff: 3
Number of volunteers: 10
Type of witness notification system: phone and
letter
Year system began: 1980
Special features: Child-care program is staffed by
volunteers. Liability insurance is provided by
the county government. Volunteer advocates
go with elderly victims throughout the court
process to provide support.

Kalamazoo County Victim/Witness
Assistance Service
Year program began: 1975
227 West Michigan Avenue, #312
Kalamazoo, MI 49007
(616) 383-8922
Contact person: Karen M. Hayter, Director of
Staff Services
Number of full-time staff: 6
Number of part-time staff: 1
Number of volunteers: 1

Type of witness notification system: phone and mail

Year system began: 1975

Special features: Crisis intervention is done in person.

MINNESOTA

St. Louis County Victim/Witness Assistance

Year program began: 1985

St. Louis County Attorney's Office

501 Courthouse

Duluth, MN 55802

(218) 726-2323

Contact person: Paul A. Gustad, Director

Number of full-time staff: 4

Number of volunteers: 8

Type of witness notification system: phone and in-person

Year system began: 1976

Special features: None reported.

Crime Victims Centers

Year program began: 1977

822 South Third Street Suite 100

Minneapolis, MN 55415

(612) 340-5432

Contact person: Dick Ericson, Executive Director

Number of full-time staff: 7

Number of part-time staff: 4

Number of volunteers: 30

No witness notification system

Special features: 24-hour crisis line. Senior citizens provided with temporary bus cards when their social security cards have been stolen. Emergency home care provide.

MISSOURI

Circuit Attorney's Victim/Witness Assistance Unit

Year program began: 1978

1320 Market Street, Room 221

St. Louis, MO 63103

(314) 622-4373

Contact person: Mary Flotron, Project Director

Number of full-time staff: 6

No witness notification system

Special features: Crisis intervention is done by phone and in person, along with outreach

letters. Work very closely with the Mayor's Department on Aging.

MONTANA

Crime Victims Unit

Year program began: 1977

Box 4659

Helena, MT 59601

(406) 444-6535

Contact person: Cheryl Bryant, Administrative Officer

Number of full-time staff: 1

Number of part-time staff: 1

No witness notification system

Special features: Help elderly in filing insurance claims.

NEBRASKA

Victim/Witness Unit

Year program began: 1981

Lincoln Police Department

233 South 10th Street

Lincoln, NE 68508

(402) 471-7181

Contact person: Shirley J. Kuhle, Administrator

Number of full-time staff: 2

Number of volunteers: 40

Type of witness notification system: phone and letter

Year system began: 1981

Special features: Crisis intervention done by phone and letter. Child care done by other facility or the program. Liability insurance is carried through the city of Lincoln. Also work with the elderly.

NEVADA

Clark County District Attorney's Victim/Witness Services Center

Year program began: 1976

200 S. Third Street

Las Vegas, NV 89155

(702) 386-4204

Contact person: Cheryl Gosnell, Administrative Assistant

Number of full-time staff: 7

Number of volunteers: 1

Type of witness notification system: subpoena
and recorded message
Year system began: 1976
Special features: Will watch children in the office when it is necessary. Served 10 children
in 1984. Liability insurance is carried by the
county.

NEW HAMPSHIRE
Victim/Witness Assistance Program
Year program began: 1979
Hillsborough County Attorney's Office
300 Chestnut Street
Manchester, NH 03101
(603) 627-5605
Contact person: Catherine McNaughton,
Director
Number of full-time staff: 1
Type of witness notification system: phone and
letter
Year system began: 1984
Special features: None reported.

NEW JERSEY
Camden County Victim/Witness Service
Year program began: 1984
518 Market Street, 4th Floor
Camden, NJ 08102
(609) 757-8462
Contact person: George Kerns, Coordinator
Number of part-time staff: at least 1
Type of witness notification system: letter
Year system began: 1984
Special features: None reported.

Victim/Witness Assistance Program
Year program began: 1982
Cape May County Prosecutor's Office
Cape May Courthouse
Cape May, NJ 08210
(609) 465-7066
Contact person: Debra Luprette, County Investigator and Coordinator
Number of full-time staff: 1
Type of witness notification system: subpoena,
mail, and telephone
Year system began: 1984
Special features: None reported.

Victim/Witness Assistance Unit
Year program began: 1979
Bergen County Prosecutor's Office
County Courthouse
Hackensack, NJ 07601
(201) 646-2057
Contact person: Harold C. Rew, Director
Number of full-time staff: 2
Type of witness notification system: mail
Year system began: 1980
Special features: Child-care program served 126
children in 1984 and is staffed by program
workers or the children are sent to a licensed
day-care facility.

Atlantic County Prosecutor's Office
Year program began: 1979
Victim/Witness Unit
19th Avenue at Route 40
Mays Landing, NJ
(609) 645-7000
Contact person: Edward Armstrong, Detective
Sergeant
Number of part-time staff: at least 1
Type of witness notification system: letter
Year system began: 1981
Special features: None reported.

Victim/Witness Assistance Unit
Year program began: 1986
Middlesex County Prosecutor's Office
P.O. Box 71
New Brunswick, NJ 08903-0071
(201) 745-3394
Contact Person: Joel M. Steiner, Prosecutor's
Agent
Number of full-time staff: 2
Type of witness notification system: mail and
phone
Year system began: 1983
Special features: Provide transportation to elderly victims.

Essex County Prosecutor's Victim/Witness
Assistance Program
Year program began: 1982
Essex County Courts Building
Essex County Prosecutor's Office
Newark, NJ 07102

(201) 621-4707
Contact person: John J. McMahon, Director
Number of full-time staff: 5
Type of witness notification system: letter
Year system began: 1982
Special features: None reported.

Sussex County Prosecutor's Office
Year program began: 1982
Victim/Witness Assistance Program
4 High Street
Newton, NJ 07860
(201) 383-1570
Contact person: Diane Brookhart, Investigator
Number of part-time staff: 1
Type of witness notification system: letter
Year system began: 1982
Special features: None reported.

Salem County Prosecutor's Office
Year program began: 1980
Victim/Witness Unit
94 Market Street
Salem, NJ 08079
(609) 935-7510, ext. 430
Contact person: Gail G. McCann, County Investigator and Co-Coordinator
Number of part-time staff: 3
Type of witness notification system: letter and phone
Year system began: 1982
Special features: None reported.

Mercer County Prosecutor's Office
Year program began: 1979
Victim/Witness Unit
Mercer County Courthouse
P.O. Box 8068
Trenton, NJ 08650
(609) 989-6428
Contact person: Mary Ethe Gunther, Coordinator
Number of full-time staff: 1
Type of witness notification system: one is present, but type was not reported.
Year system began: ??
Special features: Services to the elderly include referral for medical compensation, transportation to court, legal assistance, and follow-up sessions.

Victim/Witness Unit
Year program began: 1980
Box 623
Woodbury, NJ 08096
(609) 853-3701
Contact person: Samuel DiSimone, Captain
Number of full-time staff: 2
Type of witness notification system: mail
Year system began: 1980
Special features: None reported.

NEW MEXICO
New Mexico Crime Victim Assistance Organization
Year program began: 1979
P.O. Box 25322
Albuquerque, NM 87125
(505) 873-3833
Contact person: Martha H. Carangelo
No staffing numbers reported.
No witness notification system
Special features: None reported.

Victim/Witness Impact Program
Year program began: 1977
D.A.'s Office
415 Tijeras NW
Albuquerque, NM 87102
(505) 841-7100
Contact person: Sandra Clinton, Assistant
Number of full-time staff: 2
Number of part-time staff: 1
Type of witness notification system: phone and letter
Year system began: 1980
Special features: None reported.

NEW YORK
Crime Victim Assistant Unit
Year program began: 1976
Bronx District Attorney's Office
215 E. 161st Street
Bronx, NY 10451
(212) 590-2168
Contact person: Peter Grishman, Executive Assistant District Attorney
Number of full-time staff: 6
Type of witness notification system: phone and mail

Year system began: 1982
Special features: Crisis intervention occurs when a counselor assesses a situation and then determines what action should be taken. Special counseling is also provided to children.

Erie County D.A.'s Office
Year program began: 1981
Victim/Witness Assistance Program
City Court Bldg.
50 Delaware Avenue, Suite 350
Buffalo, NY 14202
(716) 855-6860
Contact person: Jeffrey Ricketts, Coordinator
Number of full-time staff: 5
Number of volunteers: 5
Type of witness notification system: done by D.A.'s Office
Year system began: ??
Special features: Crisis intervention is done by mail. One of top priorities is to help elderly victims.

Northwest Buffalo Community Center
Year program began: 1978
Victim/Witness Crime Prevention Program
155 Lawn Avenue
Buffalo, NY 14207
(716) 876-8108
Contact person: Elizabeth Wilk, Assistant Director
Number of full-time staff: 3
Number of full-time staff: 1
Type of witness notification system: done by D.A.'s Office
Year system began: ??
Special features: Crisis intervention is done in person. Rely heavily on referring.

Victim/Witness Assistance
Year program began: 1979
200 N. Center Court House, Room 300
Casper, NY 82601
(307) 235-9335
Contact person: Nancy Johnson, Director
Number of full-time staff: 1
Type of witness notification system: phone, in person, and letter

Year system began: 1982
Special features: Some crisis intervention done in person.

Nassau County Crime Victim/Witness Service
Year program began 1981
320 Old Country Road
Garden City, NY 11530
(516) 535-3500
Contact person: Patricia Chave, Coordinator
Number of full-time staff: 1
Number of part-time staff: 1
Type of witness notification system: Done by D.A.'s office
Year system began: ??
Special features: Crisis intervention is done in person. Also replace locks for elderly victims.

Rockland County Crime Victim/Witness Assistance Bureau
Year program began: 1984
District Attorney's Office
County Office Building
11 New Hempstead Road
New City, NY 10956
(914) 638-5001
Contact person: Susan Edelman, Victim/Witness Aide
Number of full-time staff: 1
Number of part-time staff: 1
Type of witness notification system: letters
Year system began: 1984
Special features: Crisis intervention is done in person or over the phone.

Dutchess County Crime Victims Assistance
Year program began: 1976
St. Francis Hospital
North Road
Poughkeepsie, NY 12601
(914) 431-8808
Contact person: Jean Craven, Director
Number of full-time staff: 4
No witness notification system
Special features: Crisis intervention is done at the crime scene or wherever else needed.

Monroe Co. District Attorney's Victim/Witness Center
Year program began: 1981

201 Hall of Justice
Rochester, NY 14614
(716) 428-5704
Contact person: Carol Mulhern, Coordinator
Number of full-time staff: 1
Number of part-time staff: 3
Number of volunteers: 2
Type of witness notification system: phone and letter
Year system began: 1981
Special features: Crisis intervention is done wherever the victim is.

Victim Assistance Unit—Rochester Police
Year program began: 1976
150 S. Plymouth Avenue
Rochester, NY 14614
(716) 428-6630
Contact person: Karen Kurst, Senior Victim Service Worker
Number of full-time staff: 5
Number of part-time staff: 4
Number of volunteers: 3
No witness notification system
Special features: Crisis intervention is done over the phone. Child-care program served 778 children in 1984. Provide outreach services to elderly victims. Install locks, provide compensation, counseling, and transportation.

Victims Assistance Services
Year program began: 1981
3 Carhart Avenue
White Plains, NY 10607
(914) 684-6871
Contact person: Toni Downes, CSW, Director
Number of full-time staff: 4
Number of part-time staff: 8
Number of volunteers: 2
No witness notification system
Special features: Crisis intervention is done in person or over the phone. Home visit are made to the elderly, along with emergency assistance, i.e, lock repair.

NORTH CAROLINA
Victim Assistance/Rape Crisis Program
Year Program began: 1978
825 East 4th Street, #205

Charlotte, NC 28202
(704) 336-2190
Contact person: Valerie Schmieder, Director
Number of full-time staff: 5
Number of volunteers: 25 (rape crisis only)
No witness notification system
Special features: Crisis intervention is done in person and on home visits. Phone calls and letters are sent to elderly victims.

Turning Point: Victim Assistance
Year program began: 1982
1301 N. Elm Street
Greensboro, NC 27401
(919) 373-1345
Contact person: Catherine Shaw, Supervisor
Number of full-time staff: 2
Number of part-time staff: 2
Number of volunteers: 12
Type of witness notification system: phone and mail
Year system began: 1985
Special features: Crisis intervention is done over the phone and in person. Child care is *not* babysitting. This is a drop-in nursery for families in stress. Served 250 children in 1984. One staff member/5 children. Home visits are done for many elderly victims.

OHIO
Victim/Witness Division, Stark County
Year program began: 1975
Prosecuting Attorney's Office
P.O. Box 167, D.T. Station
Canton, OH 44701
(216) 438-0888
Contact person: Pamela Goddard, Director
Number of full-time staff: 4
Number of volunteers: 10-20
Type of witness notification system: phone and letter
Year system began: 1975
Special features: None reported.

Alliance to Eradicate Victimization
Year program began: 1984
93 Versaille
Cincinnati, OH 45240
(513) 684-2851

Contact person: Jeanne F. Mays, Coordinator
No staffing numbers reported.
No witness notification system
Special features: None reported.

Seven Hills Victim/Witness Program
Year program began: 1982
701 Ezzard Charles Drive
Cincinnati, OH 45203
(513) 632-7110
Contact person: Wm. A. Alexander,
    Coordinator
Number of part-time staff: 1
Number of volunteers: 1
Type of witness notification system: phone and
    in person
Year system began: 1982
Special features: Served 100 Children in 1984.
    Child-care program is staffed by 7 people.
    Transportation is provided for elderly
    victims.

Victim Services Division
Year program began: 1984
Hamilton County Probation Dept.
Hamilton County Court House, Room 220
1100 Main Street
Cincinnati, OH 45202
(513) 632-8794
Contact person: Nancy Rankin, Director
Number of full-time staff: 2
Type of witness notification system: phone and
    mail
Year system began: 1985
Special features: None reported.

Victim/Witness Assistance Program
Year program began: 1977
Franklin County Prosecuting Attorney's Office
369 High Street
Columbus, OH 43215
(614) 462-3555
Contact person: Connie Scott or Jane Freeman,
    Victim/Witness Assistants
Number of full-time staff: 3
Number of part-time staff: 2
Type of witness notification system: letter
Year system began: 1984
Special features: None reported.

Victim/Witness Division of Montgomery
    County
Year program began: 1976
41 N. Perry Street, Room 315
Dayton, OH 45402
(513) 225-5623
Contact person: Rhonda Barner, Advocate
Number of full-time staff: 6
Number of volunteers: 50
Type of witness notification system: letters, code-
    A phone messages, telephone alert
Year system began: 1976
Special features: 24-hour crisis service. Meet with
    the victims in either the emergency room or
    the police department.

Victim Assistance Program
Year program began: 1981
P.O. Box 962
Lima, OH 45802
(419) 222-8666
Contact person: David Voth, Director
Number of full-time staff: 5
Number of part-time staff: 15
No witness notification system
Special features: Limited child care provided by
    staff. Served 8 children in 1984.

Victim/Witness Program
Year program began: 1979
Lucas County Courthouse
4th Floor Lucas County Prosecutor's Office
Toledo, OH 43624
(419) 245-4726
Contact person: Sandra Martin, Coordinator
Number of full-time staff: 2
Type of witness notification system: letter
Year system began: 1979
Special features: None reported.

Victim/Witness Division
Year program began: 1982
Greene County Prosecutor's Office
45 N. Detroit Street
Xenia, OH 45385
(513) 376-5087
Contact person: Jeannette M. Adkins, Director
Number of full-time staff: 4
Number of part-time staff: 1

Number of volunteers: 25
Type of witness notification system: mail
Year system began: 1977
Special features: Crisis intervention is done in person on a 24-hour basis.

OKLAHOMA
District Attorney's Victim/Witness Program
Year Program began: 1981
P.O. Box 428
Mangum, OK 73554
(405) 782-5069
Contact person: Linda Fletcher, Victim/Witness Coordinator
Number of full-time staff: 1
Type of witness notification system: subpoena, phone calls, and letters
Year system began: 1981
Special features: None reported.

Cleveland County D.A.'s Office
Year program began: 1983
Victim/Witness Center
210 S. Jones
Norman, OK 73069
(405) 321-8268
Contact person: Liala Mandoxr, Coordinator
Number of full-time staff: at least 1
Number of volunteers: at least 1
Type of witness notification system: phone, letters, tape recording
Year system began: 1983
Special features: None reported.

OREGON
Victim/Witness Program
Year program began: 1983
D.A.'s Office
County Courthouse
Bend, Oregon 97701
(503) 388-6525
Contact person: Marie Williams, Director
Number of full-time staff: 1
Number of volunteers: 5
Type of witness notification system: phone and subpoena
Year system began: 1983
Special features: None reported.

Polk County Victim/Witness Assistance Program
Year program began: 1984
Room 304, Courthouse
Dallas, OR 97338
(503) 623-9268
Contact person: Fran Weisensee, Director
Number of part-time staff: 1
Number of volunteers: 12
Type of witness notification system: phone and mail
Year system began: 1984
Special features: None reported.

Curry County Victim Assistance Program
Year program began: 1985
Box 746, c/o District Attorney
Gold Beach, OR 97444
(503) 247-7921, 7018, 7642
Contact person: Barbara Eells, Coordinator
Number of volunteers: 7
Type of witness notification system: phone, mail, and in person
Year system began: 1985
Special features: Support system offered to victim throughout entire ordeal.

Washington County Victim/Witness Assistance
Year program began: 1982
150 N. First, Room 307
Hillsboro, OR 97124
(503) 648-8698
Contact person: Suzanne Dudy, Director
Number of full-time staff: 2
Type of witness notification system: phone, letter, and answering machine
Year system began: 1982
Special features: None reported.

Victim/Witness Assistance of Yamhill County
Year program began: 1979
County Courthouse
McMinnville, OR 97128
(503) 472-9371
Contact person: Mary Ellen Johnson, Coordinator
Number of full-time staff: 1
Number of volunteers: 30
Type of witness notification system: phone and letter

Year system began: 1979
Special features: Crisis intervention is done at the crime scene.

Multnomah County Victims Assistance
Year program began: 1984
1021 S.W. 4th
Room 804
Portland, OR 97204
(503) 248-3222
Contact person: Marilyn Wagner Culp, Director
Number of full-time staff: 10
Number of part-time staff: 4
Number of volunteers: 45
Type of witness notification system: subpoena
Year system began: ??
Special features: Provide crisis intervention in person. Child-care program served approximately 210 children in 1984 and is staffed by Victim/Witness staff or local day-care providers. No liability insurance listed. Contact victims over the age of 60 and do a quick needs assessment and often utilize services of the elderly assurance program sponsored by crime prevention program.

Marion County Victim/Witness Assistance
Year program began: 1980
495 State Street #301
Salem, OR 97301
(503) 588-5222
Contact person: Rebecca Eqing, Manager
Number of full-time staff: 1
Number of volunteers: 35
Type of witness notification system: written
Year system began: 1983
Special features: Crisis intervention is done in person.

PENNSYLVANIA
CVC Victim/Witness Department
Year program began: 1983
P.O. Box 1445
Allentown, PA 18105
no phone number given
Contact person: Ann Cerra Pierre, Director
Number of full-time staff: 2
Number of part-time staff: 1
Type of witness notification system: subpoena and hot line

Year system began: 1983
Special features: Hot line for crisis intervention.

Women's Services, Inc.
Year program began: 1978
Victim Support Services
P.O. Box 637
Meadville, PA 16335
(814) 724-4637
Contact person: Judith H. Griffin, Executive Director
Number of full-time staff: 1
Number of part-time staff: 4
Number of volunteers: 30
No witness notification system
Special features: Staffed hot line for sex abuse victims.

Victim/Witness Assistance Program
Year program began: 1977
Office of the District Attorney
Delaware County Court House
P.O. Box 935
Media, PA 19063
(215) 891-4227
Contact person: John A. Dowd
Number of full-time staff: 8
Type of witness notification system: letter and telephone
Year system began: 1978
Special features: None reported.

Center for Victims of Violent Crimes
Year program began: 1974
1520 Penn Avenue
Pittsburgh, PA 15222
(412) 392-8582
Contact person: Mary Alice Babusci, Director
Number of full-time staff: 11
Number of part-time staff: 4
Number of volunteers: 20
Type of witness notification system: phone and letter
Year system began: 1985
Special features: 24-hour hot line; child-care program that served 175 children in 1984. Liability insurance, accident, and health policy carried. Accompany senior citizens through the criminal justice system. Home visits are also done.

The Crime Victims Center of Chester County
Year program began: 1972
236 West Market Street
West Chester, PA 19382
(215) 692-7420
Contact person: Constance Noblet, Executive
  Director
Number of full-time staff: 6
Number of part-time staff: 1
Number of volunteers: 42
Witness notification is done through the D.A.'s
  office.
Special features: Crisis intervention is done in per-
  son, at the crime scene, or over the phone.

Victims Resource Center
Year program began: 1974
132 S. Franklin Street
Wilkes-Barre, PA 18702
(717) 823-0765
Contact person: Carol L. Lavery, Director
Number of full-time staff: 7
Number of part-time staff: 3
Number of volunteers: 35
Type of witness notification system: phone
Year system began: 1979
Special features: Crisis intervention is done at the
  crime scene or wherever the victim is. Also
  have a 24-hour hot line.

RHODE ISLAND
R.I. Department of A.G.—Victim/Witness
  Program
Year program began: 1985
72 Pine Street
Providence, RI 02903
(401) 274-4400
Contact person: Beverly Horne Vieira, Director
Number of full-time staff: 4
Number of volunteers: 27
Type of witness notification system: letter
Year system began: 1985
Special features: None reported.

SOUTH CAROLINA
Victim/Witness Assistance
Year program began: 1981
Box 4046
Anderson, SC 29622

(803) 261-4046
Contact person: Doris Brown, Advocate
Number of full-time staff: 1
Number of part-time staff: 1
Number of volunteers: 2
Type of witness notification system: telephone
  and letter
Year system began: 1981
Special features: Crisis intervention is done by
  phone/outreach letter.

Victim/Witness Assistance Program
Year program began: 1978
Room 318
Greenville County Courthouse
Greenville, SC 29601
(803) 298-8647
Contact person: Jayne Crisp, Director or Mary
  Buckner
Number of full-time staff: 2
Number of part-time staff: 2
Number of volunteers: 300
No witness notification system
Special features: Housewise Streetwise, a safety
  education program for youth. Crisis interven-
  tion done either by phone or in person.
  Child-care program implemented in 1986.

TENNESSEE
Victim/Witness Unit of the Attorney
  General's Office
Year program began: 1980
201 Poplar, Suite 201
Memphis, TN 38103
(901) 576-5914
Contact person: Kenneth E. Blackburn, Director
Number of full-time staff: 3
Type of witness notification system: letter and
  phone
Year system began: 1981
Special features: None reported.

Victim/Witness Services
Year program began: 1979
Room 101, Metropolitan Courthouse
Office of District Attorney General
Nashville, TN 37201
(615) 373-1672
Contact person: Jody Schwartz, Folk Director
Number of full-time staff: 4

Number of part-time staff: 1
Type of witness notification system: phone and
   letter
Year system began: 1980
Special features: Crisis intervention provided at
   the crime scene.

TEXAS

Harris County District Attorney's Office
Year program began: 1977
Victim/Witness Program
201 Fannin, Suite 200
Houston, TX 77002
(713) 221-6655
Contact person: Gail O'Brien, Director
Number of full-time staff: 6
Type of witness notification system: letter
Year system began: ??
Special features: None reported.

Houston Police Department Crisis Team
Year program began: 1983
61 Riesner
Houston, TX 77066
(713) 222-3601
Contact person: Margaret L. Hardman-Muye,
   MSW CSW-ACP, Supervisor
Number of full-time staff: 12
Number of volunteers: 40
No witness notification system
Special features: Crisis intervention is done at the
   crime scene.

UTAH

Victim/Witness GAL
Year program began: 1983
Court Advocates for Abused Children
Weber County Attorney Office
Municipal Building, 7th Floor
Ogden, UT 84401
(801) 399-8672
Contact person: Deborah Bissell and Sandra
   Crossland, V/W Supervisors
Number of part-time staff: 2
Number of volunteers: 15
Type of witness notification system: phone and
   in person.
Year system began: 1983

Special features: Child care provided by staff.

Salt Lake County Attorney Victim Services
Year program began: 1985
231 East 400 South, 4th Floor
Salt Lake City, UT 84111
(801) 363-7900
Contact person: Karma K. Dixon, County At-
   torney, Director of Victim Services
Number of full-time staff: 10
Number of part-time staff: 1
Type of witness notification system: telephone
   and recording
Year system began: telephones, 1976; recording,
   1985
Special features: Transportation and support ser-
   vices for the elderly. Crisis intervention is
   done over the phone or in person.

VIRGINIA

Alexandria Victim/Witness Program
Year program began: 1984
520 King Street, Room 301
Alexandria, VA 22305
(703) 838-4100
Contact person: Eileen C. McGrath, Director
Number of full-time staff: 2
Number of volunteers: 2
Type of witness notification system: copy of sub-
   poena and letter
Year system began: 1985
Special features: Crisis intervention is provided for
   victims 60 and older, including financial
   reimbursement.

Fairfax County Victim Assistance Network
Year system began: 1975
8119 Holland Road
Alexandria, VA 22306
(703) 360-6910
Contact person: Anne VanRyzin, Coordinator
Number of full-time staff: 2
Number of part-time staff: 2
Number of volunteers: 37
No witness notification system
Special features: 24-hour hot line. Outreach to
   hospital emergency rooms 24-hours a day,
   and attendance of police interviews as
   requested.

Victim/Witness Assistance Program
Year program began: 1984
Elderly Victim Assistance Program
P.O. Box 15125
Chesapeake, VA 23320
(804) 547-6417
Contact person: Joyce Walsh, Victim/Witness Coordinator
Number of full-time staff: 2
No witness notification system
Special features: Emergency assistance for elderly victims.

Victim/Witness Program, County of Loudoun
Year program began: 1978
18 E. Market Street
Leesburg, VA 22075
(703) 777-0417
Contact person: Irene Wodell, Director
Number of full-time staff: 1
Number of volunteers: 42
Type of witness notification system: phone and letter
Year system began: 1978
Special features: Meet with victim at the crime scene, and give emergency support to elderly victims.

Victim/Witness Program
Year program began: 1976
Commonwealth's Attorney's Office
P.O. Box 1417
Portsmouth, VA 23705
(804) 393-8581
Contact person: Theresa J. Saunders, Victim/Witness Coordinator
Number of full-time staff: 1
Type of witness notification system: letter and phone
Year system began: 1976
Special features: None reported.

Victim/Witness Assistance Program
Year program began: 1984
Roanoke Commonwealth Attorney's Office
315 W. Church Avenue, S.W.
Roanoke, VA 24016
(703) 981-2683
Contact person: Jane P. Renick, Director
Number of full-time staff: 1

Number of volunteers: 2
Type of witness notification system: phone and letter
Year system began: 1984
Special features: Close phone and personal contact is provided to the elderly throughout the time the case is in the court system.

WASHINGTON
Lewis County Victim/Witness Program
Year program began: 1982
P.O. Box 918
Courthouse Annex
Chehalis, WA 98532
Number of full-time staff: 1
Number of part-time staff: 2
Type of witness notification system: phone and form letter
Year system began: 1984
Special features: Services for the elderly, include transportation to and from the court and assisting in the filling out of forms.

Victim/Witness Assistance
Year program began: 1982
Prosecuting Attorney's Office—Benton County
7320 West Quinault
Kennewick, WA 99336
(509) 735-3591
Contact person: Elaine Osborne, Coordinator
Number of full-time staff: 1
Type of witness notification system: letter and phone
Year system began: ??
Special features: None reported.

Pacific County Victim/Witness Program
Year program began: 1982
P.O. Box 45
Pacific County Courthouse
South Bend, WA 98596
(206) 875-6541, ext. 317
Contact person: Beth Kitselman, Coordinator
Number of part-time staff: 1
Number of volunteers: 1
Type of witness notification system: letters
Year system began: 1982
Special features: Crisis intervention is done in person.

Victim/Witness Unit
Year system began: ??
County-City Public Safety Building
West 1100 Mallon Avenue
Spokane, WA 99260-0270
(509) 456-3646
Contact person: Dorothy M. Scott, Director/
  Coordinator
Number of full-time staff: 2
Number of volunteers: 40
Type of witness notification system: phone and
  mail
Year system began: 1978
Special features: None reported.

Victim/Witness Assistance Service
Year program began: 1978
1033 County-City Building
Tacoma, WA 98406
(206) 591-7447
Contact person: Eileen O'Brien, Director
Number of full-time staff: 4
Number of part-time staff: 4
Number of volunteers: 9
Type of witness notification system: letter
Year system began: ??
Special features: None reported.

Clark County Prosecuting Attorney's V/W Unit
Year program began: 1978
1101 Harney Street
Vancouver, WA 98660
(206) 699-2008
Contact person: Amy Kendis, Supervisor
Number of full-time staff: 2
Number of part-time staff: 2
Type of witness notification system: mail
Year system began: 1985
Special features: None reported.

Victim/Witness Assistance Unit
Year program began: 1969
Room 329 Courthouse
Yakima, WA 98901
(509) 966-8906 or 575-4141
Contact person: Robyn B. Cyr, Administrator
Number of full-time staff: 3
Type of witness notification system: letter and
  phone

Year system began: 1979
Special features: Child-care program staffed by
  employees and contracted assistance. Crisis
  intervention is done over the phone or in
  person.

WISCONSIN
Outagamie County Victim/Witness Assistance
Year program began: 1983
410 S. Walnut Street
Appleton, WI 54911
(414) 735-5024
Contact person: Sheila Carmichael, Director
Number of full-time staff: 1
Number of part-time staff: 1
Type of witness notification system: phone, let-
  ters, and send police
Year system began: 1983
Special features: Services to the elderly are coor-
  dinated per the Wisconsin Elder Abuse
  Reporting Law. Crisis intervention is done
  in person.

Jackson County V/W Assistance
Year program began: 1984
307 Main Street
Black River Falls, WI 54615
(715) 284-7441, ext. 242
Contact person: Hazel Miles, Coordinator
Number of part-time staff: at least 1
Type of witness notification system: mail
Year system began: 1984
Special features: None reported.

Pierce County Victim/Witness Assistance
Year program began: 1985
Pierce County Courthouse
Ellsworth, WI 54011
(715) 273-3531, ext. 320
Contact person: Ann Gustafson, Coordinator
Number of part-time staff: 1
Type of witness notification system: phone and
  letter
Year system began: 1985
Special features: None reported.

Victim/Witness Assistance
Year program began: pre-1983
Fond du Lac County District Attorney's Office

160 South Macy Street
Fond du Lac, WI 54935
Number of part-time staff: 2
Type of witness notification system: letter
Year system began: ??
Special features: None reported.

Victim/Witness Assistance Program
Year program began: 1984
125 South Adams Street
Green Bay, WI 54301
(414) 436-4300
Contact person: Karen H. Doran, Coordinator
Number of full-time staff: 2
Type of witness notification system: telephone
and letter
Year system began: 1984
Special features: Child-care program served 14
children in 1984. Liability insurance is handl-
ed by the victim. Staff from the Brown
County Department of Social Services pro-
vides court escort, transportation, temporary
shelter, and financial assistance to all victims.
Crisis intervention is done over the phone
and in person.

Kenosha County District Attorney's Office
Year program began: 1981
Victim/Witness Services
912-56th Street, Room 312
Kenosha, WI 53410
(414) 656-6480
Contact person: Lynn M. Copen, Coordinator
Number of full-time staff: 2
Number of volunteers: 1
Type of witness notification system: phone, mail,
and in person
Year system began: 1981
Special features: Child-care program staffed by a
program worker. Served 1 child in 1984.

Victim/Witness Assistance Program
Year program began: 1981
P.O. Box 7951
123 W. Washington Avenue
Madison, WI 53707
(608) 266-1155 or 266-6470 (D.A.'s office)
Contact person: Cathi Van Ness, Statewide Vic-
tim/Witness Coordinator

Number of full-time staff: varies per county
Number of part-time staff: varies per county
Number of volunteers: varies per county
Type of witness notification system: mail and
telephone
Year system began: 1981
Special features: None reported.

Victim/Witness Unit
Year program began: 1978
Dane County District Attorney
Room 305
210 Monona Avenue
Madison, WI 53709
(608) 266-4211
Contact person: Gillian Lawrence, Director
Number of full-time staff: 4
Number of part-time staff: 1
Type of witness notification system: telephone
and letter
Year system began: 1978
Special features: None reported.

Manitowoc County Victim/Witness Assistance
Year program began: 1979
District Attorney's Office
1010 South 8th Street
Manitowoc, WI 54220
(414) 683-4074
Contact person: Brenda Guse, Victim/Witness
Coordinator
Number of full-time staff: 1
Type of witness notification system: letter and
phone
Year system began: approximately 1980
Special features: None reported.

Victim/Witness Services
Year program began: 1975
Room 412 Safety Building
821 West State Street
Milwaukee, WI 53233
(414) 278-4659
Contact person: Jo Kolanda Beaudry,
Coordinator
Number of full-time staff: 11
Number of volunteers: 10
Type of witness notification system: phone
Year system began: 1975

Special features: Utilize a court watch program for the elderly. These volunters are elderly and help the elderly victim throughout the court process.

Victim/Witness Assistance Program
Year program began: 1983
District Attorney's Office
Oconto County Courthouse
Oconto, WI 54153
(414) 834-5322
Contact person: James Newlun, District Attorney
No staffing numbers reported.
Type of witness notification system: phone
Year system began: 1983
Special features: None reported.

Racine County Victim/Witness Assistance Program
Year program began: 1983
Racine County District Attorney's Office
730 Wisconsin Avenue
Racine, WI 53403
Number of full-time staff: 3
Type of witness notification system: letters, phone, and walk-in
Year system began: 1983
Special features: None reported.

Victim/Witness Assistance Program
Year program began: 1984
P.O. Box 400
Rhinelander, WI 54501
(715) 369-7133
Contact person: Bonnie Wilcox, Director
Number of part-time staff: at least 1
Type of witness notification system: phone and subpoena
Year system began: 1984
Special features: None reported.

Victim/Witness Assistance Program
Year program began: 1983
District Attorney's Office
615 N. 6th
Sheboygan, WI 53081
(414) 459-3040
Contact person: Susan A. Hein, Coordinator
Number of part-time staff: at least 1

Type of witness notification system: in person and mail
Year system began: 1983
Special features: Have a separate waiting room for children witnesses. Work with the Office of Aging to assist witnesses and victims who are elderly.

Portage County V/W Assistance Program
Year program began: 1981
1516 Church Street
Stevens Point, WI 54481
(715) 346-1300
Contact person: Maureen Hekmat, Coordinator
Number of part-time staff: at least 1
Type of witness notification system: letter and phone
Year system began: 1981
Special features: Have an elderly abuse network where calls are made. A worker then makes contact with the elderly person to determine what to do.

Victim/Witness Assistance Program
Year program began: ??
1313 Belknap Street
Superior, WI 54880
(715) 394-0349
Contact person: Darlene Olson, Specialist
Number of full-time staff: 1
Type of witness notification system: phone and letter
Year system began: ??
Special features: None reported.

Waukesha County V/W Assistance Program
Year program began: 1979
Room G-90
515 W. Moreland Boulevard
Waukesha, WI 53188
(414) 548-7071
Contact person: Gerry Wuerslin, Coordinator
Number of full-time staff: 2
Number of part-time staff: 3
Number of volunteers: 8
Type of witness notification system: phone and mail
Year system began: 1985

Special features: Special services to the elderly include making additional contact with the Department on Aging or Adult Protective Services when appropriate.

Marathon County V/W Assistance Program
Year program began: 1984
Marathon County Courthouse
500 Forest Street
Wausau, WI 54401
(715) 847-5555
Contact person: Matthew A. Triolo, Coordinator
Number of full-time staff: 1
Type of witness notification system: mail and phone
Year system began: 1984
Special features: None reported.

About the Author

Albert R. Roberts is an Associate Professor of Social Work and Criminal Justice at the Graduate School of Social Work, Rutgers—The State University of New Jersey in New Brunswick. He previously taught at the Indiana University School of Social Work in Indianapolis. He has also served as project director or consultant on several research projects, including a National Institute of Justice-funded study of the effectiveness of crisis counseling with crime victims at the Victim Services Agency in New York City. He received his doctorate in social welfare from the University of Maryland School of Social Work and Community Planning, and is a fellow of the American Orthopsychiatric Association and an active member of the National Organization for Victim Assistance, the National Association of Social Workers, the Council on Social Work Education, and the Academy of Criminal Justice Sciences. He has published numerous articles in refereed social work, juvenile justice, corrections, and family violence research journals. He has also published eleven books, including *Battered Women and Their Families* (1984), *Juvenile Justice: Policies, Programs and Services* (1989), and *Crisis Intervention Handbook: Assessment, Treatment and Research* (1990).

About the Contributors

Arlene Bowers Andrews, Ph.D. is an Assistant Professor at the College of Social Work, University of South Carolina, Columbia, South Carolina. She also directed a statewide study of victim services and mental health services for crime victims in South Carolina.

Harriet Bemus, M.A., is the founding Director of Victim/Witness Services of Orange County and the Child Sexual Assault Network of Orange County, California.

Arnold Binder, Ph.D., is a Professor of Psychiatry and Human Behavior, and Social Ecology and the founder of the Program in Social Ecology at the University of California at Irvine. He is also the founding Executive Director of Youth Service Programs of Orange County, California.

Alan T. Harland, LL.M., Ph.D., is an Associate Professor in the Department of Criminal Justice at Temple University in Philadelphia. He also directs the Criminal Justice Semester Abroad in England program for the university.

Eric Hickey, Ph.D., is an Associate Professor in the Department of Criminal Justice at Ball State University in Muncie, Indiana.

Beverly Schenkman Roberts, M.Ed., is Project Director for Mainstreaming Medical Care at the Association for Retarded Citizens/New Jersey, located in North Brunswick.

Cathryn Jo Rosen, J.D., LL.M., is an Assistant Professor at the Department of Criminal Justice at Temple University, Philadelphia.